# What's That in Your Hand?

## God and Pool - The Gospel Trick Shot Story

by

**Steve Lillis**

PUBLISHER

Gospel Trick Shot Ministries, Inc.

What's That in Your Hand?

God and Pool - The Gospel Trick Shot Story

Copyright 2019 by Steve Lillis

Published by Gospel Trick Shot Ministries, Inc., P.O. Box 313, Hawthorne, New Jersey 07507

Website: gospeltrickshot.org   Email: billiards12@hotmail.com

Cover Illustration by Ian Grinyer taken from Photo by John Bandstra

**Library of Congress Cataloging-in-Publication Data**

Lillis, Steve, What's That in Your Hand? God and Pool - The Gospel Trick Shot Story, ISBN: 9781096544371

Published in the United States of America

# Contents

This book is dedicated to my wife Camille

and our two daughters Amanda and Sarah

Psalm 22:31 (New International Version)

"They will proclaim his righteousness, declaring to a people yet unborn: He has done it!"

# Acknowledgements

I would like to acknowledge the following people who without their many hours of help and encouragement this book might not have happened. First and foremost, my good friend and fellow church worker Dick Wells of the Hawthorne Gospel Church, volunteered to read, discuss, and help edit each chapter of the book as I wrote the manuscript roughly three chapters at a time over a three-month period. Dick also serves on the Missions Committee of the church and has followed my missionary career from the beginning in the 1990's.

Next, coauthor Devra Robledo from the first book I wrote entitled But You Must! – The Steve Lillis Story, modeled how to do the entire project from the first book and offered some key advise and suggestions for this second book. My travel partner and BCA Hall of Fame pool player Tom "Dr. Cue" Rossman, checked some of the billiard facts and names and helped edit the Gospel Trick Shot diagrams in the back of the book. Pastor Michael and Kim Hewitt of Rising Hope Church in Muncie, Indiana stood by me in prayer and encouragement while Kim took the time to produce yet another pair of valuable eyes in the editing process.

There are many others who prayed and offered advice and encouragement along the way, all to whom I would like to give a big thank you and may God bless you!

# Book Endorsements

1) **LoreeJon Hasson** – 2002 (BCA) Billiard Congress of America Hall of Fame Inductee Pool Player

"I have known Steve Lillis since I was 7 years old when he came to my Dad's pool room in New Jersey. His life off the pool table matches the messages he shares on the pool table. Steve listens to God and as a faithful servant blesses many people as they have shared that with me through the years. Who would have thought of a Gospel Trick Shot? God did and sent Steve and others all around the USA and to 26 countries to share the love of Jesus through pool! Read and enjoy what God did through Steve and Gospel Trick Shot Ministries!"

2) **Ken Vander Wall** – Campus Pastor 45 years with InterVarsity Christian Fellowship

"It was an honor to read this book and I am glad to share a few responses! I have had the privilege to know Steve as a friend and co-missionary to the campuses of northern New Jersey--in addition to serving on the GTS Board since its beginning. Two things strike me about Steve and my work with him. One, how God has used Steve in his missionary endeavors. It is amazing to me to see how interconnected Steve's ministry is! I wish I would have counted the names of all the people named in this book! Two, how far and wide Steve's ministry has been. Jesus said: "Go into all the world…." That's where Steve has gone! It was hard for me to believe how many doors have been opened by God into so many parts of the world—and Steve has been obedient to GO!! May you be blessed and encouraged to be obedient to God's calling on your life as you read this book! Serving Jesus with you, Ken"

3) **Mike Olejarz** – National Director for Chi Alpha Campus Ministries

"Steve Lillis has created a marvelous account of his personal redemption and the creation and development of Gospel Trick Shot (GTS) Ministries. Steve has invested his life in creating bridges of conversation to men and women in America and around the world about what really matters through the game of billiards. He is a gifted communicator whose brilliance on the pool table has made the name and person of Jesus Christ more famous in numerous public schools, colleges, pool rooms, and countries. Our mission organization has benefitted from Steve's ministry as he has helped us influence many college students towards knowing Jesus Christ. If you want to read a story of what God could do with one person's life surrendered to Him, this book will energize you to make yourself available to the greatest trick shot Artist of all time - God Himself! Mike Olejarz, National Training Specialist, Chi Alpha Campus Ministries"

4) **Mike Godza** – Director of RVA Chi Alpha Campus Ministries

"I've watched Steve work for the last few years on college campuses and I can say without a doubt, he's a master player with a heart to glorify Jesus. Through his story and significant research, Steve lays out the nature of the game and how it can be used for God's kingdom. An excellent read for both players and non-players alike."

5) **Jeff Ballantyne** – University of Minnesota Campus
Pastor 35 years for International Student Friendship
Ministries

"In 1980 while I was traveling as a road player, Steve shared
Christ with me. Two months later I became a follower of Jesus.
A few years later I was working in full time ministry. In 1985 Steve
called me, asking my opinion about starting a ministry of sharing
Christ through pool. I told him that it sounded like God was
leading him and he should go ahead. Now decades have passed
and God has used Steve greatly to impact the lives of thousands
of people using the very thing God put in his hand, pool."

6) **Tom "Dr. Cue" Rossman** – 2017 BCA Hall of Fame
Inductee Pool Player

"What's That in Your Hand? God and Pool – The Gospel Trick Shot
Story by Steve Lillis is an amazing reflection on the "sport gift"
(Pool) and the "sport giver" (God)! A bonded association
between the two illustrates how the divine nature of God
engages in the world of billiards, when a professional pool player
opens his heart to the Holy Spirit's leading for ministry outreach
opportunities...both on and off the table. This work will educate
/ inspire readers and encourage them to follow an adventurous
leading in the specific "gift" God has blessed them with in sport,
business, and / or specific personal endeavors they might follow.
Angelic protection, heavenly provision, and divine power are
evident cornerstones in this magnetic writing to be enjoyed by
ALL! Endorsement By: Tom "Dr. Cue" Rossman, RACK Vision /
Outreach Ministry"

7) **Pastor John Minnema** – Head Pastor of the Hawthorne
Gospel Church

"The Gospel Trick Shot Story" is a story of God's amazing,
redeeming grace! Steve tells how God transformed his own life
and how God has used and is using him and the game he loves,

pool, to bring glory to Himself. Having known Steve for many years I can truly say he loves the Lord and desires to live for Christ. Many have come to know Christ as a result of Steve's unique ministry and his story is enlightening, exciting, and encouraging!"

8) **Mike Massey** – 2005 BCA Hall of Fame Inductee Pool Player

"I did not know that when I did my first paid trick shot show at the Greenway Billiards in Baton Rouge, LA in 1976 at a pro 9-Ball event, that Steve Lillis would be in the audience to see my show and hear my testimony about what Jesus Christ did in my life to save and restore me. Years later, Steve and I became friends and brothers in Christ and not only traveled as road partners to professional tournaments in the early 1980's, but also as partners with Gospel Trick Shot Ministries in the USA and overseas in the 2000's. It has been a great joy to see God work in both of our lives using the game of pool!"

9) **Michael Hewitt** – Church Planter for the Wesleyan Church

"This gem of a book is a definite for your library. Just as God used pool to change Steve's life, God could use something unique to change yours! Enjoy the trick shots, the history and inspiring stories contained in this book as you rack up victories in life. Rev. Michael Hewitt aka *The man of the Simonis Cloth*

Founding pastor of www.NewLifeWayland.org & www.RisingHopeChurch.com"

10) **David Schuit** – Former AIM Missionary and Pastor of Missions at the Hawthorne Gospel Church

"Having traveled with Steve on a couple of his missions' trips, I have been deeply impressed with Steve's love for the game of pool, how well-networked he is with the top players in the game, and his great passion for sharing the Gospel. You put these three things together in one book and you have a very fascinating read. If you know Steve, or enjoy the game of pool, or have been touched by the Gospel you will enjoy this book."

11) **Robin Dodson** - 2005 BCA Hall of Fame Inductee Pool Player

"Steve Lillis had a vision that captured the hearts of Christians like me in the pool world. Using pool balls to share the Gospel is an amazing way to open hearts for Jesus. As time went on Steve grew in His spiritual journey and then traveled around the world to share with others. The fire to share the Gospel of Jesus Christ is as strong today as it was when he began. Many lives continue to be touched as Steve moves around the pool table performing trick shots while sharing the love of God. His life and the lives of many others who have received the Message worldwide are evidence of the power of God. Steve's unique gift has blessed the Body of Christ all for the glory of God!"

# Preface by Steve Lillis

God and Pool - What is God doing with the game of billiards?

For years I have had people misunderstand me when I mentioned that I was going to play pool, do a pool show, or go to the pool room. They thought I meant pool as in a swimming pool when I really meant pool as in playing billiards. So where did this name "pool" come from?

Exodus 4:2 (New International Version of the Holy Bible) Then the LORD said to him, "What is that in your hand?" "A staff," he replied.

In the summer of 1995, I received this verse while reading my Bible in the woods at a campground in Hershey, PA. My parents were camping with their RV and I came to visit them with my two young daughters Amanda and Sarah. They were having such a good time together that I slipped off into the woods to pray and read my Bible. As I read the story of Moses I was particularly struck by the line "What is that in your hand?" I sensed that God was talking to me about using my cue stick as I had been wrestling with God about whether the game of pool was useful for the purposes of God! I had friends that suggested that I could and I wanted to hear from God through his Word!

Acts 10: 15 (New International Version of the Holy Bible) The voice spoke to him a second time, "Do not call anything impure that God has made clean."

My Bible is marked with the date of June 23, 1999 which is the exact date when I first received this verse above in my quiet time with the Lord. I have tried for the past 34 years to make it a daily habit to be still and listen to what God is saying through his Holy Word. I had started a pool ministry using the historic game of billiards in 1996 after receiving that first verse in Exodus 4:2 above and for some three plus years continued to struggle as to whether I was doing the right thing or not. My early past haunted me as a pool hustler and high stakes gambler. Some people at my local church and others doubted that God had called me to use my gift of playing pool. I asked, was I in the will of God and did He actually call me to do this? After all, at the time in 1999, I was a respectable teacher at two local colleges, drove a school bus part time, and had been fully employed since my initial retirement from pool in 1985 when I had vowed never to play this "evil" game again.

In this book, we will briefly examine and discuss the glorious history of the European "Sport of Kings" called billiards, see the evolution of the game into the present-day culture of the pool room, and view its struggle with society and in particular the Christian Church. In his book entitled "Pool, Billiards and Bowling Alleys", Rev. John J. Phelan, M.A., Ph.D., thoroughly examines the game and its impact on American society in 1919 through extensive research and investigation. The purpose of his book was not to do away with the game, but quite the contrary, embrace pool and use it to "socialize" particularly young men to the "American way".

Phelan understood that the game had been around for centuries and it was here to stay. He insisted that pool and its use be changed through government control and regulation. His proposals went right to the desk of administrators in his native Toledo, Ohio and changed the game, at least in theory. Toledo, Ohio had 400 pool rooms for a population of 200,000 people. This was the stereotypical American city of its day. I must say that I find not much has changed since his rather extensive investigation. The study was very conclusive and the findings appear to me to be very probable. However, I think we can extrapolate his findings and conclude that government regulation has not curbed the presence of "evil" surrounding the beloved "innocent" game of billiards more commonly known as pool.

The word pool in itself is a gross miscarriage of justice when applied to the wonderful grand old game of billiards. The origin of the game is not clearly known, but many a reference can be found in European Literature over the last five centuries. Furthermore, we also know that during the European "Age of Colonialism" billiard tables traveled to the far reaches of the vast European Empires. The fingerprints of "The Age" can be found in all countries around the world with billiard tables of all kinds stationed in various cities, towns, and country sides everywhere.

In America, we owe our billiard heritage in large part to the English, French, and Spanish who at one time owned this entire country. It took wars and at least two purchases to obtain the land and the freedom to do what we want. We did what we wanted with the game of billiards! In the middle of the 19th Century, horse racing was quite popular and in particularly the western frontier of America. The poolroom was the place or room to go at the track to place your bet on the horse race. Eventually racetracks installed billiard tables in the pool room to kill time in between races and patrons placed bets on the billiard games as well. The rest is history as billiard rooms became synonymous with pool rooms and billiard tables became known as pool tables. Enter the play "The Music Man" on Broadway in the 1920's and the Hollywood movie "The Hustler" in the 1960's and the deal was sealed. Pool and pool players became synonymous with gambling, drinking, trouble, evil, and the like.

Again Rev. Phelan in his book in 1919 tried to raise the consciousness of society concerning the evils of the day being perpetuated in the pool rooms. Young American men had just returned home from World War I and it was time to get readjusted to civilian life here in the states. At that time in

American society, pool rooms were the most frequented places of amusement and social contact for young men who were on the verge of adulthood. Baseball had not yet reached its pinnacle and other sports like football and basketball were mere infants. Most prominent baseball players owned pool rooms to supplement their small salaries for playing baseball and to give them something to do in the off season. Society was being damaged as young men learned behaviors in the pool rooms that would not lend themselves to becoming productive citizens. Rev. Phelan outlined and researched this completely.

To my surprise many of the pool rooms that I visited as I traveled across the USA as a professional pool player in the late 1970's and early 1980's had not changed much since government intervention came into effect as a result of Rev Phelan and society's cry for help. The churches of the early 1900' s began to bring pool tables into their buildings to keep the young men out of the public pool rooms. The Young Men's Christian Association better known as the YMCA put pool tables in most of their buildings as well. Again, the idea was to keep young men out of the public pool rooms to avoid "evil" behavior and surroundings. The listed "evils" according to Rev. Phelan were poor sanitation, poor ventilation, inadequate toilets and poor lighting, along with closed screens and blinds to prevent observation. Additionally, there were numerous violations of the law including gambling and "treats" for minors who participated in the like. Male high school students cut class to saturate themselves in a moral cesspool complete with prolific profanity and assorted crime. Again, I found not much difference from the 1919 pool room and the one that emerged in the 70's and 80's that I observed as I traveled those same years. Although, I must admit that in the past 30 years there have been improvements in many pool rooms or as room owners would prefer billiard rooms particularly in the area of aesthetics.

The following true-life documentary that you will read will explain, in my humble opinion, what God has done to take this so called "evil" game that once was the European "Sport of Kings", and transform it into a tool to build his church. This modern-day movement of God and Pool began in my opinion somewhere in the 1970's. At that time, I was an aspiring young professional pool player setting out to become the Champion of the World. There were hundreds of like-minded young men doing the same thing at the same time. Most of us set out in response to that famous 1961 Hollywood movie called "The Hustler" with legendary actors Paul Newman and Jackie Gleason playing Fast Eddie and Minnesota Fats. This story involved fictitious pool playing characters that lived life in the fast lane. Many of my generation yearned to do the same. The results are varied, but in the following pages is my own story and those who I observed became a part of what God was beginning to do with the game of pool.

# What's That in Your Hand?

# God and Pool - The Gospel Trick Shot Story

# Prologue

After traveling to more than 20 countries around the world playing pool/billiards both in competition and doing trick shot shows while working with missionaries and churches, I have concluded that pool/billiards is truly an international sport with unique roots. God has used this sport in amazing ways in my life and has breathed new life into something that was created hundreds of years ago. You might ask how something that is centuries old can be a catalyst to thousands of people finding spiritual truth in the past quarter of a century. My only answer is that God will work out His will and make Himself known through any avenue necessary. In my ministry, He uses billiards.

Billiards originated from the Crown Heads of Europe during the 15th and 16th centuries. Hence, the game was originally called the "Sport of Kings" because of its Royal European origin. When the age of colonization/exploration started at about same time, the game of billiards was exported by these colonists to the far reaches of their empires. Lead countries like England, Spain, and France each exported their own version of the sport. Others such as Italy and Portugal had their own unique version as well.

The equipment variations are endless and vary according to the cultural origin. For example, the Spanish and French primarily played the game of carom which does not have pockets. The English were the first to cut out pockets which eventually evolved into the American game of pool. The size of the tables varies, and the cut of the pockets have also been changed according to each country. Even the size of the round object balls may vary and the cue ball itself can be a different size from the object balls. For example, the English play snooker on a big 6 by 12-foot table with the edges of the cushions rounded by the pockets and use 2 1/8-inch object balls. The Americans play pool on a 4 1/2 by 9-foot table with the pocket cushions squarer and more pointed and use 2 1/4-inch object balls. The French and Spanish typically play on a 5 x 10-foot table with no pockets and slightly bigger balls. This is the sport called carom in which the object is to strike a ball then carom a designated number of rails or cushions and then collide into another ball or go the designated number of rails first and then strike both of the other balls. The rules to the different games can change from country to country even if the equipment is similar.

To understand why there are so many cultural differences, you must go back to the days of colonization/exploration starting in the 16th century. Tracing the historical roots of how the equipment and the game came to that country will give much-needed information as to why the game became what it is today. During the age of colonization, it was very common for only the aristocrats and those given permission to have the opportunity to play the game. Limited numbers of tables were exported by ship and set up in a colony. Because this was considered initially the "Sport of Kings", only royalty and upper-class people would have had the opportunity to play. The poor and working-class people could only dream about playing the game. However, in the 19th century and particularly in America during the industrial revolution and the development of urban centers, pool/billiards became very popular and common people began to play. After the Civil War, as cities rapidly grew in America, so did pool/billiard rooms in the city. Soldiers picked up the game in the service and when they returned home, continued to fellowship around pool tables across America.

Middle-class working men now played the game and it eventually became the common man's game in America. By the 1920's, the three most popular sports in America were the three B's – billiards, baseball, and boxing.

In the middle of the 20th Century with mass production on the rise in America, tables were now exported all over the world with all social classes beginning to participate in the game. For most of the 20th century, the top players in the world were from the USA. By the end of the 20th century, America began to take a back seat to countries like the Philippines, China, and Taiwan in world championship competition. In the beginning of the 21st century, China began to crush the billiard economic engine of America. Chinese billiard companies drove many American billiard companies out of business and seriously hurt most of the rest of them. This led to a cultural exchange of not only players and their different styles but equipment and rules as well. One of the major challenges in getting pool/billiards into the Olympics is that the rules, games, and equipment vary so much. The (IOC) International Olympic Committee cannot decide on what game and what equipment would be fair to all who participate in the various cue sports! However, the cue games of snooker, carom, and pool are now part of the IOC sanctioned World Games [1]. The IOC is once again considering pool/billiards for competition at the 2024 Olympics in Paris. Since the origin of the game is France, this would be fitting if approved.

My world travels as a missionary/ambassador of pool/billiards began in 2001 when I first went to England to compete with the best Europeans and do my Gospel Trick Shot Show at the invitation of the European Pocket Billiard Federation. After playing pool for some 35 years in the USA and being ranked

---

[1] "Cue sports at the World Games," Wikipedia. Available at: https://en.wikipedia.org/wiki/Cue_sports_at_the_World_Games. 27 September 2018

as one of the top players in the world in my younger years, my eyes were opened to all the good young talent coming up in Europe. Then a few years later I was invited to Taiwan to play in the 2004 World 9-Ball Championship and to my utter shock and amazement American players ranked near the bottom as Asian players dominated the entire pool/billiard landscape. I later traveled to countries like Albania, Tanzania, Kenya, and the Philippines. Again, I saw players of all social classes and backgrounds aspiring to the best. The equipment and rules would constantly be changing, and I was forced to adapt. I became fascinated with the changes and wanted to know why. One of my quests was to follow the roots of pool/billiards around the world and share what I found. My ultimate quest is always to bring the Good News of Jesus Christ to all people that would gather at pool/billiard tables around the globe!

# Introduction

The purpose of this book is to examine the history and development of the game of billiards around the world and to trace how I believe God has and is currently using the game to advance the Kingdom of God.  Obviously if you are reading this book and are not a believer in the historic Christian Bible it might be difficult to agree with some of the views set forth.  However, if you know the game of billiards and/or the trends of business and recreation in the USA and around the world you will find this book a fascinating read.  So, my goal is not to convert all who read this book however I wish it would be so.  Also, I want to leave a record of what has actually happened in my life of more than a half a century of playing and participating in the game of billiards on a professional level.

Billiard Congress of America (BCA) Hall of Fame pool player Tom "Dr. Cue" Rossman states that he is a "Doctor of Billiardology" which he defines as the study of spheres, projectiles, and planes.  There is no formal degree issued as such to my knowledge, however in my opinion this is as good of a definition of billiards as any.

The generic game of billiards includes any game played on an upright flat table or plane usually made of slate but can be wood, marble, or any other material that will remain level and upright for a long period of time.  The projectile launcher or straight cue stick is usually made of wood with leather tips on one end.  It is used to launch the cast phenolic, plastic billiard balls, or round spheres out in a calculated direction to secure desired results.  Rubber cushions create a boundary or perimeter with colored felt (usually green) covering the table or flat surface.  This creates a combination of rebound angles and speed that must be calculated to figure out the direction and final resting place of the sphere(s) or billiard ball(s).

Billiard tables can have pockets which in that case is called a pocket billiard table. The object of that game is to pocket the balls. A table with no pockets is called a carom table because the balls can only carom around the table off the rails or cushions. Pool can be any form of pocket billiards. I will discuss the origin of the word "pool" referring to a type of billiards in chapter one!

There are many different types of pocket billiard games and again the purpose of this book is not to review the variety of rules and games or even for that matter the semantics in the use of terminology. I will leave that to other highly qualified people. However, I have personally served in the billiard industry as a professional referee, tournament director, promoter, and TV commentator many times in my career and feel qualified to speak on the subject.

There is much more to be said about the science and math of the game, but I will leave that to others as the goal of this book is to introduce a metaphysical side of the game that introduces faith and specifically my faith in Jesus Christ and how God has used this game to further the Gospel.

Some of my accomplishments as a professional billiard player are a matter of record [2]. These can be traced through various billiard publications and records [3]. Billiard Congress of

[2] "Billiard Champions and Records – 1979 BCA National Eight Ball Tournament," Billiard Congress of America - Billiards - The Official Rules And Record Book. Published by the Billiard Congress of America, Chicago, IL. 1980, p. 146. Print.
[3] "Tournaments - Bowling Green 9-Ball Open," Billiards Digest. Vol. 7, No. 5, National Bowlers Journal, Inc., May-June 1985, p. 25. Print.

America Hall of Fame promoter Charles Ursitti [4], billiard historian Michael Shamos [5], along with the deceased Conrad Burkeman's National Billiard News archives, are a few of the sources [6]. I have finished in the top ten in seven world or national championships and have won state and regional titles in the USA.

However, some of what I will share in this book has not been published, even though at times some of the billiard publications have picked up on some of my travels with Gospel Trick Shot Ministries. The content of this book has been compiled through over twenty years of record keeping and newsletters with Gospel Trick Shot Ministries, Inc (GTS or GTSM). This ministry will become the focal point of this book as GTS, to my knowledge, became the first highly recognized and respected Christian billiard ministry in the world of billiards. The incorporation of GTS occurred on June 8, 1998. I believe this was a landmark date in the history of God and pool. As you read this book, hopefully you will see what God has done around the world with this unique ministry.

An outside source I recently rediscovered was a website called BondFanEvents.com created by my good friend Matt Sherman. Matt serves on the instructional staff of Inside Pool Magazine and directed the University of Florida's Pool League which produced five national collegiate champions. He is the Guide to Pool & Billiards at ThoughtCo.com a top five website

---

[4] "Historian Charles Ursetti posts collection of historic 'Billiards Magazine' editions online," Untold Stories:
Billiards History. Available at:
http://untoldstoriesbilliardshistory.blogspot.com/2010/01/charlie-ursitti-posts-historic-pool.html. wednesday, january 20, 2015.
[5] Shamos, Mike. "Forward," The Complete Book of Billiards. Published by Gramercy Books, New York, NY. 1993, p. viii. Print. Copyright 1993 by Michael Ian Shamos.
[6] "National Billiard News," AZBILLIARDS.COM. Available at:
https://www.facebook.com/AzBilliards/. Facebook © 2019

with over 53 million visitors monthly. He has been tracking Gospel Trick Shot since 2009 by listing all of our events and adding commentary. You can go to that website at BondFanEvents.com/gts and see archival information about GTS that spans a seven-year period which will add reference to the information in this book.

At times I will refer to my first book entitled "But You Must! – The Steve Lillis Story". In that book I go into detail about my life story and particularly how God was moving me along to end up serving Him in full-time Christian ministry with GTS. In this book I will repeat some of the scenes if the reader has not read "But You Must!". I would strongly suggest that if you like this book go back and read that first one. I believe it will inspire you in your search for meaning and purpose. It is available through my website www.gospeltrickshot.org and at www.amazon.com.

# Chapter 1 – Why Pool?

Again, I would like to repeat my opening lines of my preface that for years I have had people misunderstand me when I mentioned that I was going to play pool, do a pool show, or go to the pool room. They thought I meant pool as in a swimming pool when I really meant pool as in playing billiards. So where did this name "pool" come from?

After traveling the country back in the 1970's and early 1980's as a professional pool player, I realized that this might not be a profession that would make my parents proud. I must admit that I took great pride in being a professional pool player and I highly respect all those who try to do the same thing in a respectable manner. However public opinion at that time was that being a pool player was perhaps one notch above being a professional gambler. During the late 1970's and early 1980's, I traveled around the country with my wife Camille. Although I was in my prime and a contender in every major professional tournament, it was only a subsistence lifestyle. Maybe you have heard stories of pool players who have won millions of dollars primarily through gambling on a game of pool, but what you do not hear is that they also lost millions of dollars through gambling. Even though at times I wagered fairly large sums of money early on in my pool playing career, my focus in my travels with Camille was to become a legitimate world champion tournament pool player. There have been a handful of pool players through the years who made a respectable living but usually, it was more because of endorsements and sponsors and not from just solely playing pool competitively. There simply is not enough prize money available to make a living. Of course, the dream of every professional pool player is that someday there would be enough prize money offered to make a decent living like in the games of tennis and golf.

Now let me get back to the word pool. I have personally been around most of the great players of the 20th century and always had a listening ear. From all of my research and stories handed down from the "old timers," the word pool came into being in the 1800's and perhaps somewhere in the Midwest. It was associated with horse racing and gambling. Before I tell that story about the origin of the word pool let me first mention that the word billiards came from the French word billard which is the country where the game probably began. I will address that more on that in the next chapter when discussing the history of the sport.

Back to the racetrack and the word "pool". Horse racing was very popular in the USA in the 19th century and is still popular today. It is, of course, associated with gambling. Back in the day, it was popular to play pool in between the races to pass the time. Billiard tables were placed at the racetracks. So, when two people engaged in a game of billiards other racetrack patrons surrounding the table would yell, "pool-pool!" That meant "come and place your bet on who will win the ensuing game." As the westward expansion in the USA continued, billiard tables became known as pool tables and were also placed in neighborhood saloons alongside poker tables. As you might have expected, these saloon patrons and poker players would then ask their neighbors to play a game of pool and wager on the game.

Back east billiard rooms were generally more upscale, traditional, and distinguished places of business. Gentlemen and occasionally the ladies would typically engage in a game of billiards in a billiard room where there was no gambling or alcohol permitted on the premises. These laws were passed down and remained active particularly in Northeastern USA through much of the 20th century. Signs would definitively say no gambling or alcohol permitted on the premises. This, I believe, had more to do with the European tradition of billiards as the sport of the crown heads of Europe than what Americans did in practice. This will be addressed in more detail in the history chapter coming up next.

Back east at the turn of the 20th century, the fascination with the westward expansion in the USA was personified with the Wild West shows that came to eastern cities and towns. Stories spread of pool playing prowess and how pool players won large sums of money wagering. The intrigue of fast money has always had a lure! Consequently, the American game of pool with wagering began to replace the European art of billiards. Slowly but surely as the "Music Man" on Broadway and the Hollywood movie "The Hustler" began to personify this reality through stage and screen, imaginations began to run wild. I myself, along with many of my generation, were inspired to hit the road in search of fame and fortune like Fast Eddie in the movie "The Hustler." Thus, the words "pool" and "gambling" became etched into the consciousness of the American mind. American billiard players were now called pool hustlers and hustling became a way of life! In the next chapter, we will examine through the history of pool how this mindset and the game of pool began to spread throughout the world.

Finally, even before I was serving in pool ministry which began in the 1990's, I was always fascinated with professional pool competition. My view of pool was initially shaped as a twelve-year-old boy watching the legends of the game compete in a 1960's television program which featured the billiard match of the week. Naïve as I was at twelve, my knowledge of pool hustling was very limited. I had my own pool table in the basement and imagined that I could someday be like one of these classy gentlemen on TV dressed in tuxedos performing and competing in the art of billiards. I made up my mind back then that this might be something worth pursuing. I practiced almost every day waiting to turn sixteen years old so that I would be allowed in a billiard room, or shall we say "pool room." That was the local law at the time where I lived in Northern New Jersey. So, the day finally came when I turned sixteen, and I was slowly but surely introduced to the other side of pool playing and the life of the hustler. Again, my first book "But You Must!" has many stories about that part of my life, however, I must move on to share what God was about to do unbeknownst to me as a youngster. You will hopefully see, and I truly believe, that God had a plan for my life all along using pool far beyond what I ever could have imagined as a young man aspiring to be a professional pool player.

# Chapter 2 – History of Pool/Billiards
## Part I

When dealing with the history of billiards and now I can use the word pool interchangeably, there is much information and perhaps little in terms of absolute fact. So, I will take a shot, pardon the pun, at giving you a history lesson on pool according to the Steve Lillis version. I have accumulated this information for over 50 years. It is a compilation of information from not only some of the best-written sources like Robert Byrne but also from stories and accounts that have been passed down from legends of the game like Luther Lassiter, Steve Mizerak, and Mike Massey. I have rubbed shoulders with these and many more famous billiard/pool people and have exchanged thoughts and ideas with them during my entire adult life. With that said, here is the Steve Lillis version of the history of billiards.

Many have traced the origins of billiards back as far as the Egyptians. For me, the starting point for many reasons as I will describe later was the late 1400's in France and King Louis XI [7]. He loved some form of outdoor lawn bowling and became frustrated when it rained. The idea of an indoor game on a table with green felt and rolling balls within borders evolved into perhaps the first billiard table. Many of the crown heads of Europe were related. This can be traced back to the Vikings and other related tribes who were obviously in contact with each other as European powers evolved. Furthermore, some fifty years later we note in one of Shakespeare's plays in England in the early 1500's the line, "get thee to billiards". We might be able to conclude that at least the royalty of other European

---

[7] "Billiard Room – History," Wikipedia. Available at: https://en.wikipedia.org/wiki/Billiard_room. 25 August 2017

countries followed King Louis's lead and participated in this new indoor game called billiards.

Europe began to literally take over the world in the 16th, and 17th, and 18th centuries, commonly known as the Age of Colonization or the Age of Exploration depending on your politics. This new game of billiards began to be exported on European sailing vessels around the world. There is still a billiard cloth producer, Iwan Simonis Cloth, still in existence today from 1680 [8]. Because the game was of royal descent, it is generally assumed, at least by me, that commoners in the European colonies were not generally permitted to participate in the game. It was typically reserved for the rich and privileged. Now there could be many reasons for this. When I get to the 20th century my reasons will become clearer. The USA is obviously the result of European colonization. So, the game of billiards was brought here primarily by the English along with other European countries that had a stake in this new land. Incidentally, I was born in New York and raised in New Jersey. So many of my views about billiards, at least initially, were shaped by Northeasterners, hence the English. By the way, in England to this day the cue sports are held in high esteem!

Let us pick up on our history lesson according to yours truly with the 19th century and the USA. Some fifty years after the birth of the USA the industrial revolution began. This is a very important time with respect to the history of billiards. In the USA as in other industrialized countries, cities began to form as the country moved from an agrarian or farm society to a more urban-based society. This led to the manufacturing of key products that went into the development of billiard tables and accessories. By the 1840's, the forerunner of what is now Brunswick Billiards, the largest manufacturer of pool/billiard tables in the 20th century,

---

[8] Saunders, Chris. "History Made! Iwan Simonis Cloth since 1680," Inside Pool Magazine. April 2005, p. 70-72. Print.

came into being as vulcanized rubber for cushions became the standard. With cities now forming across the American landscape, billiard tables began to appear in all kinds of urban settings including train stations, barber shops, candy stores, bars and restaurants, and just about anywhere people might gather in community and spend time with each other.

On April 12, 1859, the City of Detroit hosted the first national championship billiard match, with Michael Phelan of New York defeating local favorite John Seereiter for the $15,000 top prize—a wagonload of money at a time when even skilled tradesmen often made only a few hundred dollars a year.

The conclusion of the American Civil War in the 1860's was another shot in the arm for billiards, again pardon the pun. With servicemen returning home from the war looking for jobs, cities afforded them their best opportunity to earn a decent living with no investment. Jobs were becoming plentiful as the industrial and commercial giants of the late 1900's were literally taking over the world as in JP Morgan, JD Rockefeller, and Andrew Carnegie just to mention a few. With jobs, the urban middle class began to grow, and people had disposable income for leisure time activities. Baseball was only just beginning as billiards and boxing were crowning world champions in their respective sports in the late 1800's and capturing the public's attention. Such sports as basketball, football, and hockey were hardly ever mentioned and basketball itself was not even invented until the 1890's. For the first quarter of the 20th century it was the big three; billiards, boxing, and baseball with billiards at the top as a participation sport. Even many of the professional baseball players in that era owned billiard rooms to ensure a steady income all year round. In the 1920's the three biggest names in sports were Willie Hoppe in billiards, Jack Dempsey in boxing, and Babe Ruth in baseball.

After the great depression and World War II, things began to radically change in American society. For billiards this marked the beginning of a monumental shift as American style pool was now beginning to be exported around the world just as our European ancestors had done centuries before. This paradigm shift will be examined in the next chapter.

# Chapter 3 – History of Pool/Billiards Part II

So where did this shift in the middle to late 1900's begin? The Great Depression of the 1930's in America was a time unlike any in the history of this country as men hung around pool rooms in droves due to extreme unemployment and little hope. World War II was a wakeup call as men found purpose in uniting to go and fight a war. Ladies, please excuse men at this point as the suffrage movement only began a decade before and society was still extremely male-dominated at this point. It is true that women did play a large role in the war as they served not only in the military but also in factories at home as the men were off in the battlefields risking their lives. Truly women were unsung heroes of WWII.

Additionally, I feel very qualified to speak on this subject since I have the battle metals of my Dad, William Joseph Lillis, who fought bravely in the Pacific against the Japanese and almost lost his life as 180 of his shipmates were killed in Kamikaze attacks off the Island of Guam in a very famous naval battle. My Dad and I spent countless hours talking about the war and life in these times. He ultimately was buried at sea by the U.S. Navy in 1997 as he requested in his will to join his shipmates who died some 53 years before him. As Forrest Gump said in that famous movie by the same name when he got choked up, "that is all I have to say about that right now." I will return to this subject later in the book when I go to the Philippines in 2012 with Gospel Trick Shot Ministries, Inc.

Let us get back to our billiard history lesson according to Steve. I believe that because of WW II, the USA entered an age of unprecedented prosperity. We fully became an industrialized society because of necessity. We had to make war machines and related products to win the war. After the war, factories and manpower were available for economic expansion. When the men came back from the war, they did not exactly do what their counterparts did in previous wars in returning to the cities or the farms. Because of the new interstate highway system that exploded in the 1950's, urban sprawl or suburbia became the new phenomenon. The baby boom generation was in full bloom as men and women fled the cities and moved their families to surrounding developing towns. Billiard rooms began to disappear from the cities and with so much time devoted to work and raising families in the suburbs, the 1950's became a depressed time for billiards. World Champions and Hall of Famers Willie Hoppe, Ralph Greenleaf, and Willie Mosconi carried the sport of billiards for the first half of the century, but now in the 1950's the future of pool was in trouble.

Fifteen-time World Champion Willie Mosconi, who won most of his titles in the 1940's and 50's, was very wise as he retired from tournament competition and went to work representing Brunswick Billiards doing exhibitions and making appearances [9]. In 1961 the movie "The Hustler" came out starring Hollywood celebrities Paul Newman and Jackie Gleason with Willie as the technical advisor and a billiard revival was about to begin. The following year the Johnson City, Illinois "Hustlers Jamboree" was started by the Jansco brothers and was fueled by the new sensation, the one and only Minnesota Fats himself. His name was really Rudolf Walter Wanderone Jr. [10] but he took the name from the movie claiming that the character in the movie played by Jackie Gleason, called Minnesota Fats, was

[9] "Willie Mosconi," Wikipedia. Available at:
https://en.wikipedia.org/wiki/Willie_Mosconi. 4 September 2018
[10] "Rudolf Wanderone," Wikipedia. Available at:
https://en.wikipedia.org/wiki/Rudolf_Wanderone. 5 September 2018

really him.    Now, with billiards fueled by Brunswick the manufacturer, the network television filming of "The Hustlers Jamboree", and baby boomers catching the pool playing bug, a pool/billiards revival was underway. All this led to the development of billiard parlors in suburban towns nationwide.

I call this the "Golden Age of Pool" in the 1960's and 1970's. Some would refute that claim because the sequel movie "The Color of Money" in 1986, launched a second revival. This is simply my opinion! The word "billiards" as in Clifton Billiards or Verona Billiards, was placed on the sign outside the door to give it a classier image for the reasons I discussed in chapter two. However, it was still the game of pool that was played, you know "trouble with a capital T and that rhymes with P and that stands for pool!" (from the 1957 Broadway play called the "Music Man"). I was one of those baby boomers that entered the pool room in 1966 and was exposed for the first time to the pool room culture of gambling - American style.   At this point, I need to further mention that state and local laws usually determine the legality of wagering on pool. Many state and local laws deem it legal between individuals since pool is generally considered to be a game of skill, however when others get involved in the wagering it is generally considered to be illegal (as in pool your bets).   So, the side bet or pari-mutuel betting (calcutta style) could be illegal. As I mentioned before, I naively practiced pool in my basement on my home pool table and watched sanitized tournament competitions on TV.  I was not prepared for this cultural impact in 1966!  Nevertheless, my pool room journey began because I loved billiards. I did word that last sentence intentionally with the word billiards to continue to make my point!

In the 1970's Willie Mosconi, Minnesota Fats, and upcoming Baby Boomer stars like Steve Mizerak and Allen Hopkins (both from my home state of NJ) helped to bring the game to new heights. Billiard sales were booming, soon to become legendary cue makers were popping up everywhere, and the hopes and dreams of a whole new breed of professional pool players, including myself, began to take shape. The Billiard Congress of America which started in the late 1940's, by the 1960's had developed a Hall of Fame for Billiards and the game was starting to look like a legitimate big-time sport with future promise. Player associations like the Professional Pool Player Association (PPPA) started in the 1970's. The future looked bright as I myself began my career traveling the country playing in professional tournaments, directing and promoting professional tournaments, along with teaching and writing a column in the National Billiard News (the top billiard publication of the day). At the top of the list, I was always chomping at the bit to play and beat all the champions and become one myself. Again, after almost 15 years I did compile a respectable record of professional tournament competition mentioned before in this book which is a matter of record, but a World Championship eluded me, and so I temporarily stopped playing competitive pool in 1985, just before the second Hollywood movie "The Color of Money" came out in 1986.

"The Color of Money" again starred Paul Newman as this second pool movie fueled what I call a mini-revival of pool. In the early 1980's pool, along with the economy, was in recession and that was a major factor in my leaving the game in 1985. From a distance, I observed that the timing of the movie, along with economic recovery, the formation of new player associations fueled by ESPN, and more tournament competition all helped this mini-revival. I was absent from the game during these years and into the late 1990's. When I returned, I had friends in the industry that I stayed in contact with to get the latest information. One of those trusted friends was Hall of Famer Pat Fleming of Accu-Stats Video Productions who was always on the front lines and was also from my home state of New Jersey. Pat and I would meet in the late 80's and early 90's to discuss the state of the union or perhaps disunion of pool. As the 21st century approached pool was about to fall into a major recession.

I returned to pool as a minister with Gospel Trick Shot in the late 1990's and as a professional pool player in the year 2000 [11]. Now I could observe firsthand what was about to take place. At the beginning of the 21st century, poker, video games, smoking bans, cost of rental space, and the cost of gasoline all together was the perfect storm to lead pool into its biggest decline in a century or more. Poker became the rage as hustlers young and old realized they could make quick money playing poker and it was a lot easier than trying to pocket pool balls. Smoking bans spread across the USA as young people who used to go to the pool room to perhaps have their first cigarette now had to find somewhere else. Furthermore, they could stay home to play poker, smoke cigarettes, and not have to fill the tank with gas. Video games have been popular for decades but with the advent of smartphones in the past decade, young people would rather use their all-purpose phone to do most anything, including playing pool electronically. The final proverbial nail in the coffin might have been the cost of rental space which skyrocketed during the real estate boom that ended in 2008. This boom ended with the Great Recession of 2008 as there was also less disposable income to spend on recreation and thus the damage was done. Pool rooms across the country began to close as young people had little to no interest in playing pool. Sorry to all my billiard fans about all this doom and gloom, but there is great news in all of this! In my later chapters, I will explain how the future of pool looks better than ever as I have now traveled around the world in the 21st century playing pool and doing my Gospel Trick Shot shows. I have much good news to report!

---

[11] "UPA Men's Pro Rankings," Pool & Billiard Magazine. March 2004, p. 73. Print.

# Chapter 4 – So where is God in all this?

I have asked where God is in all this since I gave my heart and pool game to the Lord Jesus Christ in 1985. There is a short video of my life story available on the home page of my website at www.gospeltrickshot.org. This video was produced and broadcast by the Christian Broadcasting Network (CBN) and shown more than once on their very well-known television program entitled "The 700 Club." In my first book, I shared my spiritual journey of faith so here I will share what I believe God revealed to me after 1985.

The first recorded reference to the spirit world and pool that I know of goes back to the inventor of the leather cue tip, François Mingaud, in the early 1800's [12]. François served as an officer in Napoleon's army and committed such a severe infraction that he was sentenced to prison time. He requested that a billiard table be placed in his prison cell and it was granted. François experimented with leather on the end of a wooden shaft. He used some form of chalk on the leather tip to increase friction so that the tip would not slip while striking the cue ball. For probably some 300 years prior, a wooden stick or mallet had been used to push or strike the balls to move them around the table into designated positions and pockets. Now for the first time while using leather and chalk, the cue ball or white ball could be struck in such a way to create all kinds of spin, "English" as they say in America, or "screw" as they say in England. That is

---

[12] "Francois Mingaud," Wikipedia. Available at: https://en.wikipedia.org/wiki/Fran%C3%A7ois_Mingaud. 29 June 2018

another story on how those words evolved which I will leave to the reader for further research.

I have no idea of François's spiritual condition. I do know that when he was released from prison [13], he embarked on a European trick shot tour using his new discovery of spin on the cue ball being applied by the use of a leather tip and chalk. At the beginning of his tour, it was his little secret and people crowded in to see his show. To add further suspense to the show, he would come out with a black cape and black top hat in a dark theatre with illumination only around the billiard table. He would announce that there was an evil spirit in the room and would point out that it possessed the cue ball and only he could control it. He would then make the cue ball dance around the table by changing direction, swerving, and curving at his command. Audiences were amazed as never before had anyone witnessed these kinds of dives, dips, and spins of the cue ball on a billiard table. We of course now know that it was simply the laws of physics and geometry appropriately applied. It was the early 1800's and people at that time were very superstitious and religious. Later, after making a lot of money and becoming famous, François Mingaud finally revealed his secret in a published template of his shots for all the world to see.

Let us fast forward some 200 years and see what became of that template of shots made famous by the late François Mingaud. Billiard Congress of America (BCA) Hall of Fame pool player Tom "Dr. Cue" Rossman, considered by many the founder of the modern-day Artistic Pool movement, used that template, plus related format guidelines from Artistic Carom competitions, as the basis of the 40-shot

---

[13] Shamos, Mike. "Arrested Development – Francois Mingaud," Billiards Digest. March 2005, p. 80-84. Print.

program for the first official WPA World Artistic Pool Championship in year 2000 [14]. Eventually serving as Artistic Pool Chairman, sponsor, referee, and tournament director, I became very familiar with all things Artistic Pool [15]. It now became the umbrella word for all types of trick, fancy, prop, and novelty shots, and "so much more" as "Dr. Cue" would say. Prior to the year 2000, there were many attempts to stage championships and give titles. Finally, the world governing body of pool -- the WPA, (World Pool Billiard Association), gave accreditation to the first ever WPA World Artistic Pool Championship event in the Riviera Hotel in Las Vegas, Nevada in May of 2000.

So where is God now? Tom "Dr. Cue" Rossman called me the year before, in 1999, after hearing about what I was doing with Gospel Trick Shot Ministries, Inc. Since 1996, I had been focused on college campuses, churches, campgrounds, and Boys and Girls Clubs. I had essentially been away from professional pool for almost 15 years. I will discuss more on this later in the book when I focus specifically on the ministry. In our conversation, Tom shared with me that he had a RACK vision, Recreational Ambassadors for Christ's Kingdom, which had been lying dormant since first revealed to him by God in 1984. What really excited me, and I knew it was the will of God, was when he said to me, "Steve, I think the RACK Vision and Gospel Trick Shot Ministries, Inc. might partner together for the sake of the Gospel." Furthermore, Tom invited me to join him in Las Vegas in May 2000 to become part of that first ever WPA World Artistic Pool Championship. I went, and this was the start of God using

---

[14] "Official Artistic Pool Sport History / Timeline," Artistic Pool Playing Artists. Available at:
http://artisticpool.org/wp-content/uploads/2018/05/Official-AP-Timeline-12_31_17.pdf. 31 December 2017
[15] Lillis, Steve. "The Spiritual Side of a World Championship," Professor-Q-Ball's National Pool and Carom News. August/September 2003, p. 42. Print. Also available at: www.professorqball.com.

the Artistic Pool movement to help expand what He was doing with Gospel Trick Shot around the world [16].

I believe the stage was being set for this movement of God in the billiard industry in the 21st century by what happened with pool in the 20th century. As previously mentioned in chapters two and three in the history of pool, there were forces at work socially, economically, and I believe spiritually as well. For example, in 1918 the Reverend John J. Phelan, not to be confused with the billiard entrepreneur Michael Phelan of the previous century, wrote a book analyzing pool and its effects on his hometown of Toledo, OH [17]. He did an extensive survey of about 250 pool rooms in this Midwestern town of about 250,000 people. This was truly Middle America in 1918. The Reverend was concerned with the effects that hanging out in pool rooms had on young men. He noted that they were forming their morals and worldview in pool rooms, for better or for worse, and mostly for the worse. Pool, as was mentioned before, was one of the most popular sports in the early 20th century. He recorded things like how many tables were in the room, he measured the lighting in illumes, he noted what was being sold in terms of food and beverage and marked how many people were in the room along with their approximate age and sex. His conclusion was not a very bright picture as he stressed that the environment was not healthy for the social and moral development of young people. However, his final recommendation was profound. He stated that the game, in and of itself, was not evil and obviously had the attraction to lure people into the sport. He suggested an alternative should be considered. He appealed to thoughtful

[16] Lillis, Steve. "Inside Pool Column - Artistic Pool – GTS/RACK Power Team Hits the Road," Inside Pool Magazine. March 2002, p. 39-40. Print.
[17] Phelan, Reverend John J. Pool, Billiards and Bowling Alleys. Toledo, Ohio: Little Book Press, 1919. Available at: The University of Michigan Libraries.

people to bring this game of pool out of these unhealthy environments and place pool tables in churches, youth centers, and schools. There, young people could be mentored and encouraged to become wholesome productive citizens. I am not sure how much influence this book directly had but this idea quickly spread to other sections of the country.

As the years unfolded, this idea of wholesome environments collided with that of the seedy unwholesome environments. People began to make their choices accordingly! Which side would win? The 1957 Broadway play "The Music Man" remember, "trouble with a capital T and that rhymes with P and that stands for pool!", basically told adults to keep their young people out of pool rooms. Then the movie a few years later entitled "The Hustler" (1961) depicted the life of a pool hustler and made it somewhat glamorous and adventurous. Pool and billiards became schizophrenic as the former sport of the crown heads of Europe was now in the hands of rogue commoners who, in the opinion of some, had trashed the royal game.

However, there was something wonderful beginning to happen in the 21st century with pool as my travels to some 27 countries with Gospel Trick Shot began to witness. Pool was on the rise in Asia and the Arab world and by no coincidence economic development, capitalism, and democracy were also on the rise in developing countries. China became the number one producer of billiard products and began to make tables and related equipment available for less cost around the world. The Philippines adopted the game from American servicemen during WWII, and now had some of the best players in the world with the likes of BCA Hall of Famers Efren Reyes and Francisco Bustamante. Filipinos as laborers are one of the most traveled people groups in the world and wherever they go they play pool, set up their own pool rooms, and revere their hero pool players.

In the Arab world, pool became a source of national pride as countries formed teams to compete among themselves and eventually with teams in the West. In the Arabian Peninsula, world championships were held for the past decade as interest peaked and spread to the Middle East and North Africa. Even in East Africa and beyond, pool tables began to dot the landscape as aspiring entrepreneurs would purchase a pool table to begin a business. It would be placed outdoors under a tree or tarp to hopefully generate enough business to get a second table or more with the thought of eventually moving indoors with the tables to sell food, beverage, and other convenience items. This, as mentioned before, was the pattern of economic development about 150 years ago in the USA. Gospel Trick Shot went to all these countries mentioned above and more to encourage and inspire pool players worldwide with the excitement of world-famous trick shot shows along with stories of faith in Jesus Christ.

# Chapter 5 – God and Pool in my Life

There is an Old Testament Bible story of the prophet Elijah where he challenged the people of ancient Israel with these words, "how long will you waver between two opinions" [18]. The people of God had one foot in the world serving the gods of their own opinions and the other foot acknowledging that the one true God exists and is worthy of worship. I found myself in this exact place as a believer prior to the start of my ministry called Gospel Trick Shot. Previously I wanted to do things that I felt should be done my way, and in effect, I was the god of my life.

For example, in 1989 my wife Camille separated from me and had custody of our daughters, Amanda and Sarah. I was a strong believer when this happened! However, this led to a crisis of faith which I will not detail here as it is all in my first book entitled "But You Must! – The Steve Lillis Story". Simply put I was between two opinions. One was to divorce Camille and remarry someone else, which many well-meaning Christian believers suggested. The second choice was to remain single and celibate trusting God to decide the outcome since my wife did not want a divorce and neither did I.

Years later I came to respect the fact that Camille chose not to waver between two opinions. She did not let a little piece of paper stop her from doing whatever she wanted. After a few years of wrestling, praying, reading the Bible, and thinking, I concluded that God's best for me was to honor my vows, invest in my daughters, and do nothing about my marital state. This enabled me to move on in freedom to serve the Lord with a clear conscience. This was the opposite of my former life of control.

---

[18] The Holy Bible (New International Version). 1 Kings 18:21

Now God was in control and I was simply responding to God's leading, trusting Him for direction and results.

Now that you know my spiritual state before the start of Gospel Trick Shot, let me share with you some of the pioneers of pool who influenced me directly or indirectly in the right direction. In addition to the Reverend John J. Phelan and his book that I mentioned earlier, there was a Billiard Congress of America (BCA) Hall of Famer named Charlie Peterson who lived out the Reverend's suggestion in the middle part of the 20th century [19]. Charlie traveled the USA promoting billiards through his entertaining and well-mannered trick shot shows in colleges, universities, civic centers, and other positive environments across the country. This man greatly influenced Tom Rossman who years later picked up the mantle and traveled the country doing something similar and more with his entertaining "Dr. Cue" shows.

At about the same time legendary pool player and trick shot artistic Mike Massey was traveling the country competing in all billiard games and doing his own special brand of trick shots. Mike is still considered today by many as the greatest trick shot artist of all time. He played a huge role in my life as many chapters of my first book tell that story. The short version is that Mike was the first to my knowledge to publicly share his faith in Jesus Christ in a pool room after one of his trick shot shows [20]. I was there the first time he shared in 1976 in Baton Rouge, Louisiana at Greenway Billiards at a championship 9 Ball

---

[19] "Charlie Peterson," Billiards Congress of America – Hall of Fame. Available at:
https://bca-pool.com/general/custom.asp?page=31. 12 October 2018
[20] . Rosenberger, Bill. "Heaven Sent – Mike Massey and Robin Bell Dodson," Inside Pool Magazine. April 2005, p. 38-42. Print.

tournament won by "Little" David Howard, the "giant killer" as he was affectionately known.

At the time, I was trapped in a life of alcohol, drugs, and gambling at 25 years old and heard the liberating gospel message of Jesus Christ since Mike himself had been delivered a few years earlier. Mike and I became lifelong friends and we traveled together as road partners in the early 1980's and then later in ministry trips both in the USA and overseas. I eventually gave my heart to Jesus. It was Mike who initially inspired me to share my faith in pool rooms. Mike and I parted company temporarily in 1985 when I quit pool as he continued with his BCA Hall of Fame career. I believe the Lord directed me to quit because it was an idol in my life. My wife Camille leaving me in 1989 really began to shape my faith journey as I surrendered more control to God.

God placed two future female BCA Hall of Famers in my life in the 1990's to help direct me; LoreeJon Hasson and Robin Dodson. My history with both went back many years. LoreeJon and I grew up in New Jersey. I used to play pool in her Dad, John Oganowski's room called Greenway Billiards partially owned by World Champion Allen Hopkins. I would watch LoreeJon practice after elementary school not realizing that someday she would become the youngest pool player ever, male or female, to become world champion [21]. Finally, in 1993 after I was out of pool for some eight years and while managing a Chick-Fil-A restaurant in Edison, New Jersey, my Christian owner boss shared with me that LoreeJon sang in his church. My boss, Tom Walsh, was not a pool player himself but just happened to go to the same church with LoreeJon and heard that she was a professional pool player. Of course, Tom knew my background and asked me if I knew her. What are the odds of this happening? My answer now would be "God to one," or out of this world! Up until this

---

[21] "LoreeJon Hasson," Wikipedia. Available at: https://en.wikipedia.org/wiki/Loree_Jon_Hasson. 17 September 2018

point in 1993, I had not seen LoreeJon for years and had no idea she was a believer in Jesus Christ. When we reunited, along with her husband professional pool player Sammy Jones, they shared with me their amazing testimony.

LoreeJon came to faith in Jesus Christ in Hershey, PA, which is known around the world as Chocolate town, USA. She had a sister that lived out there and attended the Hershey Free Evangelical Church. My parents who were missionaries with the SOWER Ministry (Servants on Wheels Ever Ready) had their home trailer park located in Hershey. My parents and I on several occasions attended that same Hershey Free Evangelical Church. On one of LoreeJon's visits around 1990, she attended that same church with her sister while her husband, Sammy, stayed back home in New Jersey with their small children. According to LoreeJon, she heard the Gospel clearly for the first time and was radically saved and filled with the Holy Spirit. When she returned home to Sammy, he immediately noticed a dramatic change as she shared with him what had happened in Hershey, PA. They shared with me that it took a few weeks of observing Loree Jon before Sammy decided that he wanted this same relationship with Jesus for himself.

When I heard this amazing testimony, I was drawn to my old pool playing friends Sammy and LoreeJon. Sammy, a youth leader at his local church, asked me if I wanted to be a special speaker at snow camp in Vermont with the youth. The last time we were together was 9 years before in 1984 at Red's Billiard Room in Houston, Texas. It was there that we competed against each other in a major 9 Ball event won by BCA Hall of Famer and Filipino legend Efren "Bata" Reyes. Sammy beat me badly and we did not part friends as his style at that time was to intimidate and aggravate his opponents, which he did to me quite successfully. Amazingly, LoreeJon, Sammy and I now began to partner together in the work of the Lord! There is so much more

I could share about their spiritual influence on me but this was all helping me to move in the direction of full-time ministry with Gospel Trick Shot in 1996.

Another female influence on my life was BCA Hall of Famer Robin Dodson [22]. Robin and I knew each other from the early 1980's when Mike Massey and I were on the road together as professional pool players. We crossed paths several times at major pool tournaments. I shall always remember Robin's amazing testimony. In the 1970's, she was a drug addict and a mother of a small child. She reached a place in her life where she could no longer put another needle in her arm because of her motherly instincts. She heard the Gospel and knew that she had to surrender her life to Jesus. She dramatically changed as a pool player. As a drug addict, she would hustle pool for money to buy drugs. God called her to be a pool player for Jesus and the rest is history. She went on to win two world championships and let the world know that it was because of Jesus in her life. Like Mike Massey, I also did not see Robin again for many years as she went on with her fabulous pool-playing career and God removed me from the professional pool scene temporarily.

Robin called me from Los Angeles in 1998 as she had heard from LoreeJon about my new GTS ministry. Robin and LoreeJon partnered together in the 1990's on the lady's pro pool tour sharing the love of Jesus with fellow players. In our phone conversation, she shared with me that she wanted to know more about what I was doing. I soon met with Robin at a pro event in New York City in 1998. I shared with her about what God was doing in my life and she helped introduce me back into the professional pool arena. I will share more about Robin and her husband Roy later in the book as they became key partners in

---

[22] Rosenberger, Bill. "Heaven Sent – Mike Massey and Robin Bell Dodson," Inside Pool Magazine. April 2005, p. 38-42. Print.

ministry with me at many amateur and professional billiard events.

I will also mention briefly here BCA Hall of Famer Tom "Dr. Cue" Rossman and the huge influence he had on my life and ministry. As you will see later in the book, we became key partners in ministry both in the USA and around the world. Tom and I knew of each other since the early 1980's but it was not until he called me in 1999 that our relationship began to take off. In that phone conversation as mentioned earlier in this book, he shared the RACK Vision from 1984 that God gave him. After lying dormant for 15 years he felt that we might join forces and begin working together in the year 2000 at the first WPA World Artistic Pool Championship. The rest is history. We will return to Tom in later chapters on the expansion of billiard ministries!

# Chapter 6 – The Bible and Hawthorne Gospel Church

In the previous chapter, I shared how God was working through people outside of my church family and in the circumstances in my life. God was also speaking directly to me through the Holy Bible and my home church, the Hawthorne Gospel Church in Hawthorne, NJ.

In 1985 I quit pool as a full-time professional player and Camille left temporarily only to come back the following year to start our family. My second marital separation from my wife Camille began in 1989 and was a devastating blow to my spiritual journey of faith and the most difficult time of my life to date! In 1989 she took our two daughters, Amanda and Sarah, away from me. We ended up in court twice before the judge. Just before the second time, the Lord spoke to me through two Bible stories. One was the story of Abraham in the Book of Genesis in the Holy Bible. In that story, Abraham was asked by God to sacrifice his son in obedience. However, God, who was testing Abraham, provided a way out. The second story involved King Solomon in First Kings where two women claimed to be the mother of the same child. Solomon said to cut the baby in two. The real mother gave up the baby and then Solomon knew to whom the baby really belonged! God was showing me to let go and let God!

In my case, I had to let my children go for seven months without visitation to restore peace. We were not in agreement on practically anything at that point and it was very difficult for the children who loved us both! Up until that second court appearance, I knew I had the legal right to see my children in a court-appointed visitation if necessary. So, after false charges were brought up against me in the form of a restraining order, I went to court and told the judge that I was willing to let my wife have what she desired. I surrendered my rights in much the same way as Abraham did with his son Isaac. I knew Camille at this point wanted me totally out of her life and the children's life as well. She told the judge that she did not want me to see the children or her again indefinitely. Eventually, visitation was restored even though our marital separation went on for a total of 19 ½ years. When my wife Camille came back in 2009, she amazingly said to me that she believed, "God took her away from me for all those years, so we could have a worldwide ministry to partner in together".

For me to last those 19 ½ years focused on ministry and a life of celibacy, I needed to once again hear from God through the Bible. In the Book of Hosea written by the prophet of the same name, his wife Gomer left him for other lovers like my situation with Camille. As I read that book, I realized that God was asking Hosea to wait for his wife Gomer just like God waits patiently for his people to come back to Him when they stray. I felt the presence of the Holy Spirit asking me to do the same and wait for Camille. At this point in my life, I wanted God's best! I was in my early 40's and had been around the block a few times in my youth doing my own thing. I had well-meaning spiritual people suggest to me that I had spiritual grounds for divorce, and maybe I did. Yet every time I read the Bible, particularly about the Apostle Paul in the Book of Acts and in First Corinthians Chapter 7, it appeared to me that it would be better to remain single for the sake of ministry. If God wanted to bring Camille back, He would in His time and in His way and He did!

My history with my home church, the Hawthorne Gospel Church, goes all the way back to the 1950's. My parents, who are now home with the Lord, attended a Billy Graham Crusade in 1957 at Madison Square Garden in New York City. As an almost seven-year-old, I clearly remember walking down the aisles from the upper deck with my parents and sister to the front of the platform on the arena floor. My parents had decided to follow Jesus and follow they did for the rest of their lives! Back home in our little town of Waldwick, NJ they went over to the Hawthorne Evening Bible School to learn the Bible from then Pastor Herman G. Braunlin. Years later I graduated from that same school. More on that later.

Now let us revisit the late 1980's and the south. Camille and I were still living together as both our children were born in Chattanooga, Tennessee in 1986 and 1988. I worked for the Krystal Corporation as a restaurant manager starting in Chattanooga before being transferred to Albany, Georgia. Since I quit pool in 1985 and surrendered my game to the Lord, I had a strong desire to go into full-time ministry. I had read a book by George Sweeting, then Chancellor of the Moody Bible Institute, entitled "A Generous Impulse." In that book, George mentioned that Herman G. Braunlin was instrumental in him going into full-time ministry. Camille and I were wrestling, and I mean wrestling, with going back home to New Jersey at the time. I wanted to stay and Camille wanted to go home to New Jersey! She wanted to share the children with family members and also felt isolated and alone in South Georgia with two little children and me working many hours for Krystal. I had prayed and asked God to show me what to do. After reading about Herman G. Braunlin and the Hawthorne Gospel Church in the book, I decided that having a church home was most important and felt a small measure of peace about leaving the south. That decision turned out to be true and was the will of God for my life and future ministry even though I returned kicking and screaming, so to speak.

We returned to New Jersey and Camille and I began attending the Hawthorne Gospel Church. I got a new job, lost it, got another, lost it too, and began to bounce around during the soon to be recession of the early 1990's [23]. Problems began to abound in our marriage. I sought out that wise old sage, Pastor Herman G. Braunlin, who had been replaced by John Minnema in 1986 after 60 years of ministry. Pastor Braunlin was living at home and struggling with dementia. Little did I know at the time that within a year he would end up in a nursing home. I went to visit him with my problems every week for maybe two months and each time he would answer me the same wise way. He would ask, "What is the Lord telling you to do this week?" That was radical in my thinking since I was used to everybody and anybody giving me their opinions about my family problems. Pastor Braunlin would constantly direct me to the Lord! I have used this principle ever since and will never forget his wise influence on my thinking!

After that second and final marital separation that started in late 1989, my home church, the Hawthorne Gospel Church, became my lifeline. Many in my church family encouraged me each week as I served and attended the church services and Sunday School classes. I began attending the Hawthorne Evening Bible School some 32 years after my parents had attended. Pastor John Minnema was now my pastor and each week it seemed like the message was specifically designed for me. By the power of the Holy Spirit, I believe it was so even though I knew others were benefitting as well. Many of the senior adults and others at the church would take me aside and gently encourage me. It seemed like they knew exactly what I was going through. As the years rolled on, the church became the foundation for Gospel Trick Shot Ministries, Inc. More on

---

[23] "Early 1990's recession in the United States," Wikipedia. Available at:
https://en.wikipedia.org/wiki/Early_1990s_recession_in_the_United_States. 29 August 2018

Hawthorne Gospel Church will be mentioned when I share what God did through the ministry around the world in later chapters.

# Chapter 7 – Gospel Trick Shot begins to take Shape

The formalizing of Gospel Trick Shot as a ministry developed over a period of about five years beginning in 1993 and culminated with the incorporation papers in the State of New Jersey on June 8, 1998. I attended Hawthorne Gospel Church from 1989 onward. There were brief periods during all my job changes where I attended other churches, but my heart was always back at Hawthorne. Even to this day as I continue to travel and visit other churches, my home church from which I was originally sent out remains Hawthorne Gospel. In the Bible, the Apostle Paul went on missionary journeys and even founded other churches, but his original home church from which he was sent out was Antioch [24]. I have followed this same Biblical pattern with Gospel Trick Shot. During that five-year period in the mid-nineties, God brought people and opportunities to do Gospel Trick Shot Ministry.

In 1993 I attended an inner-city church in Paterson, NJ called Greater Grace, which was pastored by Bruce Wright. I worked for that church as program director for their summer camp and director of their aftercare program. The church had a small school of about 60 students called Harvest Christian Academy. In return for my services, they supplied me with room and board. The church was located in an abandon funeral home that was converted into a church with classrooms and living quarters. This was a perfect fit for me as I was paying child support while my daughters Amanda and Sarah lived in Haskell, NJ some 10 miles away with my wife Camille.

---

[24] The Holy Bible (New International Version). Acts 11:19-30

While I was serving with Greater Grace, I started my teaching career in Paterson as a 4th-grade classroom teacher in the Paterson Community Christian Schools. Pastor Dr. Frederick H. La Garde was the principal and superintendent. Dr. La Garde was very influential in bringing the Rev Dr. Martin Luther King to Paterson, NJ for a civil rights march back in the late 1960's. This school was a predominantly African-American school and I was the only Caucasian teacher. When I applied for the job, I shared my vision to help the inner-city children of Paterson.

That vision was forged a year earlier while I was working at Chick-Fil-A where my boss, Tom Walsh, encouraged me to pursue teaching. I shared this with Dr. La Garde and we instantly bonded. I believe the Holy Spirit in both of us helped forge that bond. He offered me a two-year contract as I was perusing the alternate route in teaching for the State of New Jersey. I worked my two years there as a 4th grade teacher first and then 7th grade my second year. Then, I moved on to Public School 13 in Paterson where I taught 5th grade for another two years to earn more money and secure better benefits to help my family. Altogether, there were four years spent teaching elementary school in Paterson.

During that time, pastors of various churches and ministries in Paterson encouraged me to use my gift of pool to reach young people. At first, I thought this might not be a good fit since I was then a traditional classroom teacher using conventional means to reach young people. Pastor Bruce Wright of the Greater Grace Church, where I lived as a missionary school teacher with four other workers, asked me to accompany the youth group to a local pool room. His idea was for me to get on a pool table and do some of those trick shots that I learned years before from my former road partner Mike Massey. When a crowd gathered, he asked me to share something from my heart about Jesus. I realized that this was very important.

Mike Massey had done exactly that at the Greenway Billiards in Baton Rouge, LA in 1976 at a professional tournament. I was in attendance there struggling with drugs and alcohol at the time. What an opportunity, I thought, as there might be one person like I used to be right there that night that could also have their life changed. Pastor Wright had the youth group there and after I shared on the pool table, the young people engaged the crowd. Later that night, it was reported to me that two of the young people from the pool room turned their lives and their hearts over to Jesus. That was the first time God used me with a pool cue in my hand to help lead people to Christ. To me, that was an amazing experience as I now had tangible proof that God could use me on the pool table to direct others to Him.

While living and working only one town away in Paterson, NJ, I always stayed connected to the Hawthorne Gospel Church. When able, I would attend the weekly Wednesday night prayer meetings and the Sunday Evening worship services around my Greater Grace Church responsibilities. To this day, after 30 years, I continue to attend that Wednesday night prayer meeting at the Hawthorne Gospel Church. Back then in the mid-nineties, I went to Hawthorne Gospel with a need for chairs and they graciously supplied enough chairs to fill the sanctuary of Greater Grace. Also, in the mid-nineties, before the ministry was formed, I attended a Saturday morning men's prayer meeting at Hawthorne Gospel every week with 25 to 30 other guys led by my good friend Ian Grinyer. Some of my other Hawthorne Gospel friends were there like Tony Loeffler, Eddie Mack, Mike Martin, Joe Pellegrino, Peter German, and Bruce Berliner just to name a few.

We prayed not only each Saturday morning but once a month we met on a Friday night at 9:00 pm and prayed through the night until 9:00 am the next morning. Other churches in the area heard about these meetings and asked to join in. A mini-revival in North Jersey was about to start! We then began a prayer train to connect on Fridays once a month to other churches in North Jersey. On that night, we would start at the Hawthorne Gospel Church and after three hours of prayer leave and go to another church to continue praying. During those 12 hours, we would end up praying with people from two or three other churches. The Promise Keeper movement [25] was also starting at this time and we helped fuel interest in those meetings in the region. Many of those men involved in our Saturday morning prayer meetings went on to help serve on the Gospel Trick Shot Board of Directors and/or on ministry trips, with about a dozen of the attendees even starting their own ministries. I believe that Gospel Trick Shot was born out of those prayer meetings aided by the encouragement of these men. To this day we continue to pray for each other and for God to use us for His glory!

---

[25] "Promise Keepers – History," Wikipedia. Available at: https://en.wikipedia.org/wiki/Promise_Keepers. 2 October 2018

# Chapter 8 – Was It Magic?

My parents were full-time Christian workers with (SOWER Ministry) Servants on Wheels Ever Ready [26]. They traveled around the country in their motorhome helping build churches, Christian college campuses and schools. They also built and repaired buildings on ministry properties like Teen Challenge in Pennsylvania. They partnered with hundreds of other workers in the SOWER network across the USA. I had shared with my parents all that was happening back in Paterson and with my home church in Hawthorne. They encouraged and prayed with me about the future!

In the summer of 1995, while visiting my parents at their home trailer park in Hershey, PA, two amazing things happened to me. I went into the woods alone one day to read my Bible. As I read the story of Moses, I was particularly drawn to the verse in Exodus 4:2 where God asked Moses, "What is that in your hand?" Moses in the story was finding it hard to believe God could use him to deliver the Israelites from the Egyptians. He had a wooden staff in his hand which eventually God would divinely use for His purposes. Later in the story, God did use that wooden staff to do amazing things that greatly surpassed Pharaoh's magicians. I felt God was saying to me that He would use my wooden cue stick to do amazing things. Like Moses, I was doubting at this point and was wondering if he could use me with pool to do anything for His glory. I left the woods that day feeling that God had really spoken to me even though I would still struggle with this decision for the next five months.

---

[26] "SOWER Ministry," Available at: https://sowerministry.org/. Copyright 2018 SOWER Ministry

A few days later, on a Sunday morning at the campground, my mother insisted that I attend the camp meeting. Usually, on Sundays, we went into town and attended the Hershey Free Evangelical Church services. That morning at the camp meeting a gospel magician from the area named Bob Braciliano was scheduled to perform. I offered resistance but my mother won the argument and we attended the magic show.

I went cynically to the show, as I thought it was ridiculous that magic, sleight of hand, or deception could be used in any way to glorify God. Boy was I wrong and mother right! Little did I know at the time that one year later I would be mentored by Peter Everett another Gospel Magician from my home church, the Hawthorne Gospel Church. After the show, my Mom, Ellie Lillis, tactfully pointed out that usually only about 15 people show up. On this Sunday morning, there was perhaps a hundred or more interested spectators. As the sleight of hand proceeded, I became amazed and intrigued by the way Mr. Braciliano wove stories from the Bible together with the magic tricks.

When the show concluded, a dozen or more hands flew up to ask Jesus to come into their lives. I sat there in shock! My Mom insisted that I go up to the stage and talk to him. After waiting in line to talk with him, I shared about my experience with the Moses story in the woods days before and asked him if he thought that I could use pool to do gospel trick shots like his gospel magic tricks. I will never forget when he put his hand on my shoulder and said, "But You Must!" That phrase became the name of the first book I wrote in 2013.

After hearing this Moses call in the woods in the summer of 1995 and the magic show experience, I was ready to return in the fall to teach my public-school grade 5 class of students. I would also continue to minister in the inner city to young people and now was excited to listen for the voice of God in how to use my cue stick for His glory. In December 1995 just before

Christmas, I went to visit my friend Ken Resztak, who was a deacon at the Hawthorne Gospel Church. He purchased a pool table for his basement and asked me to show him a few things. It was a Friday night and it began to snow very hard outside. By Saturday morning we were snowed in. Ken was so intrigued with my trick shots that he insisted that we sit down and began to name the shots. Not only did we name the shots, we brainstormed as to how to attach a biblical message to each shot. Thus, the first Gospel Trick Shot show outline was born. Later, my shows included life lessons, science and math principles, and other attention-getting strategies all leading to a Gospel presentation.

Armed with this outline, I prayed and asked God to show me what to do with it. Within days I received a phone call from my ex-boss Tom Walsh from Chick-Fil-A, who I had not seen or heard from in a few years. He knew my past as a professional pool player and currently was working as a youth leader at his home church. He said that the young people were intrigued by the game of pool. This was the 1990's and pool was still in a mini-revival after the movie "The Color of Money" came out in 1986. A deacon from Tom's home church had purchased a pool table and the young people enjoyed going over there to play pool. He asked if I would come over and do something. This was a direct answer to prayer and we set the date for January 21, 1996. God was giving clear direction!

There was one more missing link and that had to do with my home church Hawthorne Gospel. I knew the Biblical model of ministry was to be sent out by your home church much like the Apostle Paul was in Antioch some two thousand years ago. There was an upcoming prayer meeting on a Wednesday night. Again, I have attended this prayer meeting since 1989 and continue to do so to this day. It was now January 1996 and I wanted my church to not only approve of my pool ministry but also pray and send me out as they did for many of their missionaries. This prayer meeting on Wednesday, January 19 was two days before my first show with Tom Walsh and the youth group.

I went to that meeting with much excitement and apprehension. I planned to ask the church to pray for my show coming up on Friday, January 21st. Pastor Howie Van Dyk, the associate pastor, was giving the message that night. During his message about using your gifts and talents for the Lord, he paused and remarked that he thought that I could use my gift of pool to bring glory to God. He did not know that I was about to ask for prayer that evening, and he did not know my show was scheduled in two days. I spoke right up about what I was doing, and Pastor Howie and the church prayed for me on the spot.

Was it magic? No, it was the mind of God working in just the right order, with just the right people, to bring me to a place where I could start the ministry and have confidence in Him to lead and guide all the way. God is sovereign and works uniquely with different people. He does not need a magician, a cue stick, or a Moses experience to work in the lives of people who sincerely want to know His will! However, in my case, he did exactly that! Praise God!

# Chapter 9 – The Broken Table

In my mind, the ministry began in 1996 even though it was not incorporated until June 8th, 1998. God began to bring other opportunities to do my Gospel Trick Shot shows. After that Hawthorne Gospel Church Wednesday evening prayer meeting and that first show on January 21st, things began to speed up. Word got around and I started doing shows for groups at my home church and then other local churches. That first show outline is still listed on the ministry website to this day even though it is not used. In the spring of 1996, I did other shows in and around the Paterson, NJ area as I continued as a public-school teacher.

Another Paterson-based ministry that was instrumental in the development of Gospel Trick Shot was Star of Hope Ministries. Jay Sinclair was the executive director and we developed a friendship after a series of encounters at the Hawthorne Gospel Church back in the early nineties. Jay was married to Barbara Paolino. Her Dad, Ray Paolino, was my boss at my first full time job back in 1970 at Allied Chemical Corporation in Haledon, NJ which ironically is across the street from where I now live. I was struggling in the early 70's to make sense of life as I was in and out of college, hustling pool, and looking for meaning in life. God had a plan that I would someday meet Jay Sinclair some 20 years later through Hawthorne Gospel Church and Barb's family. Furthermore, Jay came from a Salvation Army background and later I would partner with the Salvation Army on some of my Gospel Trick Shot travels.

I went to see my friend Jay Sinclair in the Spring of 1996 after visiting my parents in Phoenix, Arizona where they set up a home base after years of traveling on the road with the SOWER Ministry. I had heard a message at my parents' home church,

Phoenix First Assembly, by well-known Pastor Tommy Barnett [27]. He shared how they started this huge church of over 10,000 members by first reaching out to the poor. I thought of back home in Paterson and how I needed to use Gospel Trick Shot to help the poor. I had no pool table in Paterson at the time and wondered how I could help the needy. So, I went to speak to Jay because I knew he was serving the needs of the Paterson community through Star of Hope. They receive money and resources from suburban churches to help urban churches. I thought Jay would know where I could find a church with a pool table and he directed me to Pastor John Algera of the Madison Ave. Christian Reformed Church, right in the heart of Paterson.

Pastor John Algera [28], who retired in 2018 after 40 years of serving the needy people in that section of Paterson, is an unsung hero of the faith. Although he had never met me before, he graciously greeted me that day and genuinely thanked me for my willingness to serve the community. He said that he had a pool table, but I might be disappointed. He directed me to the youth leader of the church Sharif Bugg who took me to the youth center across the street. Up on the second floor, there was indeed a pool table, a broken pool table! I instantly replied that the table was perfect! God had put in my heart in Arizona that I was to give and serve the needy. This would be a perfect opportunity to give as I had to repair the table before I could use it to do my Gospel Trick Shot shows.

I now was on a mission to figure out how to get this pool table fixed. It had a broken leg, ripped felt, broken rails, and

[27] "Tommy Barnett," Wikipedia. Available at: https://en.wikipedia.org/wiki/Tommy_Barnett_(pastor). 30 August 2018
[28] "Madison Avenue CRC," Available at: https://www.crcna.org/churches/4561. Copyright 2018 CRC in North America

damaged and missing pool balls. By most standards, this table was ready for the garbage. This pool table represented the damaged people in this difficult inner-city area and I became even more determined.

I went to see some of my old pool room friends in the area that I have known since I was a teenager. Remember, I was indoctrinated into the pool room culture at 16 years old and became one of them. I thought this might not only be a good way to get good qualified help and advice, but I could share my new relationship with Jesus Christ with my old pals. So, I went to former pool room owner Pat Fleming and we talked, and I asked him if he could help. Pat donated cue sticks, a triangle rack, and pool balls. Then I went to pool room owner Carmine Lombardo and he donated some beautiful green felt in exchange for me to do a Gospel Trick Shot show at his pool room. Carmine had never seen my trick shots, so he was intrigued. I did a short show and there was a local pastor's son in the pool room that day who immediately ran up to me after the show with something on his heart. He said to me that he was running away from God, his home church, and his father. He said that he was hanging around in the pool room with no direction in life. He also said that he knew God had sent me to the pool room to help bring him back to his heavenly Father, earthly father, and his church. I never saw or heard from him again, but I believe he meant it! This experience motivated me even more to get that pool table fixed!

Finally, I went to see my old pool playing pal Skip Weston who lived only one block from where my children grew up in Haskell, NJ. I would stop over and visit many times after visiting my children who lived with my wife Camille. Skip and I used to gamble on pool games against each other back in the day and now he was an excellent cue stick maker. He was really handy and could fix anything. I asked him if he could come and see the broken pool table in Paterson. I told him that Pat and Carmine had donated supplies to help. Skip and I went to Paterson. He took one look and determined that it could be done in stages one rail at a time. There are six rails and each one needed a new cushion and then had to be covered with new felt. The bed of the table also needed to have a new cover of felt. The broken legs needed to be fixed and secured before the leveling process. The six pockets also needed some patchwork. The bed of slate is the most important part of the table and it was not cracked or broken, thank God! With a good bed of slate, you can work around it and refurbish almost any pool table. It took Skip about two weeks and the table was ready. My next step was to go to Pastor John Algera and youth leader Sharif Bugg to set a date to do a Gospel Trick Shot show for the kids in the neighborhood.

The first show was set for a Saturday morning and about 60 neighborhood young people came that day. These young people live in difficult circumstances as many a night they go to bed with the sound of gunshots as neighborhood gangs and drug dealers roam the streets outside their homes. The pool table performed beautifully, and I was able to speak to the hearts of these young people through the Gospel Trick Shots. When I got to the end of the show, I could see in their eyes that they were asking, "what is next?" I began to challenge them to trust Jesus for everything and about a dozen of them truly did. I received feedback from the leadership of the church that the young people truly made a commitment that day to follow Jesus and it became evident in their actions. I was so excited and thankful that God had used a broken pool table to help touch and heal broken lives.

Word spread around the City of Paterson about that pool table and I was then asked by Director Mike Melendez to do another show for the men of The Good Shepherd Mission [29]. This

---

[29] "The Good Shepherd Mission," Available at: http://gsmpat.org/. Copyright 2016 The Good Shepherd Mission

is a homeless shelter that has been serving the needs of homeless men in Paterson since 1930. Mike sent two van loads of men over to the Madison Avenue Christian Reformed Church to see a Gospel Trick Shot show. Again, the pool table performed brilliantly and the message in the show touched many of the men's hearts. I remember many hands going up in the air to ask Jesus to help them change their lives. I know it was real as I went back for years to that mission on Broadway to meet and speak to the men. Each time, I was greeted warmly and felt like one of them.

God was not yet done with that repaired pool table. After those two shows, one for the youth and the other for the homeless men, an amazing encounter with college students was about to happen. Pastor John Algera of the Madison Ave Christian Reformed Church shared with Rev. Ken Vander Wall, a campus pastor for InterVarsity Christian Fellowship (IVCF), about the previous shows. Ken went to that church and was a campus pastor at William Paterson University in Wayne, NJ one town away from Paterson. A college retreat was scheduled in that same building of the church since Ken worked alongside of other IVCF campus leaders at other local colleges. The second floor of that building had a gym and the pool table we repaired. Ken contacted me and asked if I would like to do a little demonstration for the college students. He had scheduled over 100 college students to be there for a local InterVarsity campus ministry conference representing about a dozen colleges in the New York Metropolitan area. Ken said that maybe some of the students might invite me to their campuses to do my Gospel Trick Shot show for their fellow students. I was totally amazed as after the demonstration, students lined up to ask me to come to their respective campuses. I ended up not only going to most of those colleges that were represented that day but as word spread around the country, Gospel Trick Shot was soon to go nationwide on college campuses. Praise God and thank you InterVarsity

Christian Fellowship! And to think it all started with a broken pool table! God had a plan and I was starting to see bigger things!

For me, the message behind the story of the broken pool table is that God can use everyday things. He can use anything and anybody who is willing! This important lesson served me well in my future travels as I played on many a table that was not in good condition. I would also partner with different people who had a heart for God but not much else to offer except themselves. One such person was Tony.

I met Tony at a Passaic County Community College billiard club organizational meeting. Tony did not know how to play pool but wanted to learn. He lived in Paterson across the street from my house. He would show up at my doorstep unexpectedly and we would talk for hours. I could see Tony wanted to help the ministry and all he really had to offer was his love for stand-up comedy. One of the main reasons he loved comedy was because it was an escape from the reality of a difficult childhood. My heart would break as he would tell me stories about how his mother had to give him up because she struggled with mental illness. His father was a hard worker and because of his upbringing did not know what to do with a son. Since the age of five, Tony lived with his grandmother, who was now dead. He was living alone in his grandmother's house when he met me. We became friends and partners in ministry. He would travel with me to major billiard events particularly in Las Vegas and different colleges. He became a confidant and helper and when times were tough, he knew how to make me laugh. Tony even accompanied me overseas and became a Gospel clown. He was a kid magnet and God used Tony to not only bring children to see Gospel Trick Shot shows but their parents too. Yes, God uses everyday things and everyday people and He can use you!

# Chapter 10 – Beginnings and Expansion Nationwide

My Christian growth was being noticed by my pastors at the Hawthorne Gospel Church. After the incorporation of Gospel Trick Shot on June 8th, 1998, I was invited to do a Gospel Trick Shot show for the folks of the church at the 1998 Annual Summer Bible Conference. My good friend Tim Braunlin, the son of HGC Church Founder Herman G. Braunlin, was the head of the maintenance department. He designed and constructed an arena in the open floor of the church pavilion. Using risers and bleachers, the arena could hold about three hundred people with the pool table in the center of the floor. My daughter Amanda, 12 years old at the time, sang two gospel songs while my other daughter Sarah, 10 years old, worked the Gospel Trick Shot table in the back. We had a good crowd that night and the show was like a coming out party for me. That was the first time I did a show for the church and it was well received. By the year 2000, I was accepted as a missionary by the church. I not only received support from the church, but many individuals in the church became the backbone of support for what God was about to do nationwide and then later around the world with Gospel Trick Shot (GTS).

My work and ministry continued to expand in and around Paterson. The initial InterVarsity campus ministry contacts that I made with the "broken table" kept me busy in the New York Metropolitan area. I also served as President of the InterVarsity Christian Fellowship (IVCF) at Passaic County Community College during my two year stay as a student earning my Associate of Science Degree in Computer Science. Each May, I would travel to Lake Saranac in upstate New York, to attend Basileia which is an

InterVarsity leadership training conference for the New York/New Jersey region [30]. At the conference, I would do a Gospel Trick Shot presentation and meet campus ministry leaders from various New York and New Jersey colleges and universities. They would invite me to their respective campuses for the following school year and again by word of mouth the ministry expanded. IVCF played such a vital role in the initial expansion of GTS Ministries that I even considered at one point to go full time with them. However, as you will see God had different plans! My appreciation and loyalty to IVCF always remained as I attended Urbana in 2009 as a booth exhibitor to share my ministry with some 17,000 IVCF students from all over the world. In 2012, I started and led an IVCF faculty Bible study on the campus of William Paterson University while serving there as an adjunct professor until retiring from teaching in 2016.

All these college experiences required different approaches in presenting Gospel Trick Shot shows. For example, at one college the director of the student center met me at the front door and insisted that I not do the show as planned. He realized after approving the paperwork for the InterVarsity campus ministry that I was going to share the Gospel on a pool table in a public access area. Even though this was perfectly legal, he did not want me too. I represented the campus ministry as their guest speaker and they rightly reserved part of the pool room which was in a public access area. All student-led organizations had that right! Anyway, I asked him if I could do a generic show and invite the students who are interested to hear more in a private room away from the public access area. He promptly agreed and thanked me for understanding his viewpoint. The show went on as scheduled and the crowd was

---

[30] "InterVarsity Basileia," Available at: http://ivcfnynj.org/events/basileia/. Copyright 2018 InterVarsity Christian Fellowship

invited to a private room after. Most of the students came to that room to hear the rest of my story as on the pool table I shared about my hustler lifestyle in pool and that my life changed [31]. They wanted to know what happened. When we got to the room, I was able to share about Jesus and what he did in my life. At the end of my talk, I invited these students to make that same change and many did. That day taught me that God is not limited by obstacles and that He will provide what is needed for the show to go on to give Him glory!

Word began to spread to other campuses around the country, such as the University of Minnesota in Minneapolis. My first time there was in 1999 [32]. God was about to teach me something new. Campus pastor Jeff Ballantyne was an old pool-playing buddy that had come to Jesus years before I started Gospel Trick Shot. He claimed that God used me to help him make that decision.

Back in 1980 right after Camille and I got married, I was playing in a world class billiard event called the Rocky Mountain 9 Ball Open in Colorado Springs, CO. I was almost 30 years old and playing the best competitive pool of my career. The tournament had 64 of the best players in the world with many pool players and fans in attendance. I finished 4th in the tournament and Jeff was one of the pool-playing spectators. After the event, he asked to meet with us to hear more about our travels. Camille and I were road warriors traveling 85,000 miles the previous three years playing professional pool all over the

---

[31] Garcia, Ernie. "In the Name of Jesus, He Walks Softly and Carries a Cue Stick," Herald News. An Edition of The Sunday Record, One Garret Mountain Plaza, West Paterson, NJ 07424. Front Page A1 and "Pool: Billiards Player Makes Trick Shots for Jesus," on p.6. Sunday July 1, 2001. Print.

[32] "Holy Roller," The Minnesota Daily. Volume 100, Number 61, The University of Minnesota – Twin Cities Campus, Minneapolis, MN. 14 January 1999, Front Page. Print. Also available at: www.mndaily.com.

country. Jeff wanted to hear stories about our pool playing and the people and places we had been to. He thought that he might go to some of those same places and win money too playing pool.

Camille and I took Jeff to a restaurant in a local mall and all we wanted to do was share about Jesus. We were feeling blessed in our new marriage and current billiard successes. Jeff listened intently, and we parted. He headed west and picked up some hitchhikers who shared more about Jesus with him. About one month later, Jeff called me to share that he just became a Christian and was headed to Bible school in Minneapolis, MN to go into full-time Christian ministry. When I got the phone call, I was struggling in a tournament in Port Angeles, WA. I was getting weary after playing three tournaments in a row against the best players in the world. That phone call got my mind back on God and where he would have me go next. Jeff would call me years later after he finished Bible school and remind me of the story. Every time he would call, I would be amazed at how God used Camille and me in Jeff's life!

Now let us fast forward again this time to 2003 as Jeff was excited to bring Gospel Trick Shot to the University of Minnesota and had big plans [33]. He wanted to do a campus-wide outreach and have multiple shows at multiple sites on campus. He got six different campus ministries to partner together. They were InterVarsity, Cru (formally known as Campus Crusade for Christ), Campus Ambassadors, The Navigators, Chi Alpha, and International Student Friendship Ministries. Each ministry would be responsible for the follow-up in the dorm where they held meetings. Each dorm had a pool table. Every night we would go to a different dorm and hold a Gospel Trick Shot Show with pizza and soda. We also did shows in the two large student centers on

[33] "Preachin' Pool Shark," The Minnesota Daily. Volume 104 Issue 110, The University of Minnesota – Twin Cities Campus, Minneapolis, MN. 12 March 2003, p. 4. Print. Also available at: www.mndaily.com.

campus where all the ministries could be seen working together as the Body of Christ. This turned out to be a tremendous success as over 1,000 students attended the shows with hundreds of response cards collected for follow-up. This helped to expand their ministries as students responded by either trusting Christ for the first time and/or agreeing to attend the ministry meetings on campus. The University of Minnesota became a regular stop each year for about a decade.

After one of those large University of Minnesota outreaches in Minneapolis, Jeff arranged for me to go to a little Catholic campus called Saint Mary's University in southeastern Minnesota in Winona population 27,000 on the Mississippi River. I was about to get another ministry lesson about the heart of God! When I got to the campus there was only one pool table in the middle of the student center. Then Jeff introduced me to the new Chi Alpha campus ministry with only six students. They were excited to meet me and exclaimed that they had been praying for five months in anticipation as to what God will do with this outreach. My initial thinking was focused on the one pool table which I assumed does not get much use and the six students in this small university of about 1,000 students. I had just finished another fantastic outreach at the University of Minnesota which had 55,000 students. The show was even scheduled for late afternoon which I thought was way too early.

I arrived early for the show to warm up, but God was there long before me. There was a crowd of people surrounding the pool table so I that could not even see it. I worked my way through the crowd and sensed the excitement in the room even before I hit one trick shot. The six campus ministry students were there and just smiled. I did my show, or should I say God did the show, and the results were amazing. Almost every student there decided for Jesus in some way or another. After the show, the ministry leader invited me around campus to see what was going on. I went to a few different food and beverage locations on campus and everywhere I went students were talking about Jesus and reading their Bibles. They were thanking me from the bottom of their hearts for coming. I felt ashamed for thinking those early thoughts when I arrived on campus, but God brought two Bible verses to mind. One was from Zechariah 4:10 KJV, "do not despise the day of small beginnings." The other verse was from I Samuel 16:7 ESV, "man looks on the outward appearance, but the Lord looks on the heart." To this day, I treasure what happened on that campus because of the prayers of those six faithful believing students. From then on, prayer became a more important part of the ministry.

My friend, Jeff Ballantyne, at the University of Minnesota, had many Chi Alpha connections. In the year 2000, he took me to Los Angeles to the World SALT Conference [34] to meet more campus pastors. One such pastor was Mike Olejarz who was ministering at MIT. Going to MIT opened new ways to share the Gospel. I realized that I was now dealing with a different type of student. Most campuses that I had been to before were more liberal arts oriented. MIT students were not only under a lot of stress to perform academically but were totally immersed in math and science. I knew that pool was a game with many math and science principles. I did take college level physics and calculus years before and remembered that the first five chapters of my old physics book had many billiard examples. I got that book out and began to study it from a trick shot show perspective. When I did my show at MIT, the students were fascinated. After one show I had a student ask me if he could build an instrument to measure the amount of humidity in

---

[34] "Chi Alpha – How We Got Here," Available at: https://chialpha.com/about/our-story/how-we-got-here/. Copyright 2018 Chi Alpha Campus Ministries

the room to calculate the angular momentum on the object balls after being struck by the cue ball. I could go on and on about all this as I do in my math and science Gospel Trick Shot show, but for now I will refrain. While doing trick shots, I present about 25 math and science principles. Just as I did that first time at MIT, I do this to lead up to the most important principle of all and that is to have a relationship with the Creator.

Campus ministry has always been a major focus of Gospel Trick Shot, but God had some other work for me to do. My Mom and Dad were there back at the beginning of the ministry in 1996 and lived in Phoenix. As mentioned earlier, they attended the Phoenix First Assembly Church with Pastor Tommy Barnett. He envisioned a Dream Center in Los Angeles shortly after the Watts riots in 1993 [35]. Most of the churches had moved out of the area. Pastor Tommy and his Phoenix church purchased the Queen of Angels Hospital in Los Angeles. Many of the births in Los Angeles in the prior 50 years were in that hospital. Pastor Tommy turned that facility into a huge ministry complex to house hundreds of people and disciple them to go into ministry. He also mobilized an army of workers to minister in the Los Angeles area. This was very successful and now there are other Dream Centers in other major cities.

Mom and Dad had helped to get that initial Dream Center ready when they worked with the SOWER Ministry. My Mom presented an idea to Pastor Tommy who immediately passed it on to his son Pastor Matthew Barnett, who was now the lead pastor at the Dream Center in Los Angeles. Mom knew there was a pool table available in the rec center and suggested they bring me out there to do Gospel Trick Shot. Plans were set and street gangs from the City of Los Angeles were invited. At one show, there were 45 gang bangers and 12 gave their hearts to

[35] "Dream Center," Wikipedia. Available at: https://en.wikipedia.org/wiki/Dream_Center. 19 October 2018

Jesus. One of those former gang members was in a wheelchair and I asked him to get up and shoot a special trick shot called the "Railroad Shot." He did and made the shot. He decided right then and there that he would go into billiard ministry just like me. I lost track of him until some six years later when he found me in Las Vegas at a professional billiard event. His name is George Layton and he had a love for pool since he was a little boy. I will share more about George later when I share about Gospel Trick Shot at major billiard events around the country. He is part of Gospel Trick Shot to this day.

# Chapter 11 – School to Pool

My teaching career, mostly as an adjunct professor of English at William Paterson University, went on for 23 years until retirement in 2016 and by no coincidence coincided with the Gospel Trick Shot ministry. In my teaching career, I also taught at Passaic County Community College, Kean University, the Paterson Public Schools, along with my first teaching assignment at the Paterson Community Christian Schools. I came to Paterson in 1993 to start teaching in the inner city and as a result, the ministry of Gospel Trick Shot grew out of my desire to teach and encourage young people. I saw the need to meet them outside of the classroom and so did others. This was a wonderful union of school and pool!

After my first four years of teaching elementary school, I spent the remainder of my teaching career on college campuses. With all my college contacts, I thought it would be a good idea to start billiard clubs on college campuses. Since I was already working with college campus ministries doing Gospel Trick Shot shows all over North Jersey, I now had a network of students to help start the billiard clubs. I began with William Paterson University and Passaic County Community College where I had contacts with the school administration. Once those two campuses were up and running, I presented the idea to Newark Rutgers, NJIT (New Jersey Institute of Technology), Essex County Community College, and Montclair State University. At this point, I had already done multiple Gospel Trick Shot shows at each campus and knew many people to help start billiard clubs.

To form a billiard league with college campuses, I needed a venue to hold the weekly college billiard league and the students needed transportation. I went to my friend Carmen Lombardo who owned Crown Billiards in Wayne, NJ. I asked him if he would be interested to host the league each week on a Tuesday night in his upscale pool room. He was more than happy to have 60 college students come and play each week during the school year. Now that we had a venue it was time to go back to the school administrators and get permission to transport the students. They agreed to send the students as a club team sport and took care of all the finances.

The billiard clubs were student-led organizations and had access to SGA (Student Government Association) funding. Van loads of students would arrive each week at the pool room in Wayne. I not only ran the league which we called the (MIBL) Metro Inter-Collegiate Billiard League, I also taught them how to play the game, and challenged them with life lessons through Gospel Trick Shot shows [36]. Two of our student athletes placed in the top 10 nationally at the annual ACUI College Championships [37].

The league lasted for three years until I no longer could continue to do all the administration and networking needed. We even had requests from other college campuses to join us. Looking back, my only regret was not mentoring someone to take over the league. It was more than I could handle at the time as I was now going overseas with the ministry. Years later, I would meet some of those students who would remind me of the good times we had in the college pool league.

God taught me an amazing life lesson at (UTEP) University of Texas at El Paso. This story entitled "Spiritual Warfare" is an excerpt taken from a **Gospel Trick Shot**

---

[36] Davidson, Janice. "Billiard Clubs Wraps up Semester," The Beacon Weekly. Vol. 67 No. 14, William Paterson University, Wayne, NJ. 11 Dec. 2000, p. 5. Print.
[37] Quinian, Laurie. "WPU crowns two billiard champions," The Beacon. Volume 66 No. 26, William Paterson University, Wayne, NJ. 3 April 2000, p. 22. Print.

**Newsletter** dated **March 2011**. This is one of many examples of lessons learned to help equip me for further use in God's Kingdom.

"**Spiritual Warfare** - There is a battle for the souls of men and women happening on planet earth and Gospel Trick Shot was privileged to be a part of it in two outreaches this past month. The scene was El Paso, Texas in the beginning of February, 2011. With Northern New Jersey being hit yet again with another severe snowstorm Steve Lillis had a seemingly impossible date to keep at the campus of the University of Texas at El Paso. Newark Airport was shut down with 1,500 flight cancelations, however Steve's Texas flight was one of the first to leave after the airport was reopened.

After digging out of snow and ice and driving to the airport, Steve made it to El Paso only to find that the worst winter storm in over a decade in El Paso was well under way [38]. Half the city was experiencing a blackout with the university completely shut down. Steve's baggage was lost in transit and his room on campus was not ready in time because of the school closing. At this point it became obvious that God was up to something big as host Charlie Wolcott, the President of the IVCF campus ministry, and Steve both agreed that God did not bring Steve safely and on time from Newark, NJ to El Paso, TX to do nothing and just turn around and return home. What was God up to they asked?

Over the next few hours the plan of God became a little clearer. IVCF helpers Bobby and Lorena Maddox put Steve up at their house and entered into what God was about to do. Steve and Charlie agreed that having a dorm show would be the way to go

---

[38] "Severe winter storm paralyzes the Sun City," Borderzine, by Omar Perez on February 17, 2011. Available at: http://borderzine.com/2011/02/severe-winter-storm-paralyzes-the-sun-city/.

as the school was closed and the students were trapped in the dorms with nowhere to go. Bobby printed up the flyers and Lorena gave needed suggestions. The following day Steve retrieved his luggage from the airport and picked up Charlie at his dorm and together they headed back to Bobby and Lorena's house.

There were many obstacles along the way but God's grace was obvious. After a hearty breakfast with Bobby's famous homemade waffles, it was off to the dorm for a three o'clock show. It would be nice to say that everything went smooth from there, but again God's grace in ordering the pizzas, setting up the room, and getting the word out last minute with everything shut down, was obvious to all.

The Gospel Trick Shot show was anointed in a special way as about 70 students attended and towards the end of the show you could hear a pin drop while the Gospel was being presented. It seemed so natural at that point to break out in an invitation to trust Christ, which was done and about 20 students received Christ as Savior and another 18 were interested in attending the IVCF Bible study group.

The following night we did another GTS Show but this time it was in a local pool room with IVCF campus ministry helping to reach out into the community. Again, there were many obstacles and obvious resistance as we invaded happy hour in a local pool room with the Gospel of Jesus Christ and yes, we had the owner's permission to do this! Half way through the show it became obvious that people turned from hecklers to serious listeners. At the end of the show the 10-year-old son of Bobby and Lorena walked up to Steve and said, "God won". The chief heckler at the bar who yelled out sarcastically in the beginning of the show that he wanted to go to Hell, became the most interested as after the show he shared his heart with Steve and was led to Christ.

Indeed, hearts had been transformed by the power of the Gospel and God only is to be praised!"

**End of Article.**

Those experiences with college campuses taught me a very valuable lesson in my relationship with God. Many times, people look at what they can do for God and become a worker FOR God. There is a big difference in being a fellow worker WITH God than a worker for God. I was teaching on college campuses out of necessity. At the time, I was still separated from my wife Camille and had a child support order where I had to make monthly payments. I needed the steady income from teaching to make my payments. God knew my heart for ministry and pool. He presented me many wonderful opportunities like the college pool league and other invitations both locally and nationally and I simply responded to His leading. Looking back, I realize that having to hold a steady job as a college professor was truly a blessing. Under different circumstances, I might have gone back to the road life of being a professional pool player. I was in my early fifties and could still compete with the best players in the world. By obeying God in providing for my wife and daughters, He began to orchestrate circumstances and people so that I could continue in pool and be a blessing to others.

In many ways and at so many times, I felt like the student with God as the teacher. As a teacher and administrator, God had to constantly remind me who was in charge. He was so gracious and kind as he would bless me even though I made mistakes. For example, at times I would demand too much from my students and ministry volunteers. I found it hard to give grace and forgive other people's mistakes even though I had received it myself from God. I tend to be a perfectionist with a type A personality. People would try to gently point this out to me and I would become defensive. God put up with me and had wonderful ways of showing me that I needed to change while continuing to bless me. My teaching responsibilities expanded while Gospel Trick Shot eventually became a worldwide ministry. School and pool would prosper for the glory of God! My heart's goal was to please God and looking back I realize that this is most important. We are not perfect as humans but are forgiven because of Jesus!

# Chapter 12 – Back to Big Time Pool

After my initial contacts with my pool playing buddies Loree Jon, Robin, and Tom prior to the year 2000, God was about to launch a spiritual revival in the billiard industry. In May 2000, we all came together and agreed to hold daily Bible studies at the Riviera Hotel in conjunction with the world-famous BCA (Billiard Congress of America) amateur pool league event and the first ever WPA World Artistic Pool Championship [39].

Our Artistic Pool event was held in one of the Riviera ballrooms. There was a total of 18 different billiard tournaments with 6,200 pool players and 240 pool tables all assembled under one roof. When I got to the hotel, I was met at the door by Mike Massey, whom I had not seen for 15 years. What a grand reunion with my former road partner! He took me around to about 100 vendors and key people in the billiard industry. When Mike approached a vendor or a big shot in the billiard industry they would stop and take notice. Mike was a genuine big-time billiard celebrity and probably had been on TV and in Hollywood movies more than any pool player in history. When we approached people together, Mike would announce, "Look who's back, it's Steve Lillis and he is a pool-playing preacher!" I had been away from the billiard industry for 15 years so this was a great encouragement to me that I was in the right place. There were many new people in the industry and they did not know me. God

---

[39] "Artistic Pool Playing Artists – Official Artistic Pool Timeline History," Available at: http://artisticpool.org/wp-content/uploads/2018/05/Official-AP-Timeline-12_31_17.pdf. Document compiled / updated by Tom "Dr. Cue" Rossman (Artistic Pool Foundation Historian) December 31, 2017.

used Mike Massey once again, not only to help me but also help launch Gospel Trick Shot.

Every day at the Riviera, twelve of us would meet for Bible study at 9:45 am in a Steak House that was closed during the morning hours. The owner gave us permission not only for that first year but for many more years to come. I led a devotion from the Bible and we prayed asking God for direction. Tom Rossman had asked one of the administrators if I could do a public Gospel Trick Shot show in the main arena and he said no. This probably happened because it was our first time attempting to do Gospel Trick Shot with major pool leagues, big-time promoters, and top professional pool players. We were all searching for God to lead us. He did!

The first WPA World Artistic Pool Championship was a success. Mike Massey won the tournament and Tom "Dr. Cue" Rossman took second and was the tournament director. I participated in that tournament and had planned to continue competing. Some of our fellow competitors thought that it would be better if Tom would not run the tournament and compete at the same time. Tom came up with a wonderful idea and asked me if I would be willing to give up competing and take over as director of future Artistic Pool tournaments. This was a perfect fit for me as I was more interested in promoting Gospel Trick Shot than competing for trophies and prize money. I could now serve the billiard industry in many practical ways.

In 2001/2002 I was appointed Chairman on the newly formed WPA Artistic Pool "General Committee" and continued as Chairman of the renamed WPA Artistic Pool Division from 2002 to 2004. Since 2000 these Artistic Pool umbrella structures have been recognized around the world by all of the WPA continental billiard federations. Little did I know at the time that this would eventually help connect me to travel around the world with Gospel Trick Shot. More on that in later chapters.

In 2001 we all returned to the Riviera Hotel in Las Vegas for another BCA Pool League event and WPA World Artistic Pool Championship. The BCA event was one of the most prestigious events of its time and the largest. This time things were vastly different. I was not only the tournament director of the Artistic Pool event, but Gospel Trick Shot was now a corporate sponsor. The good people at the Hawthorne Gospel Church had given me enough money to pay for eight volunteer helpers to staff a Gospel Trick Shot booth and help staff the Artistic Pool event. The Gospel Trick Shot booth had four people every day handing out helpful Christian material and meeting and greeting all the pool players who came by. We even had a prayer corner where we encouraged pool players to come and share so we could pray for them. That year the WPA Artistic Pool World Championship expanded to more players and we had more spectators. The year before we were not permitted to do a public Gospel Trick Shot show but this year, we were given permission to do whatever we wanted.

The stage was set for God to launch a revival in the billiard industry. We invited Steve Geller, a fantastic Gospel singer and a former BCA National Trick Shot Champion, to join us in a big Gospel Trick Shot show. We flew in Jeff Ballantyne, my pool-playing pal turned campus pastor at the University of Minnesota, to be the master of ceremonies. Jeff and I had worked together on his campus with Gospel Trick Shot for the past three years. Together with Loree Jon, Robin, Mike, Tom, Steve Geller, Jeff, and myself, we were excited about what God would do. We did two major Gospel Trick Shot shows at halftime at the two major Artistic Pool events. The North American Artistic Pool Championship for the BCA was first, followed by the WPA World Artistic Pool Championship. Those who qualified from the BCA event would directly move on to the World Event. Other competitors flew in from around the world to join them.

What an opportunity to share the love of Jesus with so many wonderful people.

The shows were landmark events in the history of Gospel Trick Shot. Steve Geller and Loree Jon sang beautiful Gospel songs which were amped up so that people could hear them in other ballrooms in the Riviera Hotel. There were thousands of pool players within earshot and hundreds who witnessed the show in person. Robin shared her amazing testimony about being a former drug addict and pool hustler who turned in desperation to Jesus. It seemed like there was not a dry eye in the house. Robin was a world champion and future Hall of Famer, but people did not know the rest of the story behind her fame.

Tom, Mike, and I for the first time did a tag team show of assorted trick shots mixed in with the joy of the game, testimonies, and a Gospel invitation. Tom would start with his hilarious globetrotter/tabletrotter style of trick shots to break the ice and open the hearts of the people with joy. Mike would follow with his powerful stroke trick shots that at the time no other human being could do. Then he would share the source of his power in Jesus and share his own personal testimony. I would follow with an assortment of Gospel Trick Shots containing life lessons and principles that would lead to a Gospel presentation. My years in the classroom as a teacher helped me to clearly articulate and connect with people. These two shows at the Riviera in 2001 would become the first of many [40]. Tom, Mike, and I would do over 100 shows at dozens of other events around the world in the years to come.

Here is an article written by a good friend of the ministry Roger Long who eventually became a GTS board member. It

---

[40] Lillis, Steve. "Darling Defeats Massey by One Point," Inside Pool Magazine. January 2004, p. 54-57. Print.

reflects an initial view of someone who came to Las Vegas early on and objectively viewed all that God was doing. This article was published back in **2001 in Arizona billiard publications** and a Gospel Trick Shot newsletter.

**Gospel Billiards, Anyone? Christian Pool Players Are Uniting to Become "God's Team" By Roger Long**

"In its simplest form, the word gospel means good news. In Biblical accounts, the good news began when the Son of God, Jesus Christ, miraculously rose from the dead after being crucified and buried in a tomb for three days. The good news that Christian believers have continued to spread since that event of 2000 years ago is that anyone, regardless of nationality or circumstances, can be spared from eternal condemnation by simply calling on the name of Jesus Christ and asking Him for forgiveness.

In the last few years, it has become quite common to hear high profile sports figures publicly giving Jesus Christ credit for their success. Boxers, golfers, baseball players, basketball players, and football players have all made televised statements glorifying God and Jesus. Most notably was an instance that happened last January when St. Louis Rams quarterback, Kurt Warner, loudly and proudly on national television, gave Jesus Christ the credit for his team's Super Bowl win.

The sport of pocket billiards (or pool, if you prefer) has also picked up its share of Christian believers. In 1992, Christians dominated the U.S. Open 9-Ball Championships in Chesapeake, VA when Tommy Kennedy won the men's division and Robin Dodson captured the women's division, in what their Christian fans believe was Divine Providence. Kennedy gave praise to Jesus Christ during his post-tournament interview with ESPN. A couple of other well-known Christian pool players, Loree Jon Jones and

Mike Massey, have also helped spread the Gospel during their careers.

In May of this year 2001, a group of Christian pool players were brought together for daily Bible studies at the BCA Nationals in Las Vegas by Steve Lillis, founder of Gospel Trick Shot Ministries in Hawthorne, NJ. In his promotional literature, Lillis refers to himself as *"God's Pool Player."* Lillis was at the Nationals to compete in the Professional Artistic Pool event, and as long as he was there, he thought he would see if there were any other Christians present who would like to join for morning Bible study and prayer. To Lillis' pleasant surprise, some of the most prominent people in pool came by to participate in the Christian Fellowship. Not only did the aforementioned Robin Dodson and Tommy Kennedy show up, but Belinda Campos, Darlene Stinson, and Tom Rossman joined in. Several other lesser known players heard about the meetings and ended up in attendance, as well.

Since the time of the Nationals, there seems to be a real Christian pool players' movement afoot. Members of the original Las Vegas Bible Study group have reported that they have been in almost daily contact with each other through email. They have been supporting each other with fellowship and prayer. Now, they desire to reach out to other players who have become trapped by the vices that always seem to accompany the game of pool. They want to share the Gospel with those players. They also want all of the other pool players that are already Christian believers to know that they do not walk alone. They want to invite all Christian's players to become members of their newly formed pool team, *"God's Team."*

Robin Dodson put it like this; "I would like to open the lines to more Christian pool players. I know this is helping me already with my own walk. Just being able to fellowship is awesome! It is just that one lost sheep out there that I want to be there for." Steve Lillis added, "Can you picture no one in the pool industry standing in the gap for Christ? There would be CHAOS! I can remember 25 years ago being a road player and going to the most ungodly places on planet Earth. There were pool halls with no restraint. There were players with no vision or revelation from God. Now we have a group of godly players who will stand up for Christ and keep His law."

One of the avenues for uniting the Christian pool players is through Steve Lillis' Gospel Trick Shot (GTS) Ministries. Lillis has recruited fellow Christian trick shot artists, Tom Rossman and Steve Geller, to join GTS as National Board Members. Rossman and Geller are both highly skilled trick shot artists and pool players who have become motivated to use their talents to spread the Gospel. Rossman (better known as "Dr. Cue") has actually been promoting Christian play since 1984 when he started an informal organization called RACK, which stands for Recreational Ambassadors for Christ's Kingdom.

Steve Lillis has also been encouraging a few of the professional Christian tournament players, like Robin Dodson, to develop trick shot routines and begin using their talents in this different method of spreading the Gospel. Dodson has accepted Lillis' challenge and is now working on her own trick shot routine. She plans to call her show "Gospel Glorious" whenever she feels it is ready to be taken on the road.

Another thing God's Team has decided to do is start a web site of their own. The proposed name for the new site is www.BilliardsChurch.com (note - eventually became Christian Pool Players Association). Once the site is established, pool players from all over the world will be able to contact the founding members of God's Team to gain access to Christian counseling, encouragement and support.

So why are all of these Christian pool players going to so much trouble? Well, Jesus said, "Go therefore and make disciples of all the nations, baptizing them in the name of the Father and the Son and the Holy Spirit, teaching them to observe all things that I have commanded you." That's what spreading the Gospel is all about, so you can be sure that's what God's Team will be doing.

**End of Article.**

# Chapter 13 – Expansion and Revival

After that 2001 BCA Event in Las Vegas, Gospel Trick Shot ministry began to expand rapidly [41]. In the next few years Gospel Trick Shot booths, Bible studies, and GTS shows appeared at most of the major billiard events around the country. Some of those major events included the Hopkins Expo, (APA) American Poolplayers Association Championships, (VNEA) Valley National Eight Ball Association, and of course the BCA pool league - Mark Griffin later used the official name of BCA Pool League. Teams of volunteer helpers, mostly financed by Gospel Trick Shot, would come and find different ways to serve. Bible Studies at the events grew to as many as 35 people. Those that went to the Bible studies were usually very serious about serving God in the billiard industry. They would come at 9:00 am in the morning before the vendor booths would open at 10:00 am.

Other billiard ministries began to spin off from Gospel Trick Shot (GTS). Cue4Christ was one of the first. Prayer warrior and GTS helper Elizabeth Hayes from Beaumont, TX, came up with a great idea. She had a trademarked logo and began to make shirts, hats, and towels displaying Cue4Christ with John 3:16 attached. GTS purchased hundreds of these items. Soon a small army of GTS/Cue4Christ pool players was wearing the apparel, thus proclaiming Christ. Another ministry that developed was (CPPA) Christian Pool Players Association founded by Jim Mazzulla. He became a regular at the events in the early 2000's and people began to sign up to become part of that

---

[41] Lillis, Steve. "Inside Pool Column - Artistic Pool – GTS/RACK Power Team Hits the Road," Inside Pool Magazine. March 2002, p. 39-40. Print.

ministry. Hundreds began to be mobilized across the USA by the internet and state and area leaders were appointed.

One story that involved CPPA occurred in May 2003 at another BCA Pool League event. Early in the book, I mentioned "Wheelchair" George Layton who met me at the Dream Center in Los Angeles back in 1996 after coming out of a street gang. George had decided after a Gospel Trick Shot show back in 1996, that he would use his love of pool for ministry. He had heard that Gospel Trick Shot was in Las Vegas and thought that I might be involved, but he had forgotten my name. He claimed that he had been looking for me by the name of "The Master of the Railroad Shot," since that was the shot that led him into ministry. On that shot seven years before I asked him to get up out of his wheelchair to shoot the shot and he did. Now Back to CPPA and Jim Mazzulla the Founder.

One morning during the event, I had to put out Cue4Christ apparel, Christian literature, videos, tapes, along with autographed cue balls and other materials. We also had my testimony on a glossy page with CPPA information on the back to contact Jim Mazzulla for counseling and be plugged into the CPPA network. This would enable pool players to find another Christian pool player and perhaps a church close to them. We were in Las Vegas with most of the thousands of pool players scattered from all 50 states and Canada.

On that day, George picked up the glossy Steve Lillis page. He recognized my picture on the front although he had forgotten my name. As George put it, "I finally got you." He called the number on the back which was Jim Mazzulla's with CPPA. He insisted Jim must be Steve Lillis because of the picture on the front. I was preparing the booth nearby and tuned in to the phone conversation between George and Jim. As soon as I heard the word Dream Center, I went over and taped George on the shoulder and the rest is history. We had a grand reunion. In the next few Gospel Trick Shot shows that day, George became a part with his amazing testimony from the gangs of LA to Gospel Trick Shot. George continues to this day to minister with Gospel Trick Shot to many pool players at major billiard events and back home at his local pool room in Los Angeles called Hard Times Billiards.

Also, in 2003, we went to Hard Times Billiards in LA to hold the North American Artistic Pool Championship with host and owner Kenny Thomason. Hard Times was one of the most famous pool rooms in the world. Internationally known Filipino players like Efren Reyes and Francisco Bustamante made that their home when not in the Philippines. I was the tournament director of that event and again Mike Massey and Tom "Dr. Cue" Rossman were with me as competitors. This was the home pool room of World Champion and GTS helper Robin Dodson, who lived in nearby Anaheim. Tom, Mike and I did another one of our Gospel Trick Shot shows during halftime of the event. After the show, Robin, a close friend of Kenny, shared the Gospel with him in his office and he received Christ. Kenny would go on later to become a great partner and sponsor of Gospel Trick Shot. Francisco Bustamante, who had recently lost a child, would go on to help bring Gospel Trick Shot to the Philippines years later. More on that in the Philippines chapter.

Other ministries began to spin off GTS. Tom "Dr. Cue" Rossman's RACK Vision was resurrected as pool players who were active with Gospel Trick Shot became RACK Team members. Pool rooms that had a RACK team member would become a RACK room as Bible studies and even church services would take place in that pool room. Dominic Esposito created "The Drill Instructor" with a series of pool teaching techniques. He would use his booth at major billiard events to not only sell his materials but also make it a safe place to share the Gospel and talk about Jesus. Dominic had a church in a pool room back home in Florida and is a Christian author and preacher. "Playing Safe" with Eddie Richardson came along later. He would rent booths at various major billiard events to hand out Chick Gospel Tracts and sometimes partner with Gospel Trick Shot to draw a crowd with a show.

Various billiard manufactures also began to join the movement. Longtime Christian friend and legendary cue maker Bob Meucci, who was at the first Bible Study in 2000 at the BCA Pool League event, was my cue sponsor at the time and a Gospel Trick Shot supporter. Bob had been sharing Jesus Christ long before GTS was formed. I played with one of his cues as a professional staff member back in the early 1980's. Only the top players were selected back then as Bob was the number one cue maker in the world. He gave much back to the game and would always say that the Lord gave him everything.

Other cue makers began to see what Gospel Trick Shot was doing and wanted to help. Even though some of them were not Christians, they wanted to help support us as they would say that we were helping to raise the standard of the billiard industry. Predator Cues, OB Cues, Tiger Cues, Stealth Cues, and Schuler Cues all would donate cues to give away at Gospel Trick Shot shows. This helped them to get more visibility for their products as it helped Gospel Trick Shot reach more people with the "Good News." Many other industry vendors would also donate items to be a part of what God was doing with Gospel Trick Shot. Later, McDermott Cues would become a major sponsor of Gospel Trick Shot to go around the world. More on that in future chapters.

In addition to billiard industry sponsors, various major Christian ministries became part of this expansion and revival. Radio Bible Class (RBC) Ministries was one of the first. For many of those formative years, GTS would use RBC's "Daily Bread" for devotional material at Bible studies and as free Christian literature to be given away at GTS booths. I was invited to share my testimony on the RBC worldwide broadcast entitled "Words to Live by." I talked about the separation from my wife Camille and how I was willing to wait for her return while doing GTS ministry. The broadcast was such a success that it was aired two more times. RBC's "Sports Spectrum" magazine also did a piece on the ministry. Another article on the ministry was published by the (BGEA) Billy Graham Evangelistic Association's "Decision Magazine." In 2007, the (CBN) Christian Broadcasting Network's "700 Club" did a made for TV story about my life entitled "The Pastor Shoots Pool" which was broadcast several times [42]. At the end of the broadcast, the host would make an appeal to the TV audience and invite them to trust Jesus. The phone lines would be opened for the people to respond. CBN claimed that many people came to Jesus after those broadcasts.

Billiard publications started to print articles about Artistic Pool and Gospel Trick Shot. I wrote a column for a few months for "Inside Pool" magazine about the Artistic Pool movement and Gospel Trick Shot. In March 2002 the article entitled "GTS RACK Power Team Hits the Road" was published. Professor Q-Ball's monthly national newspaper featured many articles on the Artistic Pool movement and the Gospel Trick Shot RACK Team including a front-page story in June 2004. I began to interview some of the team members and wrote articles that were published. One long article I wrote told the fascinating life story of cue maker Bob Meucci and what God did in his difficult life journey.

Amazingly God brought all this together. It was not me as too many things were happening that were totally out of my control. I realized that I did not have the time, talent, or treasure to do all this. I simply obeyed the Lord in working as an adjunct

---

[42] "Steve Lillis – The Pastor Shoots Pool," CBN.com by Will Dawson. Available at:
http://www1.cbn.com/700club/steve-lillis-pastor-shoots-pool.

professor in a local college. This enabled me to pay my child support for my two daughters and my personal living expenses. I also served my wife in whatever way she would allow me even though we were separated. God knew what He was doing, and I trusted Him knowing that He had only the best for me. God opened the doors in the proper time with just the right amount of money to go and do ministry. My motto was trust and obey -- for there is no other way to be happy in Jesus but to trust and obey!

# Chapter 14 – Professional Pool and Campus Ministry

I continued as WPA Artistic Pool Division Chairman, and Mike Massy and Tom "Dr. Cue" Rossman battled for the top two positions in many of the major Artistic Pool events. Probably the highest rated billiard show on ESPN in the early 2000's was "Trick Shot Magic". One of Mike Massey's shots, called "The Machine Gun Masse," made the top 10 weekly highlights for all sports on ESPN. The eight selected competitors for "Trick Shot Magic" were chosen by their WPA World Artistic Pool ranking and/or special invitation by the host promoter.

The format was taken from the 40-shot Artistic Pool program in which Artistic Pool players from around the world contributed trick shots. A special shot selection committee under the WPA Artistic Pool Division would constantly update and edit the program shots, as the sport was quickly evolving. "Trick Shot Magic" was seen by millions as Mike and Tom would be center stage competing. As WPA APD Chairman, I would sit in the front row and be acknowledged by broadcasters Allen Hopkins and Mitch Laurance.

After 2004, I would resign as Chairman and serve as tournament referee because of my knowledge of the shots and the players. Those TV appearances with all the popular reruns led to much airtime and visibility. As a result, Gospel Trick Shot got invited to many college campuses.

Most of the time, I went alone to college campuses as it was easier for just me to schedule Gospel Trick Shot shows around my college teaching schedule. In 2006, I invited Mike Massey to join me at Southern Illinois University. Ironically, this campus was located only about 30 miles down the road from the original site of the "Hustler's Jamboree" in Johnston City, Illinois. In the beginning chapters, I discussed the negative influence of the gambling that took place at this event back in the 1960's.

Mike and I arrived as guests of Chi Alpha Campus Ministries to promote the beauty of the game and to share our faith. We sensed that this would be a big event for two main reasons. One was that Mike was easily recognized by students as many of them had watched ESPN and Mike was a multi-time "ESPN Trick Shot Magic" Champion [43]. Additionally, the campus ministry students met every morning at 7:00 am for an hour of prayer. They met 365 days a year as they had a ministry house and a campus church pastored by Chi Alpha director Dale Crawl. We attended those morning prayer meetings and the students not only prayed for us, but also for their campus and for the world. They had a large map on the wall and routinely went around the world by prayer asking God for the nations (Psalm 2:8 NLT).

The night of the Gospel Trick Shot show was exciting. The student center director Bill Null, who was a Christian, took care of all the arrangements. He moved one of their beautiful Gold Crown pool tables and placed it in the center of a large ballroom in the student center. He circled the pool table with risers and bleachers to seat about 400 students. He had audio and visual set up to amplify the sound and record the show [44]. The campus ministry team who had been handing out invitations during the day came one hour before the show to lay hands on Mike and I

[43] "Mike Massey – Titles and achievements," Wikipedia. Available at: https://en.wikipedia.org/wiki/Mike_Massey. 7 September 2018
[44] "Mike Massey and Steve Lillis with Gospel Trick Shots at SIU in 2006," YouTube. Available at: https://www.youtube.com/watch?v=NlUpFyn-Yp0&t=13s. Published on Sep 20, 2018 by Steve Lillis

and pray. That night the room was full. There was a special presence of God in the room.

Mike and I tag teamed with each other and did two shots each until Mike stopped towards the end and gave his riveting testimony. I followed with some select Gospel Trick Shots and an invitation to trust in Jesus. On that night, out of 400 response cards that were filled out, 80 students indicated they wanted to trust in Jesus. After the show, I realize that it was all the prayer and the Body of Christ working together for the same goal that brought so many people to Jesus. It was an amazing lesson in the power of prayer and unity among God's people.

Mike Massey was elected to the BCA Hall of Fame in 2005. After our college show at Southern Illinois University in 2006, Mike had a great idea. He asked me if I would like to do a special Gospel Trick Shot show with him at his old high school back in Loudon, TN. He knew that everyone back home had seen him on ESPN for years. He wanted to have a homecoming and most of all he wanted to share his love for Jesus and the source of his fame. He purchased 900 Bibles and decided that after the show everyone would have an autographed copy. The gym was packed that night and his calculations were correct as every Bible was given out after the show.

Back home in New Jersey, my local college pool league called the Metro Inter-Collegiate Billiard League had peaked and I developed fall and spring college tours. My appearances on ESPN helped me get on more campuses. My return to competition playing 9 Ball on the UPA tour, the top professional tour in the USA [45], also helped secure invitations as students loved to challenge a top 32 ranked pro [46].

By 2006, I had connections with dozens of college campuses through the major ministry networks of IVCF (InterVarsity), Cru (Campus Crusade), Chi Alpha, and others. After that first "broken" pool table show for IVCF NY/NJ metro college students back in 1996, I had done well over two hundred Gospel Trick Shot shows on many campuses around the USA in the following decade. Just like at SIU when 80 out of 400 students made a commitment to follow Jesus, response cards came back at most Gospel Trick Shot shows with about that same 20% response rate. I do not know why but it was consistent!

Campus ministry teams would be kept busy long after I left to follow-up with each student that responded. The students would be invited out for coffee or to a special campus ministry event. There were also special investigative Bible studies that were set up for new believers. I would check back with each college and ask how the follow-up was going. However, just like Billy Graham was quoted more than once that he felt like perhaps only 10% of those who made a commitment would stay with Jesus, I too was realistic enough to know that many would not make it. Sometimes the campus ministries did not follow-up and other times the people did not show up. If there were thousands of responses through the years to GTS invitations, which there probably was in total, that would mean perhaps that hundreds are now living for Jesus. I had learned early on in ministry that

---

[45] "Official United Sates of America Rankings Released," UPA – United States Professional Poolplayers Association. Available at https://upatour.com/official-united-states-of-america-rankings-released/. Phoenix, AZ (May 6th, 2008)
[46] "UPA Tour Rankings," Pool & Billiard Magazine. October 2004, p. 116. Print.

without follow-up there would be no discipleship. Jesus told us to go into all the world and make disciples not converts.

Every August, I would send out invitations by email to campuses ministry contacts in my database and line up college shows for the coming fall. During the Holiday Season, I would again send out email invitations to campus ministries to join the spring college tour. I was teaching four college courses on two campuses each semester as an adjunct professor. I was still separated from my wife Camille and visitation with my daughters Amanda and Sarah was infrequent as they were now 20 and 18 years old respectively and in college.

Those years were perhaps the busiest and I really do not know how I kept up that hectic pace, except for the grace of God. I missed my daughters as they now had their own lives. Maybe I compensated by doing more ministry. I did not know that by 2009 my wife Camille would return to me. Looking back, I believe one of the reasons God brought her back was to help me slow down as I was constantly taking on too much during those years as financial giving to the work of the ministry reached the highest in 2008. All along, I was acting in faith and unaware of potential health risks. God surely knew what was needed and came to my rescue just in time with Camille's return.

# Chapter 15 – The World Opens Up

I mentioned at the beginning of this book that I would eventually share good news about the future of the game of pool. In the early chapters on the history of pool, I mentioned many reasons for the decline of pool and outlined historically what happened particularly in the USA.

To review, there was bad news concerning pool in the United States. By the end of the first decade of the 21st century, pool was in sharp decline in the USA. Pool rooms had closed due to high rents and the results of the Great Recession of around 2008 [47]. Smoking bans, the popularity of poker, rising fuel costs, and video games, sent people elsewhere or they simply stayed home. The best players in the world were now clearly not from the USA. By the early 2000's, the Chinese were tops in the manufacturing of billiard products and were turning out great players as well. Countries like the Philippines and Taiwan had already proven in World Championship competition that they were superior.

Europe, with countries like Germany and England leading the way, was producing top players and began to prove that they were superior to the USA. Every year the annual Mosconi Cup, put on by Matchroom Sports of England [48], became the most popular televised event in the world of pool. It featured a team of top European players against the top team of American players in head to head competition. For well over the past decade, the

---

[47] "Great Recession," Wikipedia. Available at: https://en.wikipedia.org/wiki/Great_Recession. 12 November 2018
[48] "Mosconi Cup," Wikipedia. Available at: https://en.wikipedia.org/wiki/Mosconi_Cup. 28 September 2018

American players won only once. Willie Mosconi from the USA, the greatest pool player of all time, must have been turning over in his grave as the quality of play in the USA hit an all-time low when compared to the rest of the world.

With billiard industry corporate sponsors, my connections established through serving on the WPA Artistic Pool Division board, and my home church missionary connections and financial support, I began to travel internationally in 2001. I first went to England, the country I believe was probably most responsible for bringing the cue sports to every corner of the globe. Once, it was said that the sun never set on the English Empire, and as far as billiards is concerned, I believe it is still true. You will see in later chapters as I travel that I will continue to observe this English influence. Only God could have arranged that I would go in 2001.

American 9-Ball pool was becoming popular in England. After I became Chairman of the WPA Artistic Pool Division, the (EPBF) European Pocket Billiard Federation invited me to Hull, England to the Mosconi Cue Club to do my Gospel Trick Shot show and compete in a 9-Ball event. This was a landmark event for 9-Ball in Europe as well over 100 players came from many European countries. There were many young players there that would go on to become future stars and play on European Mosconi Cup teams.

At this 9-Ball event, I had a wonderful opportunity. I did a Gospel Trick Shot show sharing about the history of American billiard artists through my trick shots. This show gives credit on each trick shot to the American performer who made it famous. Mike Massey had taught me that years before as he always gave proper credit. Years later, Mike wrote a book entitled "Mike Massey's World of Trick Shots" where he did exactly that. At this time, I would guess that most of these young European players had never seen a show like this. In addition, I added my own brand of Gospel Trick Shots that I am sure they had never seen. It has been 17 years since that show at the Mosconi Billiard Club and some of those European players still remind me about it with a smile and some kind words. I also networked with The Salvation Army and a local church while there. I did a show at the Salvation Army headquarters in Hull and brought some of the local church people back with me to the Mosconi Cue Club to help share the Good News about Jesus with the pool players. God alone knows how He was glorified that week in England.

The next country I was invited to was Germany. I was the tournament director of the 2002 WPA World Artistic Pool Championship which was held in the mountaintop resort area of Willingen, Germany. As WPA APD Chairman and tournament director, I also was initially permitted to display my Gospel Trick Shot banner in the arena. Mike and Tom, who of course where in the tournament, had planned to join me in a special Gospel Trick Shot show at the end of the event. Just as the event was about to start someone filed a complaint about the GTS banner. After much discussion, the President of the WPA Ian Anderson approved the banner. Ian and I had driven up the mountain together from the airport and he knew that Gospel Trick Shot Ministries, Inc. was a corporate sponsor and had a right to be there even though it was a religious organization.

Mike Massey won his second WPA World Artistic Pool Championship title in three years, and then we proceeded to do a special Gospel Trick Shot show for German TV. Tom would start with his unique brand of trick shots and humor and Mike followed with his amazing display of shots. I concluded with my Gospel Trick Shots and the crowd grew silent. I knew this was a hard group to reach spiritually and asked if anyone out there loved Jesus. To my pleasant surprise someone from the back of the crowd yelled out I DO, I DO!! I sensed that people began to warm up to the message. After the show, I met that young man who broke the ice! His name is Marcel Kaiser and he began to share his amazing testimony with us. Marcel became part of the Gospel Trick Shot RACK Team and began to travel with us all over the world.

Next was Kiev, Ukraine in 2003 for the 4th annual WPA World Artistic Pool Championship. We received a phone call that Marcel Kaiser was under house arrest at the airport. He forgot to bring all his legal paperwork. This was a serious problem as he could not leave or return to Germany until they verified who he was. It was a weekend and the border agents were off. Through a series of events that only God could have orchestrated, prayers were fervently prayed, phone calls were made, and hearts were moved to let him go to meet us at the tournament. When Marcel arrived, we celebrated and gave thanks to God!

Before the event, I contacted Morgan Morgulis, who had a Christian ministry in Russia called The Bridge International. He had connections with the largest church in Kiev. One of my other missionary contacts, Art Williams of (BOAM) Bible Open Air Ministries, gave me his name and Morgan was delighted to work with me. Morgan translated my Steve Lillis Gospel Tract called "God's Pool Player" into Russian as he explained that billiards was very popular in Russia. The church in Kiev gave permission for us to use their one-hour time slot to broadcast on Russian television our Gospel Trick Shot show at the end of the tournament. This broadcast had the potential to reach 290 million people in the former Soviet Union.

The tournament ended with Mike Massey winning his third WPA World Artistic Pool Championship title in four years and now the stage was set for a televised Gospel Trick Shot show. Pastor Sunday Adelaja [49], who was from Nigeria, Africa had a

---

[49] Sunday Adelaja," Wikipedia. Available at:
https://en.wikipedia.org/wiki/Sunday_Adelaja. 6 October 2018

church of thousands in Kiev and sent some of his congregation to make up our TV audience. Tom, Mike and I were in our fourth year of doing Gospel Trick Shot shows and we were able to take 20 minutes each to fit into the one-hour time slot. Morgan reported that the show was aired more than once and was a great success for the glory of God. He wanted me to expand my Steve Lillis Gospel Tract into a full-length book, so he could translate it into Russian and bring me back for a Russian book tour.

I eventually wrote that book ten years later in 2013 which was my first book entitled "But You Must – The Steve Lillis Story!" Morgan and I began working on plans to translate my book into Russian in 2014 but the war in Ukraine [50] broke out and we stopped. Tom was going to join me on that trip and we were going to Donetsk in the Ukraine which turned out to be the center of the war. Much of the conflict was over language as many Ukrainians wanted to speak Ukrainian and some Ukrainians and the Russians wanted them to speak Russian. The book was going to be translated into Russian which would have placed us in a very unpopular position with many in Donetsk. God protected us, and the trip was postponed until God reopens the door! I learned another valuable lesson. Be willing to go wherever God opens a door and continue to trust that He will guide and protect. When I go, I go in God's power, with God's provision, and with God's protection!!!

In 2004, I resigned from my position with the WPA Artistic Pool Division and went out on my own internationally [51]. Tom, Mike and I, along with other GTS/RACK team members,

[50] "War in Donbass," Wikipedia. Available at:
https://en.wikipedia.org/wiki/War_in_Donbass. 7 November 2018
[51] Timko, Sally. "The BCA International Expo Goes the Distance," Inside Pool Magazine.
May/June 2005, p. 50-52. Print.

continued to do outreach and produce Gospel Trick Shot shows at major billiards events in the USA. However, for the next eight years, I traveled with others and used my church and missionary connections to network with people on the ground in other countries.

In that same year, 2004, I traveled back to Germany to meet Marcel Kaiser for a Gospel Trick Shot tour of Germany. My Mom and her new husband Ron (my Dad had passed away in 1997) went with us as my Grandfather on my Mom's side was born and raised in Stuttgart, Germany. Marcel had arranged Gospel Trick Shot shows in billiard rooms and pubs in six different cities as he knew all the top players in Germany and the places where they played. Germany has a network of billiard rooms with club teams that go and challenge other clubs in other cities.

I also had a church contact through Operation Mobilization (OM) from my home church, the Hawthorne Gospel Church. OM started in Hawthorne, NJ area more than 60 years ago and now was worldwide. They were very active in Germany and held many street outreach evangelistic campaigns. I became part of one such outreach as young people went out into the streets to invite people into a partner local church to see a Gospel Trick Shot show. A pool table was set up in the main sanctuary with plenty of surrounding seats. We had a good crowd of over 200 people and God was glorified! I felt additionally blessed as I had the privilege of taking my precious Mom around the country that was her father's homeland.

The year 2004 was a milestone year in my professional pool playing career. I had been practicing and playing professional pool for the past three years and particularly the game of 9-Ball as it was the most popular pool game worldwide. I was making a comeback at 53 years old. I felt the Lord wanted me to play again to get more visibility for Gospel Trick Shot and ultimately to "make Jesus famous." I like this slogan, as I have heard it used by other ministries. This reminds me that it is all about Jesus. I knew Jesus did not need me to make Him famous, but pool is the gift that He gave me to use and I believe He fully expected me to use it!

The last time I played in a World Championship was the early 1980's. As I mentioned earlier in the book, I had several top 10 finishes in world championship tournaments which are a matter of record. Now it was about twenty years later, and I was selected to represent the USA in the WPA World 9-Ball Championships in Taipei City, Taiwan. I returned to professional pool playing mostly 9 Ball on the (UPA) United States Professional Poolplayers Association tour and maintained a ranking in the top 32 from 2003 -2008. In 2004 at number 21, I was invited to represent the USA in the World 9 Ball Championship as one of 128 total players selected from around the world. Years later, I was humbled when my name was given honorable mention in an article about the greatest 9 Ball players of all time [52]. I put in a lot of hard work practicing and it paid off!

I knew I could not go and just play pool as I had a much higher calling with Gospel Trick Shot. My buddy, now Gospel Trick Shot Vice President Pastor Jeff Ballantyne from the University of Minnesota, said that Pastor Dale Crawl from Chi Alpha Campus Ministries at Southern Illinois University in Carbondale, Illinois had a contact in Taiwan. I called Pastor Dale and there was a former student turned missionary serving in Taipei City and another missionary that had attended his campus church was now in Incheon, South Korea. There was a professional pool tournament in South Korea right after the event in Taiwan. I contacted Charlie Williams, the promoter of

---

[52] "The HyperTexts – Who was the best nine-ball player of all time?" Available at:
http://www.thehypertexts.com/Who%20was%20the%20best%20nine-ball%20player%20pool%20billiards.htm. Complied by Mike Burch

the South Korean tournament, and he not only gave me a formal invitation to play but also permission to do one of my Gospel Trick Shot shows. I had done some Gospel Trick Shot shows for Charlie at some of his major pro events back in the USA and he liked them since he had a Christian background himself. Charlie was becoming a big-time world pool promoter and I knew I could count on him.

Plans were now coming together for my first Asian Gospel Trick Shot tour. I had a partner church with an American missionary in Taipei City and another missionary contact in South Korea all from my connections with Chi Alpha Campus Ministries back in the States. In Taiwan, we did an outreach and Gospel Trick Shot show in the main pool room in Taipei City where all the pro players practiced. In the tournament, I met many of the young players who had seen me perform in England just three years earlier. I traveled with 12 American players who were also in the tournament. Every day I held Bible studies in my hotel room. Some attended and were curious about what I was sharing about Jesus. A few were touched and to this day continue with their faith. I won a couple of matches and eventually got knocked out of the event.

Now it was time to go to South Korea. I was welcomed at Incheon, South Korea by a missionary family who would partner with me at the professional tournament. Once again, I played and won a couple of matches before getting knocked out. I had plenty of time to prepare for my Gospel Trick Shot show which was to be held before the finals of the event. My missionary Korean translator and I rehearsed for the show so much that I was able to do all the trick shots without saying a word. She knew the storyline for each trick shot and continued speaking as I shot until she gave a Gospel invitation at the end of the show. I was the hands and she was the mouth. We were in unity as the Body of Christ. What a life lesson!

People responded and received Christian literature and contact information from a local church in Incheon, South Korea. One young man stated that God put on his heart to do Gospel Trick Shots even before seeing the show. He told me that he would work on his show and trust God to guide him how to use his gift for pool in South Korea. He updated me a few times after I left the country and I believe God really did something special that night in his heart and in the lives of others who were there. I learned that the same God who spoke to me in the USA was speaking to other pool players around the globe to use their gift of pool for His glory! I was not alone!

In the following year, 2005, I returned to Asia once again, this time China. Back in the USA, I had secured a new sponsor called Yalin Billiards of China. We became friends the year before at the Hopkins Expo. Patrick Tran, their sales rep in the USA, was trying to introduce their new line of pool tables to the thousands of people in attendance at the Expo. Their name was unknown at the time, and nobody seemed to notice them. I had an idea! I always was looking for a vendor booth to do my Gospel Trick Shot show and draw a crowd to share Jesus. I asked Patrick if he would be interested in me doing my show and then give away a cue stick as a door prize to help attract a crowd. He said the most amazing thing, "Let's give away the pool table." This was a major prize and was sure to attract a crowd. The rest is history as the crowd was huge and I shared Jesus. We gave away the pool table and people picked up all the Christian literature I had with me. Yalin became my new sponsor and the company sent me to China the next year.

The trip to China was intense on many levels. I had only 5 days as I had to return to teach my classes at William Paterson University. I was scheduled to do 14 trick shot shows in 3 ½ days at the 16th Annual International China Sport Show in Shanghai,

China [53]. After a 24-hour flight, I went right to the arena. The shows were high energy as crowds gathered around our vendor booth. Chinese TV interrogated me, cleared me, and then recorded one of my shows. Customers came to my sponsor's booth from all over the world and purchased literally boatloads of pool tables.

Every night there was a celebration feast for the top customers. Food, alcohol and women were available to all who sat at the table. My sponsor wondered why I would not drink alcohol and I explained to him that it would hurt my pool game. Then he offered me a woman and I refused. When he asked me why I said that I am a Christian and I follow Jesus. I politely dismissed myself from the table and told my sponsor that I was going swimming in the pool. I was alone in the swimming pool praying and thanking God for bringing me to China and asking him to touch my sponsor and my personal translator who I had been sharing Jesus with in English.

To my surprise about 30 minutes later, my sponsor, that very wealthy owner of the pool table company, showed up at the swimming pool and asked me to teach him how to swim. I knew this was a breakthrough. At the final meal before boarding my plane to go home, I asked my translator if she wanted to follow Jesus as she was the only person in the group who spoke English. She had been observing my behavior for days. At that last meal, she said to me that she would follow Jesus. She then asked my sponsor, the boss, in Chinese, if he would like to follow Jesus too. He looked at me with a smile and said maybe in Chinese.

I met him again back in the States at another event in Texas the following year. He had become one of the top pool

[53] "China Sport Show," Available at: http://en.sportshow.com.cn/index.html. Copyright 2008-2018 CHINA SPORT SHOW, All Rights Reserved

table distributors in the world. Through his translator, he asked me what the source of my energy and vitality was since I was 54 and almost twice his age. He saw me take vitamins and asked if I would take him to the store to get some for him. I took him and told him that vitamins are good for the body temporarily, but Jesus is what he needs for his soul and eternity. We had a language barrier, but we did not have a heart barrier. To my knowledge, he did not fully accept Jesus. However, I learned through my interactions with him and all my Chinese friends that I needed to be a witness all the time and when necessary use words. Another valuable life lesson from God!

# Chapter 16 – The Albania Project

I went to Albania for the first time in December 2003. Little did I know that I would return three more times over the next 15 years and befriend Albanians both in the USA and abroad. Eli Mema, the Director in Albania for Every Home for Christ International at the time, contacted me in the summer of 2003. She was introduced to the popularity of billiards in Albania by her father who was quite the cue artist according to her. She wanted to bring me to Albania to do a Gospel Trick Shot tour of the entire country. The country is small enough that it could be well traveled by automobile.

Eli arranged to put me up in the internationally known Stephens Center hotel [54] in downtown Tirana, the capital city of Albania. I went alone. She rented a van from a German Christian based ministry to take a team of Albanian helpers with us. Eli was the translator. She put together an itinerary which included a college campus working with Campus Crusade for Christ and billiard rooms in various villages and towns. She knew mayors and politicians and secured some local TV coverage to assist. Her goal was to increase the size of local Christian churches and plant new ones.

At the University of Tirana, students packed around the pool table to see the Gospel Trick Shot show. Television cameras were there and soon video footage and my interview with Eli as translator flashed across the country on TV news channels. In some of the villages, they now knew we were coming and prepared. The mayor and other town officials were there to greet us and make public proclamations before the shows. The

---

[54] "Stephen Center Albania," Available at: http://www.stephencenter.com/. Est. 1994

local churches and the helpers traveling with us took names and other information for follow-up. Sometimes in one day, we would cover hundreds of miles and do GTS shows in three different villages before returning at night exhausted to the Stevens Center in Tirana.

Edmund Loku, the President of the Albanian Billiard Federation [55], got word that an American professional pool player was in Albania. To my knowledge, I was the first and only American professional pool player to go to Albania at the time. I heard later from Mr. Loku that one other professional pool player from Europe had been there before me. Of course, he was English. Mr. Loku offered me a challenge to play two of his professional Albanian pool players. Eli Mema, my ministry hostess, cautioned me about taking the challenge. She said that it might be viewed by some as my God against their God as Mr. Loku was a Muslim. Eli asked me to pray and I did. I decided that this was just a pool match and it would be fun. I viewed it as a sign of disrespect if I turned down his offer. This later turned out to be true and I thank God for leading me in this direction.

I accepted the challenge and the stage was set for a showdown. Eli and the other ministry helpers stayed back at the Stephens Center and prayed. They felt uncomfortable about going because they did not understand the rules of the game and were not familiar with professional competition. I went alone, and the arena bleachers were packed and loud. This was obviously not a pro-American crowd. We warmed up before the match and the first player was ready to challenge me. It turned out that their best player was waiting on deck as he wanted to see my pool skills before playing.

---

[55] "Edmond Loku," Available at:
https://www.linkedin.com/in/edmond-loku-0478529a/detail/recent-activity/posts/. LinkedIn Corporation copyright 2018

We played American 9-Ball on Albanian tables where the pockets and balls are much smaller than American pool. This type of pool table was inspired by the English as they use similar equipment. This was the final day for me in Albania, and I had been playing on their equipment for the past 10 days, so I was somewhat comfortable. The rules were standard WPA World 9-Ball rules. I was so glad my ministry partners back at the Stephens Center were praying because I sure did need prayer under these adverse conditions. The format was that the first player to win seven games wins the match. I had to play two different players.

In the first match, we played close to even for the first few games as we were both feeling each other out. There are both offensive and defensive strategies in the game of 9-Ball. About halfway through that match, something amazing happened that I had not experienced in many years. We were playing the winner of the previous game breaks the balls open for the next rack. With the score tied at 3-3, I broke the rack of balls and the winning ball, which is the 9-ball, fell into the corner pocket. This is considered somewhat lucky as I did not plan it and is an automatic win of the game for the player breaking open the rack of balls. I broke the next rack and the winning 9-Ball fell in the pocket again. This is very rare, and my opponent was so shaken that he did not win another game. I won that match 7-3.

In my next match with the better player, the pro-Albanian crowd was expecting a different outcome. The match started off about the same as the previous one. With the score tied 3-3 once again, I stepped up to the table to break the rack of balls. At this point, the crowd appeared nervous and grew quiet. Then the most amazing thing happened that I had seen only once before in my pool playing career. It happened at my first professional tournament back in 1975 at the Hi Cue Billiard Lounge in Elizabeth, NJ against one of the top players in the country "Neptune" Joe Frady. It helped launch my pro career back then as I won that match years ago and ended up in 4th place in a tournament that had about 10 future BCA Hall of Fame players like Jim Rempe, Mike Sigel, Steve Mizerak, Allen Hopkins, Pat Fleming, and others.

Here in Albania decades later I did the unthinkable and broke the 9-Ball in the pocket three straight times! This propelled me to a 6-3 lead which led to a 7-4 match victory. After the match, my opponent and the crowd kept looking at my cue stick thinking it was magic. However, I knew it was the prayers of my ministry friends back at the Stephens Center that caused me to break the 9-Ball into a pocket a total of 5 times in two matches against the two best players in the country.

In January 2006, Mr. Loku, the President of the Albania Billiard Federation, invited me to come back to Albania right after the 2005 Christmas Holidays to teach Team Albania at a billiards training academy. This would be my second trip and the first year that Albanians could celebrate Christmas as a legal holiday. The Apostle Paul was there almost 2,000 years ago and churches were established [56]. Albania was a Christian nation for 1,500 years until the Muslim Turks converted the people to Islam about 500 years ago [57]. Then, after WW II in 1945, the country became communist and banned all religion under dictator Evander Hoxha. I thought the Christmas season would be a wonderful opportunity to return to Albania with the Good News of Jesus Christ.

---

[56] "Early Christianity in Albania," © 1988, Dr. Edwin E. Jacques, Reformation for Albania and Kosovo, Available at: https://reformation.edu/albania/pages/early-christianity-albania.htm.
[57] "Islam in Albania - History," Wikipedia. Available at: https://en.wikipedia.org/wiki/Islam_in_Albania#Conversion_and_Consolidation_(15th-18th_centuries). 30 November 2018

Mr. Loku had planned for me to come and teach the WPA Artistic Pool 40-shot program to his 12 professional pool players and their coaches. The government subsidized these players and coaches by helping them with housing and a salary. Their hope was to develop a billiard team that would be competitive with other European nations that were already in the (EU) European Union. Albania, to this day, is still not officially in the EU. They also knew from my former position on the WPA APD board that I had connections with the (EPBF) European Pocket Billiard Federation officials. Mr. Loku planned a TV special on their widely watched sports station called TeleSports. This show would feature the 12 professional players in addition to my show. He expected me to choreograph the entire show since he was unfamiliar with Artistic Pool and wanted to showcase what the players had learned.

From my previous trip to Albania in December 2003, I developed connections with other ministries. I worked with Athletes in Action, which is part of Campus Crusade for Christ now called Cru, and went to the International Protestant Assembly Church in Tirana right across the street from the Iranian embassy. The Fellowship of Christian Farmers International with George and Julie Holmes went to that church. I planned to stay in Tirana at their ministry team house. This way, I did not have to take any money from the government of Albania to teach their professional pool players. I also asked Mr. Loku if I could do my Gospel Trick Shot show on TV and he said yes.

We had a Gospel Trick Shot team of five. Scott Pruiksma of the Hawthorne Gospel Church was my personal assistant on the trip. Tony "The Clown" Anthony from Paterson, NJ came along for obvious reasons. Christian pool players and now GTS/RACK team members Marcel Kaiser from Germany and Christian Coffey from Canada came to lend their expertise. The night before the TV special we had a Bible study in the kitchen of the team house. I was reading in the Bible from Matthew 10:33 (ESV) where Jesus said, "Whoever denies me before men, I also will deny before my Father in heaven." As soon as the words got out of my mouth dishes fell out of the closet on to the kitchen floor. I stopped the group and said I believe God is speaking to us right now. We need to pray not knowing what we will face tomorrow in that TV special. It turns out that we needed those words from the Bible the next day.

The stage was set, and all was in place to start the show. Mr. Loku asked me not to mention anything religious even though he had previously agreed that I could do a Gospel Trick Shot show. With his background in communism, I could understand his view, but I was there for one main reason and that was to share Jesus. It was also still the Christmas season. I told him that we had an agreement and that if I cannot do my show then I would do nothing as I remembered the Bible Scripture from the night before. He became frustrated and I became more resolute! My translator, Edvin Dashi, was one of his 12 pool players who I had been sharing the Gospel with all week and he had already trusted Jesus. Edvin said to me, "I will do what you say and say what you say on the TV set." He later lost his job as a pool player for taking that stance. He remains a Christian servant to this day. After about a five-minute pause filled with tension, which Scott captured on our video camera, Mr. Loku agreed to let the show go on as planned.

We were not out of the woods yet. Mr. Loku told the translator in the TV sound booth not to translate anything religious even though Edvin Dashi on the studio floor would. There was also a large live TV studio audience. I had a partner with the Fellowship of Christian Farmers who reported back to me that much of my show was not being translated into my intended words. I had a special shot prepared called "The Candy Cane" Gospel Trick Shot. I brought a large three-foot candy cane from the USA in honor of Christmas. I planned to give it away in the show to a special person. Suddenly, the Holy Spirit gave me a great idea about who should be that special person.

There was a billiard hero in Albania. He supposedly kept billiards alive when the communists outlawed the game years ago as they thought it represented Western culture. I met him at my billiard training academy that I just finished teaching. God placed in my mind to bring him forward and honor him with the candy cane. Tony "The Clown" Anthony had been clowning around with the live audience in his clown outfit and everyone was in a good mood.

When I brought out our hero, I began to share the meaning of the candy cane as it tells the complete story of the Gospel. The shepherd's staff shape of the candy cane with all the stripes and red colors illustrate the life of Jesus and his death on the cross for our sins. Both translators, Edvin with me down on the studio floor, and the translator in the sound booth translated the candy cane story word for word to a live audience both in the arena and on TV. The President of Albania was watching the broadcast live and called Mr. Loku immediately after the show to tell him it was fantastic. I am sure he had a large part in getting Christmas to be a legal holiday in Albania. Mr. Loku proudly reported to me that the President not only liked the show but instructed him to play it over and over for the entire week. I was then given the honorary name in Albanian "Professor of Bilardo Artistica".

The next week was amazing as the show was broadcast 40 times on TeleSports, perhaps the most watched TV station in the country. We had planned with all our ministry connections to do shows all over the country and we did. We came to towns as celebrities as people recognized Tony the Clown first and then flocked to where we did the Gospel Trick Shot shows. We made sure to make "Jesus Famous". This was so successful that we went home and began to plan a return trip.

My love for Albanians grew and I wanted to do more on the third trip. While home in New Jersey, I went to a special training program where my good friend and fellow missionary Paul Troper, from the Hawthorne Gospel Church, was the Director. Paul was a Christar missionary and the one-month program was called (STOP) Summer Training Outreach Program which was designed for missionaries going to Muslim countries. With a large population of Muslims here in Northern New Jersey, it was the perfect place to train. There were 30 hours of classroom instruction per week and then 20 hours out in the field.

Students were taught about the principles of Islam and the life of Mohammad and then went out into the surrounding neighborhoods to meet Muslims. The neighborhoods were: Turkish, Pakistani, Iranian, Syrian, Palestinian, Jordanian, and of course Albanian. We were instructed to knock on their door and explain that we are in a training course and would like to learn more about Muslims and their culture. We were told that they would receive us as a gift from Allah and welcomed us in for coffee, tea, and food. We went to many homes and I felt so welcomed. After my training, I got a vision for not only Albania but for the rest of the Muslim world which you will see later in the book.

I began to envision teams of other Gospel Trick Shot artists being trained and sent out to do what I was called to do. I shared this vision with GTS supporters and began to receive funding to raise up a team in Albania for this project. My Gospel Trick Shot Board of Directors came alongside me in the vision. Edgar Reich, one of the board members, drew up a plan to launch teams on every continent. Albania would become a pilot program as I knew enough people in Albania to find and train our first Gospel Trick Shot RACK Team.

In July 2007, we were ready to go back for the third time. We had a new purpose and the vision expanded. From our partnership with George and Julie Holmes of the Fellowship of Christian Farmers, we now had many church connections as they had a church planting ministry. They would go into unchurched Muslim villages and set up Bible Clubs for children and give to the adults needed supplies such as eyeglasses, prosthetic devices, and seeds to plant.

Gospel Trick Shot had gone into the villages with them before to do shows. We knew that the billiard rooms in the villages were for men only but most of the church attendants in Albania were women. We came up with the idea of equipping churches with pool tables to launch coffee house billiard cafes to draw men. Our Gospel Trick Shot team would then go around to those churches and create RACK (Recreational Ambassadors for Christ's Kingdom) rooms by introducing billiards and Bible studies.

We found our GTS team with the help of our ministry friends. We hired Albanians Gysi from Athletes in Action, Fation from the Fellowship of Christian Farmers, and Edmond from the International Protestant Assembly Church in Tirana. Scott Pruiksma from the Hawthorne Gospel Church filmed us doing a Gospel Trick Shot RACK Team training video. This video had a sample Bible study and 12 GTS shots showing not only how to shoot but also a message about Jesus related to each shot. Along with our new Albanian GTS/RACK team, we compiled a list of 15 churches to receive the shipment of pool tables. The Christian Farmers had access to a truck and a place to store the pool tables after delivery by boat to Durres, Albania.

We arrived home and considered this trip a success. We secured a donor to finance a shipment of Chinese pool tables from my sponsor at a reduced price. We began to make shipping arrangements, but something came up that we did not anticipate. We were informed that to get the pool tables in the country we would have to submit to a bribe. At the dock, we would be expected to turn over five of the pool tables to government officials. We had heard about things like this in third world countries and unfortunately it was true in Albania. I began to search for other alternatives of shipment.

I contacted a Dutch ministry called Hope for Albania in the Netherlands who I knew shipped needy items to the country by truck near the mountainous region of Korce where I had ministered before. We had a church there willing to help us. The consensus opinion was that upon inspection those same government authorities would be contacted and activate the bribe. I even had a friend connected with the military who tried that option, since the U.S. had a military base in Tirana. Nothing worked, and the project was postponed in 2008. A decade later in 2018, we would return to Albania. More on that later in this book as God was not finished with our work in Albania.

# Chapter 17 - Operating on Three Fronts – International, USA Billiard Events, and Schools

Since that first international trip to England in 2001, Gospel Trick Shot has been operating on three fronts: international, college campuses, and billiard events. The previous two chapters discussed international travel to Western Europe, Eastern Europe (Albania), and Asia. By 2008, I had been to dozens of different college campuses over the past 13 years and performed more than one hundred GTS shows working with different college campus ministry organizations [58]. I was still teaching about four college courses per semester as an adjunct professor in two different colleges.

We would also return each year to major billiard events on the east and west coasts with our Gospel Trick Shot booths, Bible studies, and GTS shows. I was still playing professionally full time as much as possible and managed to maintain a top 32 ranking which afforded me some invites to pro events. My professional pool playing career was put on hold in 2009 when my wife Camille came back to me. More on that later!

Here are three stories that were published in 2003 in our Gospel Trick Shot newsletters to give specific examples of what God was doing in my life and ministry at a retail billiard industry event, a professional billiard tournament, and a college campus.

**GTS News March 2003** - The scene was in Valley Forge, PA and the event was the annual Hopkin's Super Billiards Expo. Tom "Dr.

---

[58] Lillis, Steve, with Devra Robledo. But You Must! Gospel Trick Shot Ministries, Inc., 2013, pp.180-181

Cue" Rossman, former U.S Open 9-Ball champion Tommy Kennedy, and I did a series of GTS/RACK presentations along with Bible Studies and ran a Gospel Trick Shot booth. I did one of my favorite shots at the time called the "911 Shot".

The shot is very visual with the red ball representing fire and the black ball representing smoke. The white cue ball is the plane and two other balls are placed up table representing the Twin Towers. The shot is performed with the "towers" crashing down and moving out of the way as the nine ball slides quickly up the table after being struck by the plane (cue ball) with the fire and smoke balls included in the combination. The shot has been appreciated and applauded literally all over the world. I had been using this shot for two years since September 11, 2001. On this day, there were some people in the audience that thought the shot was totally disrespectful and insensitive to people who suffered through 911. Later after much thought, I realized why.

The shot is not the focus, it is the message! The "911 shot" is to pay tribute to the policemen and firemen who gave their lives to save others. My Grandfather was a New York City fireman. This point of "sacrifice" leads to Jesus Christ giving his life as the eternal Son of God to save the lives of humans from eternal separation from God. The purpose of this shot is to share the Gospel.

One result of the shot, was that the people who were offended began complaining to others and the Gospel message was lost. Perhaps they only heard certain parts of the message and emotions kicked in! My two good friends and brothers in Christ, Tom Rossman and Tommy Kennedy, approached me with obvious concern. I became defensive and frustrated because things were going well up to that point as 40 people prayed to receive Jesus, and many were pleased with the shows all week.

Things got so frustrating for me that it became obvious to Tom that I needed prayer immediately. Tom took me behind a "pop cooler" (as they say in Indiana where he is from, "soda machine" in New York and New Jersey) and prayed for me with tears in his eyes. All I remember is that when we came out from behind the pop cooler everything seemed different and an obvious weight was lifted. We went out and had our final and best GTS/RACK presentation and God was glorified. I learned once again the power of prayer and to be more aware of how to present sensitive material to a hurting world. End of article.

**GTS News September 2003** – I was not headed in the right direction on Saturday morning August 31, 2003, on the Pennsylvania Turnpike. This was just a symptom of a much larger issue in my life. I was on my way to a very important professional pool tournament match in Philadelphia, PA. I had just won four matches the prior few days and was becoming a serious contender for the Capital City Classic UPA 9-Ball Championship. This was the third stop on the UPA Tour (top pro pool tour in the world at the time).

In my other two events in New York City and Las Vegas, I was showing promise but more so in this Philadelphia event. I also had a new pro tour sponsor called Billiard Capital, Inc and I really wanted to make a good showing for my sponsor as well. Furthermore, I had just finished with successful GTS shows out west in Las Vegas and Los Angeles, and another the night before in this tournament in Philadelphia. In the more than two weeks of travel, we had many Bible Studies and saw dozens of people accept Jesus Christ as Savior.

Back to my story! I was headed west instead of east on the PA Turnpike on that Saturday morning August 31, 2003. For three days, I had headed east from my brother Bill's house in PA to get to the tournament on time. On this morning, I headed in the "wrong direction" and did not realize it until I reached Lancaster,

PA one-hour round trip in the "wrong direction!" Immediately, I turned around and had to race back.

My match was scheduled for 1 P.M. and it was already 12:10 P.M. with one hour of driving to go. Arriving a few minutes late I attempted to play my match with almost no warm-up and ended up taking a "good" beating. I was now out of the tournament with a respectable but disappointing finish and headed back on the PA Turnpike to go home. I asked for directions, but the toll booth person unintentionally misled me, you guessed it, in the "wrong direction!" Quickly, I tried to exit the highway to avoid a bridge in the "wrong direction" and low and behold a police officer appeared in my mirror flashing his lights. I stopped and received a ticket for crossing over two lanes to exit without using my blinker. Getting back on the highway, I asked the Lord what He was trying to show me.

Back in New Jersey, I checked into a local poolroom to explain to the owner that I would not be in town for his tournament this October because my pro tour sponsor wants me to go to China. The owner was very disappointed as I gave him my word to play. I thought he would understand that the trip to China was a chance of a lifetime, but he saw it as a question of honor.

Getting back in my car, I sensed in my spirit that God had been saying to me all day long, "Steve you are headed in the wrong direction!" I knew what I had to do. I called my sponsor and canceled the trip to China, and then called the poolroom owner and told him I was wrong and that I wanted to honor my word. What about you, are you headed in the wrong direction? If so stop and make things right! God will bless that decision. End of article. I went to China two years later in 2005! Praise God!

**GTS News November 2003** - This past Spring, while on the campus of Texas A&M University, a very "strange" thing happened. I was working with a group of students from the RES

(Resurrection Week) staff doing campus outreach the week before Easter. My job was to do a series of Gospel Trick Shot shows to raise the level of awareness of Christ on campus.

The first show was poorly attended as the word did not get out due to advertising challenges. Furthermore, during that first GTS show, the prayer tent across campus blew over and the concert with Christian Artist Chris Rice had to be canceled due to a lack of ticket sales. This signaled a time for action! I went with a group of students to the "prayer tent" to pray. The campus would not allow us to put up the tent on the grass, so we tried again on the concrete with weighted buckets, but to no avail. We then decided to pray on the grass without the tent and risked, being ridiculed in the open by the many students passing by.

We began praying responsively to Psalm 91. I picked that because, before I left, my Pastor's wife Jean Richmond gave me that Psalm to read. When we got to verse 9 and 10, we read, "If you make the Most High your dwelling, even the Lord, who is my refuge, then no harm will befall you, no disaster will come near your TENT" (NIV). Right then and there a revival broke out. One of the RES students took out her guitar and we began to praise the Lord. We had students passing by and joining with us in praise and worship.

The next two Gospel Trick Shot shows had many students attend as a blackout occurred on the campus the next day and classes were cancelled. They tried to cancel the GTS shows as well, but God would not let that happen. As a matter of fact, because of the blackout, we were able to do one extra GTS show and give God all the glory. The RES students became bold for Christ as we all learned how God can easily change our plans and cause "no disaster to come near our TENT".

**End of articles.**

In addition to billiard events and GTS work on college campuses, international GTS missions was expanding. Through my home church, the Hawthorne Gospel Church, I had many contacts all over the world. My church had about 80 missionaries serving around the world and another 20 people serving on the mission's committee.

A GTS worldwide network was forming through my billiard contacts developed from WPA World Artistic Pool movement, my home church, and worldwide campus ministry organizations like Cru, InterVarsity, Chi Alpha, and others. In the years to come, there would be trips to the Arabian Peninsula in 2009, Africa 2010, Egypt 2011, a return to China 2012, and more after that. Altogether, Gospel Trick Shot has been to 27 countries with some more than once. In later chapters, I will focus on the larger outreach trips to Africa, the Philippines, and the Arab World.

On the local front, Gospel Trick Shot remained busy in the New York/New Jersey metro area similar to when it first started back in 1996 with campgrounds, retreat centers, churches, schools, and local pool rooms. One of those local shows took place at the Hall of Fame Billiards in Brooklyn, NY owned by the Balukas Family featuring BCA Hall of Fame pool player Jean Balukas. I had known Jean since she was a young girl and watched her grow up to become a champion.

Her Mom was an active Christian and had the idea to bring me to reach people in their area of Bayside, Brooklyn. We partnered with four other ministries. Teams of young people from the New York School of Urban Ministry, the Grace Baptist Church of Brooklyn, and students from two college campuses in the Midwest went out into the parks and playgrounds to bring people back to the pool hall to see a Gospel Trick Shot show.

As the show started, a street gang walked in. The leader was carrying a baseball bat and was looking at me as if he wanted to take a swing. Right in the middle of a Gospel "trick shot", I grabbed the bat out of his hand and let him know that it would be waiting for him behind the counter at end of the show. He was so stunned that he froze and listened to every word as I ended the show with an invitation to trust in Jesus. He and four members of his gang prayed to receive Jesus on the spot and the church people that were there welcomed them into the family of God. I learned to be bold for Christ no matter what the situation, knowing the will of God was my protection. This truth would serve me well later when I went to dangerous countries.

Another exciting story, from a GTS newsletter dated March 2007, was about the start of a Christian pool league in conjunction with an (APA) American Poolplayers Association franchise in Upstate New York owned by Scott Packard. Tom "Dr. Cue" Rossman did his famous "Dr. Cue" show at Hippos House of Billiards in Utica, New York which is in Scott's area. Tom could not talk about spiritual things during this show because of his contract with the APA, but Scott picked up his "subtle witness" during the show. After the show, Tom shared his personal testimony and Scott was excited and wanted more. Tom told Scott to give me a call. We talked, and I led Scott in a prayer to give his heart to Jesus. Scott wanted to serve Jesus with his APA pool league, so the two of us planned how. Here is the March 2007 newsletter explaining how the plan unfolded.

**GTS Newsletter March 2007** - The Mohawk Valley in Upstate New York spans from slightly west of Albany to slightly east of Syracuse. Scott Packard is the owner-operator of the APA franchise in this region and has been recognized as an outstanding league operator by the APA (American Poolplayers Association). The APA has the largest membership enrollment of all national pool league associations in the USA.

Scott and I began to collaborate last August on the idea of Christian pool leagues working in conjunction with the APA and Gospel Trick Shot Ministries, Inc. After I did a GTS show, sponsored by Scott's home church called Mt. Zion Ministries last August, the idea to promote the league became a reality when Mike Massey and I did a Gospel Trick Shot show at Hippos House of Billiards in Utica, NY. Mike is also a regular performer with the APA and I was once again sponsored by Mt. Zion Ministries.

Mike and I did a tag team GTS show and at the end of the performance, an invitation to sign up for the Christian Charity Pool League was extended to all. Dozens of people signed up on the spot after they realized that they could play pool in a nationally recognized pool league and compete for prizes and prestige. They also could be part of a worthy cause. Part of the money would be given to the Compassion Coalition Food Bank which is administered by the Mt. Zion Ministries Church of Utica, NY.

The APA has recognized this opportunity as a pilot program to tap into the community, particularly churches, to fuse together the fun of playing organized pool and reaching people who want to give back to their community. GTS will hopefully be partnering with other APA franchise owners around the country to launch more Christian Charity Pool Leagues. Of course, in true Gospel Trick Shot style, Jesus Christ is always presented.

Additionally, that GTS show last August helped give birth to an investigative Bible Study led by Scott Packard and held in Hippos House of Billiards in Utica, NY. I will be going back up to the Mohawk Valley later this month to do some trick shots for local TV to help promote the launching of the new APA Christian Charity Pool League. Please pray that God would bless!

**End of article.**

Later, I created a DVD of 12 Gospel Trick Shots that not only has the trick shots but the Bible scriptures and messages that are associated with each shot. This was used in the investigative Bible study held by Scott Packard which ran for 12 weeks as they used one shot per week. I learned from this that just one Gospel Trick Shot can change a life for eternity. This principle was introduced to me by one of my former mentors, Peter Everett from my home church, who used Gospel magic tricks or sleight of hand. Another friend, who is a chemist, can change water to different colors to illustrate the Gospel. What is in your hand that you can use?

Eventually, when the portable pool table came in 2013, outdoor venues became possible. Places like city parks, boardwalks in New York and New Jersey, and even outdoors on college campuses were sure to draw a crowd! The next chapter will tell that story.

# Chapter 18 – The Portable Pool Table & Bobble Ball

The story of the Gospel Trick Shot portable pool table goes all the back to December 2002. Gospel Trick Shot friend and helper Tommy Kenney invited me to Southwest Florida to do a GTS tour. Tommy ran the Southeast Pro 9-Ball tour and I was invited to compete and do my GTS shows. We held Bible studies in pool rooms for the pool players and Tommy joined me in the shows doing his world-famous pool ball juggling act. Tommy can juggle up to 12 pool balls at the same time by rolling them off the cushions around the pool table and at different speeds. Tommy has done his juggling many times in GTS shows through the years as he is a bold Christian and top professional pool player.

During this Florida trip, I visited a local billiard supply company that featured selling outdoor portable pool tables. I had gathered information before the trip and searched on the internet all over the country for a portable pool table. It appeared that the best one on the market was in Florida. I went and tried out the table by hitting pool balls off the cushions and checking the roll of the balls on the table. I looked at the construction of the wood table bed (pro tables have a slate bed) and found that underneath was a system of brackets to adjust in case the table bed began to warp. Wood is used to reduce the weight and keep the table portable as the total weight was about 300 pounds. Slate tables usually come in three pieces of slate each weighing 150-200 pounds. With the wood frame and other pieces, the total table weight is about 900-1,000 pounds. This table did not feel solid and I did not want to take a chance that it would warp being outdoors. I decided that it was not worth the $3,400 price tag and let the idea go.

Six and one-half years later in June of 2009, I was at the annual BCA Trade Show in Las Vegas. This show featured on display some of the finest billiard equipment in the world. I had been to the previous seven years' worth of shows as my pro billiard sponsors would invite me to do my Gospel Trick Shot shows in their booth to help attract a crowd. There were many buyers and sellers in the building doing business and it was always difficult to keep their attention. I usually did 10-minute mini GTS shows during the day around the business activity. This was also a good opportunity to network with industry people for possible future sponsors and most of all to share Jesus.

After one of my mini shows, a booth vendor who had been watching came over to speak with me. She introduced herself as Devra Robledo from Anaheim, California and informed me that she and her husband Fred own a company called "Wildlife in Wood" that primarily produces wood carved legs and components for pool tables. This was the beginning of a beautiful Christian relationship as Fred and Devra would later help make my first book and portable pool table possible.

Fred and Devra had been in business about 25 years and had a factory building in Anaheim. They began to design and experiment with different combinations of materials for the portable pool table. Different composite wood materials were tested in the bed of the table which is most important to prevent warping. Pockets were cut to the pro standard size. Cushions were put in place that played as well as any available on the market. Waterproof felt was placed over the bed of composite wood and the six rail cushions. The portable pool table was tested in the sun and out in the rain. They figured out how to transport the table with a dolly and bracket system that truly made it portable and easy to set up. They even had pro player Robin Dodson, a GTS friend and helper, come over and test her famous jump shots.  Robin said that she could easily jump balls. The final table played like a professional table.

While Fred was attending to the assembly of the portable pool table, Devra and I worked on the book of my life story.  By 2012 both were near completion.  The Gospel Trick Shot Board and I decided that we should have a book launch with the portable pool table.  The book was released in March of 2013 and the portable pool table was delivered from Anaheim to New Jersey that same month.

The date was set for April 11, 2013, for a Gospel Trick Shot show, book signing, and fundraiser at the Calvary Temple Church in Wayne, NJ.  That partner church had elevated seating in the sanctuary to view the show and a foyer to accommodate a buffet style reception and book signing.  My partners Mike Massey and Tom "Dr. Cue" Rossman both flew in to do the show with me.  We also announced plans to expand Gospel Trick Shot internationally and displayed by video 10 possible countries where we felt God wanted us to go and minister.  The night was a success as about 175 people invested in the vision of GTS by donating money.

With the portable pool table broken in by Mike, Tom, and myself, I was off and running in the New York/New Jersey metro area.  Four more shows followed in local churches that did not have access to a pool table.  The table rolled in and was set up in about 15 minutes, with another 15 minutes to load it back up and leave.  I could now consider outreaches and locations that previously were not possible.

That same year 2013, I received an invitation to go to Central Park in Manhattan.  Nine years before at a UPA professional pool event in Grand Central Station in Manhattan, I did GTS shows before thousands of people passing by.  Now I could do Gospel Trick Shot shows outdoors in the park in conjunction with bands as thousands of people once again would pass by. My portable table went in front of the 72nd Street bandshell in the park and when the band would take a break I would start. We stayed all day from 10:00 am to 5:00 pm as people listened to the Gospel music and stopped by to see the portable pool table and listen to me share about Jesus. Over the next two years, we did this same thing three more times.

My dream was to do Gospel Trick Shot shows on boardwalks at the New York and New Jersey shore. Having grown up in New Jersey I knew that the boardwalks were the place to go in the summer. Dale Wilden, the President of the (OGCMA) Ocean Grove Camp Meeting Association saw an article in a billiard publication on Gospel Trick Shot and contacted me. Ocean Grove is a Christian retreat center on the ocean right next to Asbury Park, NJ. Dale was an avid pool fan and had his own personal pool table in his home. He asked me to come and do a show for the youth and when he found out that I had a portable pool table our plans expanded over a period of the next three years. Multiple GTS shows were done indoors on Dale's pool table and in the youth building. Then we moved outdoors on the Ocean Grove boardwalk with the portable pool table.

Every morning while staying in Ocean Grove, I would jog over to Asbury Park on my three-mile run. As I jogged through the streets, I began to feel a burden for the people of this shore town. I knew that the Salvation Army and the Market Street Rescue Mission were there as this town was known for having people facing challenging life situations. Here I was staying in Ocean Grove with all my Christian friends enjoying the sun and fun. The burden became intense and I had to do something. The Lord reminded me that I could go anywhere with that portable pool table. I decided that I would bring it to Asbury Park the next time down. I discussed the idea with the OGCMA and the Hawthorne Gospel Church. They both got behind the idea and we planned an Asbury Park portable pool table boardwalk outreach for the summer of 2014. I shared the idea with my partners Mike Massey and Tom "Dr. Cue" Rossman and they made plans to join me.

Just prior to the Asbury Park outreach, I did a one-hour GTS show at Jones Beach in New York City. I worked with the same outreach team and bands that had invited me to Central Park. This was a success as the portable pool table was placed in the band pit and the people walking on the boardwalk had a perfect elevated view, enjoyed the shots, and clearly heard the message of Jesus. I was excited about the Asbury Park outreach as my home church in Hawthorne brought van loads of church helpers with us every day for two weeks to assist in the outreach. However, I did not realize that four hours of shows in the sun with all the set-up and tear down each day for two weeks would be too much for me.

At the time, I was too concerned about the set-up of the portable pool table and tried to do it all myself even though people were willing to help. After the first week in Asbury Park, I began to experience blackouts from exhaustion and dehydration. I ended up in the hospital and Mike and Tom finished that last week without me. Slowly, I began to realize that I had to trust people more and let them take over the set-up. Fellow GTS board member Robert Tenny took that job over and became more than a helper. He would get volunteers and take over the set-up and all I had to do was the show. In the next few years, portable pool table shows were done at the Alexander Hamilton Public School in Paterson, twice at the Preakness Health Care Center in Wayne, many local parks in New Jersey working with different churches, and other churches and school venues. I also did shows with the portable pool table at the Hawthorne Gospel Church which had a Christian school of about 500 students.

In May of 2015, I flew out to Anaheim, California and did a special GTS show for the public-school program called "Released Time" for religious instruction. This was an end of the year banquet celebration. Devra made the initial contact as it was in her hometown. This was a perfect fit for me since I started a "Released Time" program at my public school in Paterson when I was teaching back in the mid-1990's. Fred and Devra Robledo had made more portable pool tables after that first one they made for Gospel Trick Shot. I was the featured speaker and did my Gospel Trick Shot show. They set up three portable pool tables at the banquet with one for me, and the other two for the students to introduce them to a new game called Bobble Ball.

The idea for Bobble Ball came to Fred and Devra as they went around the Anaheim area to Senior Centers, YMCA's, Boys and Girls Clubs, and saw that the pool tables were not being used nearly enough. This might have had more to do with the fact that it was hard to keep cue sticks in one piece and especially hard to keep cue tips on the end of the shaft. They saw an opportunity to introduce people to the pool table with a new game called Bobble Ball which did not need a cue stick when playing the hand rolling version. Two players would stand at the head of the table with six pool balls each.

The egg-shaped (when it rolled it would roll unpredictably) Bobble Ball would be placed strategically in one of six different spots at the foot of the table. After each round, the Bobble Ball would move to the next spot. Each player would take turns rolling one ball per turn until all six were rolled by each player. The object is to bounce off one or more cushions first, and then try to roll up to the Bobble Ball as close as you can. You can hit the Bobble Ball but only after you strike at least one cushion first. Players would then learn the speed of the felt and the angle that the balls come off the cushions.

We call this the "kindergarten of pool" as children young and old, seniors, and even the handicapped can play. My Mom Ellie who had a stroke in 2002, years later would learn how to play Bobble Ball from a wheelchair with her one arm that could move. It was her favorite game.

Fred and Devra went out to visit my Mom in Phoenix to introduce the game to others in her senior citizen community. I attended and of course did a Gospel Trick Shot show. The union between Bobble Ball and Gospel Trick Shot began. In the years following, I would take Bobble Balls to college campuses to get students interacting in fellowship. I would also bring them to billiard events and introduce other versions of Bobble Ball with a cue stick.

For example, we would play Bobble Ball 9-Ball. It would be standard 9-Ball but with the Bobble Ball addition. Before players could strike the lowest numbered ball on the table (standard 9-Ball) they would have to hit the Bobble Ball after hitting a cushion first. Remember the Bobble Ball is egg-shaped and unpredictable. Players must proceed with caution and be very precise. This would not only make 9-Ball more difficult, but players would be improving their banking and kicking skills in the process. It would now take twice as many stokes of the cue stick to run all 9 balls. Even the pro players loved the challenge of this new game. This allowed more interaction in the Gospel Trick Shot booths to share the love of Jesus.

Bobble Ball continues to be part of Gospel Trick Shot as we now have some trick shots using the Bobble Ball. On one trick shot, we apply maximum spin to the Bobble Ball and cause it to rise on its side and continuing spinning for 30 seconds or more. We use this shot to illustrate that with Jesus you too can rise up no matter what difficulty you are facing. Fred and Devra even have a ministry section on their Bobble Ball website called (GUET)

God's Uses Everyday Things [59]. Devra wrote an article called the "Egg and the Scorpion" which represents the Gospel. I continue to marvel at how God uses an everyday thing like the game of pool to bring glory to Him!

---

[59] "The Egg and the Scorpion," Guet: God Uses Everyday Things. Available at:
http://www.guet.me/guet1eggscorpion.html. Copyright 2016 by Devra L. Robledo. All Rights Reserved

# Chapter 19 – From the Streets of Paterson, New Jersey to the Jungle Interior of Africa

Gospel Trick Shot started from the streets of the inner city of Paterson, NJ in 1993. I was working as a 4th-grade classroom school teacher in an Afrocentric Christian school called the Paterson Community Christian Schools. I also worked as an after-school and summer camp director for the Greater Grace Church. I did my first GTS show with a youth group outreach as mentioned earlier in the book. Little did I know at the time in 2010, I would end up in Tanzania with the Hawthorne Gospel Church and in Kenya because of a (CSRM) Christian Sports and Recreation Ministry Summit in Phoenix, AZ. God had been moving the pieces together in His time over a 17-year period.

I continue serving in ministry in the Paterson area to this day. My 23-year teaching career ended when I retired in 2016. After teaching elementary school for 4 years starting in 1993, I attended the (PCCC) Passaic County Community College, also located in Paterson, to increase my computer science skills. While there, I was the President of the InterVarsity Christian Fellowship as a student. Because I had already earned a master's degree from St. Peter's College by 1996, they offered me a position as an adjunct professor of English at PCCC in 1997. I began Gospel Trick Shot in 1996 full time, even though it was not incorporated until 1998.

Upon PCCC graduation in 1999 with an Associate of Science Degree in Computer Science and my Master's Degree (MA) in Education, I was offered an adjunct position in Computer Science at (WPU) William Paterson University. The campus is only about one mile from the Paterson border in nearby Wayne. I spent the rest of my teaching career at WPU.

My African experience roots were deeply planted as the largest people group in Paterson are African Americans. There is even a designated "Underground Railroad" [60] location. It was used before the American Civil War and is a national historical landmark. Even as a young high school boy in nearby Wayne, I always had a special place in my heart for my black brothers and sisters of Paterson. My favorite major league baseball player, Henry Aaron was black. I wanted to grow up and play in the big leagues just like him.

I played semi-pro baseball until age 20 against some the best players from Paterson. Larry Doby became the first black professional American League baseball player in 1948 [61]. He was from Paterson and I knew the history. I played on the same ball fields and always was awed with the history of Paterson. Because of all my work and ministry in Paterson, I lived in the city for 17 ½ years which is longer than any other place. I also had a bus route, driving students from Paterson to (PCTI) Passaic County Technical Institute in Wayne. They call people from Paterson, "Patersonians", and even though I was not raised in Paterson, I am one of them.

Even with all my love for African Americans, I had no prior intention of going to Africa. The closest I came to Africa was meeting African missionaries from Nigeria who came to our Paterson church where I was serving in the mid-1990's. Back

---

[60] "Underground Railroad Monument Unveiled on Broadway," Paterson Times. Available at: http://patersontimes.com/2014/11/21/underground-railroad-monument-unveiled-on-broadway/. Copyright 2012-2018 Paterson Times all rights reserved
[61] "Larry Doby," Wikipedia. Available at: https://en.wikipedia.org/wiki/Larry_Doby. 9 November 2018

then, they ministered to me and strengthened my faith as I was about to launch GTS. God was weaving together experiences and people to make a trip to Africa possible. My head Pastor, John Minnema, at the Hawthorne Gospel Church, went on a trip to Tanzania, Africa with our new mission's pastor David Schuit in 2009. At that time, I already had been a missionary with the church for 9 years. Pastor John came back from Tanzania and remarked, "We should send Steve Lillis to Africa." He noticed all the pool tables dotting the landscape in East Africa.

While Pastor John and the team were in Africa in 2009, God was preparing me that same year. I went to a (CSRM) Christian Sports and Recreation Ministry Summit in Phoenix, Arizona. They later changed their name to Church Sports and Recreation Ministries [62]. CSRM brings together over 100 Christian sports ministries each year from around the world to meet at different locations in the USA. It was convenient for me to go to Phoenix as my Mom lived there. The large church, where the meetings were held, had a pool table. I set up a GTS information booth and demonstrated on a pool table what I do. During those meetings, I received an invitation to Africa from Pastor Kennedy Salano of Kariobangi, near Nairobi, Kenya. He said that many of the young people play pool and that he could use it to help build his church and Christian school.

I began to pray and ask God to provide for a possible trip to Africa. Back home, my missions pastor David Schuit gave me a formal invitation to join him and a Hawthorne Gospel Church team to go to Tanzania in 2010. He said that I could provide the recreation through billiards, while the medical teams minister to the people on the Islands of Lake Victoria. Pastor Dave

---

[62] "CSRM," Church Sports and Recreation Ministries. Available at: http://www.csrm.org/copy-of-home.html. Copyright 2018 | The Association of Church Sports and Recreation Ministries | All rights reserved

envisioned that I would do a Gospel Trick Shot show as part of a Sunday morning service while he serves as my Swahili translator. Now half of the trip was covered and now I prayed for Kenya and Pastor Kennedy Salano in Kariobangi, near Nairobi. My home church was not going to Kenya at that time, so I was on my own, at least financially, as they always cover me in prayer wherever I go.

God had three more special provisions in mind for that Kenya part of the journey in 2010. In 2008, at the BCA Trade Show where I first met Fred and Devra, who made our portable pool table, I met Greg Knight the new owner of the McDermott Cue Company. He is a Christian and when he heard what I was doing with Gospel Trick Shot, he offered to help me with my travels internationally. Also, that same year, I met Jason "The Michigan Kid" Lynch who was an outstanding professional Artistic Pool player and plays with a McDermott cue stick. Jason gave his heart to Jesus at one of our Las Vegas events and publicly shared his faith in Christ. With his knowledge of trick shots, he began to come up with his own brand of Gospel Trick Shots. Jason offered to accompany me to Kenya with McDermott providing his expenses.

A final piece to this puzzle was getting a pool table delivered to Kariobangi. I had a new pro tour sponsor, Thomas Aaron Billiards, who replaced my Chinese sponsor. The owner was Thomas Cartwright and the company was in Florida. He is a Christian and wanted to help with the ministry so he donated a pool table to be shipped to Africa. My mission's pastor David Schuit informed me about containers that were packed and shipped by (AIM) Africa Inland Mission each year in Pearl River, New York which is near our church. The container is shipped from there to Africa. AIM was the organization that was making all the arrangements for us in Tanzania, so this was truly a blessing.

Again, I was reminded that when God wants me to go somewhere for His glory, He will provide all that is needed. Below are two Gospel Trick Shot Newsletters that were published in 2010 reporting on the results of this trip to Africa.

**GTS Newsletter July 2010** - On May 30th, we left New Jersey for Nairobi, Kenya for a two day stop over. We rested and planned for a return trip to Nairobi ten days later. While there, the team stayed at the AIM Mayfield Guesthouse and conducted a series of meetings with the Kenya Pool Club with the "Sport for Good" Campaign, the Kariobangi North Kenya AG Church, and TJ Ministries.

Plans were set for a return trip to Nairobi after ministry on the Islands of Lake Victoria in Tanzania. The team arrived in Mwanza, Tanzania on the shores of Lake Victoria and met with short-term missionaries from the Hawthorne Gospel Church and permanent missionaries stationed on the islands. Our goal was to conduct various athletic competitions with me directing a pool tournament, conducting challenge matches, and performing GTS shots to share the Gospel of our Lord Jesus Christ.

After two days of competition, I had the privilege of being the closing speaker on the third day at the Sunday morning service and we had an altar call with the GTS shot called "TRUST". Dozens of island natives came forward near the pool table to put their trust in the Lord Jesus Christ. Praise God! The Hawthorne Gospel Church team spent four more days in the interior of Tanzania visiting the Nassa Theological College (NTC) and Majahida Bible Training School (MBTS). GTS proposed a "Gospel Trick Shot" Scholarship Program at MBTS and hopefully, our first student will be one of the pool competitors who came to Christ on the island of Iramba in Lake Victoria during the sport's crusade.

The Hawthorne Gospel Church Short-Term Mission Team and I parted company in Nairobi as they prepared to return home while I stayed on to minister in Kenya. Jason "The Michigan Kid" Lynch met me at the Nairobi Airport as Pastor Kennedy Salano of the Kariobangi Kenya AG Church picked us up. Pastor Kennedy arranged all the accommodations. Jason had recently joined me in partnership with GTS as he is also a world-class trick shot artist. We welcome Jason with all the various gifts and talents the Lord has given him to be used for God's purposes. Jason and I spent much time training local Africans Nelson Mathiu and John Mburu. Together, they make up our GTS/RACK Africa Team. They are students at the East Africa School of Theology (EAST) and both answered the call of God to do GTS ministry when Pastor Kennedy Salano, our host, who is a professor at the school, shared the GTS vision.

The two young men both have backgrounds with pool and have answered God's call to be trained as evangelists with pool in Africa. GTS gave them over $1,000 in equipment and supplies including brand new McDermott Cue Sticks. They were given hands-on knowledge and experience in setting up the Thomas Aaron pool table that was shipped from America to the (KAG) Kenya Assemblies of God Kariobangi Church. The young men will report to Pastor Kennedy Salano who oversees the team.

Nelson and John now have the tools of the trade to make money as pool tables are plentiful in Kenya. Nelson remarked, "I can get married now because I have a source of income". GTS shows and tournaments were done with the GTS Team of Jason, Nelson, John, Teresa, Pastor Kennedy, and myself. Locations included the Mathare and Kariobangi North slums and the EAST college campus. A special GTS show was done for the Kenya College Pool Championships in the upscale "Village Market" shopping center in conjunction with the Kenya Pool Club and the "Sport for Good" campaign.

Two churches in Nairobi invited me to preach and I taught classes at the EAST Bible College on "Leadership" and "Cross-Cultural Communication." Jason, myself, and Teresa of TJ Ministries had the privilege of dining with the Bishop who oversees 3,500 Kenya AG churches. He has given his blessing for us to work with all under him in the country of Kenya. They invited GTS to work with some of their missionaries next year on the ground in North Kenya near Somalia where it is mostly Muslim.

There was a terrorist attack on a Christian prayer meeting in Nairobi close to where we were staying as seven people died and hundreds were injured. We considered going! Please pray for God's protection for the Christians in Kenya. We would like to thank all our many supporters and prayer partners. We did not have the time or money to take a safari and still ended up $800 over budget. We trust the Lord to continue to supply through His people. God bless you!

**GTS Newsletter October 2010** - Pastor Kennedy Salano of the Kariobangi North KAG Church leads the Gospel Trick Shot team of Nelson Mathiu and John Mburu who are students at the East Africa School of Theology in Nairobi, Kenya. This past Spring 2010, Africa Inland Mission delivered a beautiful Thomas Aaron pool table to Pastor Kennedy's church in Kariobangi which is a slum area of Nairobi. Pastor Kennedy reports from his church about the pool table:

"I chase the boys away at times as they stay playing pool till night. The Mathare boys yesterday asked me when the next tournament is. We will arrange with Nelson on how we can plan for another evangelistic tournament soon. Thanks"

The "boys" are the young men in the Kariobangi and Mathare slums in Nairobi where GTS worked this past summer. We need Nelson and John, who were trained by Jason Lynch and me last June, to work with all these young people as they are clamoring for more pool with supervision. Nelson and John were trained to run outreach events and have all the tools needed. GTS is supporting them partially and we need help. John recently had to leave Bible school. This puts him out of the area to do GTS ministry. John recently wrote:

"I am pleased hearing from you once again. I am currently writing this from my brother in law to be's house who is programmed to wed on the 25th. An encounter I am honestly excited about. It feels nice in my spot, trust me. Meanwhile, I take this opportunity to thank you for all what you are doing for Christ's sake, and for the extension of His kingdom.

About school, it would cost a lot even if I wasn't boarding in school. It would cost even more just in case boarding is a thought worth thinking about. I am freely flexible on any account of the above two encounters.

And now about the table. I am finding it hard forming a procedure before I make a shot, and remember you say that it was necessary. I was just wondering if you would share what you personally prefer right before you go down into the shot. Plus, probably a couple of steps after the shot. Your assistance will be of tremendous help.

Mum says hi, at least she can now stand up straight and probably walk a little bit. On a similar account say hi to your family, especially your wife. And have a marvelous time serving God and His household. There is not a job as important. I make myself useful for I have tasted and found it is not worth turning back."

As you have read above John is sold out in serving God and is excited about being on the GTS/RACK Africa team. The amount of money needed in American dollars is about $1,100 per semester and is needed before January 2011 for him to return to school. Nelson is presently in school and working without John.

They were trained as a team to serve under Pastor Kennedy who is a professor at their Bible college.

**End of articles.**

Nelson and John went on to serve the Lord in other ways after helping Pastor Kennedy establish his billiard ministry at the church and school. The school located in the Kariobangi slums had only 30 students when we arrived in 2010. It now has 175 students and traveling soccer teams. This work continues to go on in the Kariobangi slums of Nairobi. GTS helped raise money and gave oversight to the building of an extension on the classroom building and a kitchen to provide two meals a day for each student. Additional staff was hired, and financial support continues to be an ongoing need.

Later, there was a mass murder terror attack by an Islamic terrorist organization in the upscale Westgate Shopping Mall in Nairobi [63]. We walked those very halls just three years before and visited many of the shops where 71 people were shot dead with about 200 more people injured in 2013. As I looked at the images on my TV back home, I grieved for the victims and once again marveled at God's protection.

As mentioned before, there was a bombing at a prayer meeting we thought of attending while there in 2010. I also remember the many years serving in ministry on the streets of Paterson in some of the roughest sections of town where gunshots still ring out many a night. I remember the faces of those Paterson children in my elementary school classrooms who must live in those dangerous neighborhoods. While I was living in Paterson, someone was shot dead across the street. I learned through all this that the safest place to be is in the will of God.

[63] "Westgate shopping mall attack," Wikipedia. Available at: https://en.wikipedia.org/wiki/Westgate_shopping_mall_attack. 6 October 2018

God led me from the streets of Paterson to Africa. His power caused lives to be changed for eternity, while He provided and protected every step of the way.

# Chapter 20 – The Philippines and Souls

Two years after Africa in 2012, God put together one of the most amazing trips for Gospel Trick Shot to the country of the Philippines. This trip was 10 years in the making as I began dreaming about it in 2002. I had been competing against the best Filipino players in the world for 10 years and built friendships and connections. Many of those players saw my Gospel Trick Shot shows and called me Pastor. That is one of the main reasons I got the name Pastor of Pool. With my ministry connections growing, it was time to put together that long-awaited trip to the Philippines.

I also had a special personal interest in going to the Philippines because of my Father. Dad served in World War II (WWII) and helped set the Filipino people free from bondage to the Japanese. He was on an aircraft carrier as a first-class machinist's mate helping prepare the fighter planes for battle. He fought in about a dozen Naval battles in the Pacific around the Philippines. His ship was hit by Kamikazes and 180 of his shipmates died off the Island of Guam. Dad requested his remains be buried at sea so that he could rejoin his shipmates.

His remains were buried at sea in 1997. I have some of the bullet shells from the gun salute and the American flag that were part of the ceremony. Little did I know before I left that I would go to some of the same places his ship maneuvered in battle 70 years ago. As I stood on the shore looking out at the possible locations where Dad's ship might have been, I heard the still small voice of the Holy Spirit whisper in my soul, "I sent your Dad here to help set the Filipino people free physically, and now I am sending you to help set them free spiritually."

Here is the story of what happened on that first trip in the Summer of 2012 taken from the GTS newsletter files.

**GTS Newsletter August 2012** - Lead ministries that served as Gospel Trick Shot hosts in the Philippines were: (WOL) Word of Life Ministries headquartered out of Schroon Lake, NY, the Fellowship of Christian Athletes (FCA) which is perhaps the largest Christian sports ministry in the world, and World Intent Ministries headquartered in the State of North Carolina. These exciting ministries would serve as the framework for all that God would do during our Philippines tour. The first stop was Manila with Word of Life located in Laguna with full-time missionaries Jon and Sheila Abraham providing the accommodations and transportation.

Jon and I first met and shared our respective ministries at a mission's conference last summer at the Ringwood Baptist Church in Ringwood, NJ which supports both of our ministries. Jon and Sheila worked tirelessly with the GTS Team to provide all that was needed to help make this leg of the journey successful. They stopped their regular activities of running the campgrounds and helped to coordinate activities at the Word of Life Bible Institute in Laguna to ensure that all GTS needs were met [64]. Thank God for devoted missionaries like this willing to serve and plug into what God is doing!

The first GTS Show was done on the WOL campground property on the first Sunday of the trip after church. After I spoke during church service, Mike Massey, Tom Rossman, and I performed pool shots and presented the Gospel on one of the two campground pool tables. One WOL female staffer remarked, "For years we have tried to get the husbands of some of our

---

[64] "Laguna Camp," Word of Life Philippines. Available at: http://www.wolphils.org/laguna-camp/.

women here for church and Bible studies, and with one Gospel Trick Shot show they came to hear the Gospel for the first time!"

Later, that first week legendary pro Filipino pool players Francisco Bustamante [65], Dennis Orcollo [66], and Marlon Manalo [67] helped provide venues, pool tables, and other accommodations. Mike, Tom, and I were honored guests at the Filipino Independence Day celebrations in Manila on June 11 and 12. After meeting with various mayors, congressmen, and other officials, Gospel Trick Shot shows were performed with students being dismissed from school early to attend.

We presented gifts to many public officials which included Tom "Dr. Cue" Rossman's seven world championship medals. When the gift was presented, we would express our appreciation for the invitation to share the Gospel in their areas of jurisdiction. Then, sometimes with TV cameras rolling, we would read I Peter 4:10 (ESV), "As each has received a gift, use it to serve one another, as good stewards of God's varied grace." We would then pray for the official and his people. Finally, we would share with him that we are entrusting the medal to him as a symbol of God's grace and at such a designated time in the future, he is free to pass on the medal and the Scripture.

GTS helper Scott Pruiksma is a fireman and town councilman in his hometown of Midland Park, NJ and came along to help the team. Scott brought a fire helmet from his hometown of Midland Park, NJ and presented it to a Fire Chief in Manila. Again, the GTS team presented the gift, read I Peter 4:10, offered words of

---

[65] "Francisco Bustamante," Wikipedia. Available at: https://en.wikipedia.org/wiki/Francisco_Bustamante. 15 August 2018

[66] "Dennis Orcollo," Wikipedia. Available at: https://en.wikipedia.org/wiki/Dennis_Orcollo. 5 September 2018

[67] "Marlon Manalo," Wikipedia. Available at: https://en.wikipedia.org/wiki/Marlon_Manalo. 5 September 2018

encouragement and exhortation, and then closed with prayer. Each time there were members of the press and other government officials on hand to witness all that God was doing. One show was done for the cadets in training for the fire department, police, and rescue workers. Other shows were done in the Manila area included various shopping malls, upscale pool rooms, gymnasiums, and community centers. In some areas, schools were let out early so the students could attend the shows.

Next stop on the tour was the Island of Bacolod were Mike, Tom, Scott, and myself met with public officials from much smaller towns than Manila before performing Gospel Trick Shot shows. Again, gifts were exchanged as the team shared. In one town, 250 people jammed into a local five table pool room to see a GTS show. It turns out, that the pastor of a local church fled that exact pool room years ago to leave a life of sin and then go into ministry. This same pastor joined us in reaching the people of this town with the Gospel and now is committed to going back into that pool room to rescue souls that are perishing. Additionally, we presented this pastor with a brand-new McDermott cue stick as he is an avid pool player and now a new Gospel Trick Shot RACK Team member.

The Fellowship of Christian Athletes (FCA) a large U.S. based sports ministry with a presence in the Philippines led by Filipino Pastor Gary Vistacion, helped provide other contacts and venues [68]. Churches, community centers, pool rooms, and universities were the sites of many shows on the Island of Bacolod. It was on this leg of the journey that both Tom and I got sick for a few days

---

[68] "International – Philippines," FCA. Available at: https://www.fca.org/international/globalregions/south-pacific/philippines. Fellowship of Christian Athletes © 2018

each with stomach viruses and dehydration as Mike soldiered on, living up to his famous nickname, "Tennessee Tarzan".

Another local pool room was involved with the selling of drugs and idols that included religious-themed statues which supposedly represented luck and good fortune. We specifically preached during the show to put away idol worship and trust only in the finished work of the Lord Jesus Christ. The local pastors with us indicated after the show that this was the first time, they had an opportunity to penetrate this area with the true Gospel.

Again, the team had another opportunity to minister at a local church for a Sunday service for the third time. Each time I would preach, Tom Rossman would share his testimony, and 17-time international pool champion Mike Massey would sing his country Gospel songs. At each church service salvation bracelets made by the Serving Hands group back at the Hawthorne Gospel Church were given out to the congregations as witnessing tools. We rejoiced in the fact that we left behind all these salvation bracelets to help equip the people to take the Gospel to their streets.

The third and final leg of the journey came on the Island of Cebu where the tour continued to pick up even more momentum. Already the team had been on television twice with the worldwide 700 Club in Manila and a local station in Bacolod. Now, in Cebu, a press conference with twelve members of the media was awaiting us in one of the fastest growing cosmopolitan areas in the Philippines called Cebu City. Newspaper articles and two more television appearances took place with one a worldwide broadcast and the other local. The shows were in an upscale mall in Cebu City called the J Center Mall.

Rob and Roma Boswell with World Intent Ministries are full-time missionaries and served as gracious hosts. I first met Rob at a

Legacy Minded Men's meeting with Founder Joe Pellegrino, our GTS webmaster, last summer as Rob was there to share about his Filipino ministry. I attend two men's groups in the North Jersey area with one being the (LMM) Legacy Minded Men which meets in Lincoln Park in Passaic County [69] and the other (NCS) New Canaan Society of Bergen County which meets in Wyckoff [70]. Having grown up attending churches in both Northern New Jersey counties, it is wonderful to still be part of what God is doing locally. Both groups feature many different ministries and people dedicated to the Lord's work around the world. God continues to provide many ministry contacts through these two men's groups.

Rob and Roma Boswell run an upscale Christian themed coffee cafe in the mall in Cebu called the Malakius Art Kaffe. Some of the local Christian businessmen who help Pastor Rob partnered with the GTS team to help with various costs and amenities like hotel, food, and transportation. ESPN Asia and Puyat Sports made their way down from Manila by flying in a pool table mechanic. They also provided a professional pool table. An ESPN Asia representative stayed with the team most of the week to help us with a series of shows in this upscale mall. The coffee cafe served as a meeting place for members of the media and for follow-up with all those involved in the mall ministry.

Hundreds of response cards were filled out during the Gospel Trick Shot shows with information on attending Bible studies in the coffee cafe and an invitation to attend the mall church led by

[69] "Joe Pellegrino – Founder," Legacy Minded Men. Available at: https://www.legacymindedmen.org/. Copyright by Legacy Minded Men. All Rights Reserved 2018
[70] "Bergen County Chapter," New Canaan Society. Available at: https://newcanaansociety.org/bergen-county/. Copyright 2018 New Canaan Society

Rob Boswell. Again, more salvation bracelets were given out to help equip those involved with the mall ministry to share the Gospel with those they come in contact.

The GTS team was taken to "Garbage City" to see where the poorest of the poor live. World Intent Ministries led by Pastor Rob in the Philippines is doing a great work there as they have built a schoolhouse right in the garbage dump and purchased an off-site large house. This house takes in the malnourished to nurse them back to physical health and help them spiritually.

The GTS team was treated at the end of the trip by a local Christian businessman to a weekend vacation out on the ocean at his seaside resort in North Cebu. There we went to a fourth Sunday morning service marking four weeks in the Philippines. The team ministered again with me doing the preaching, Tom sharing a testimony, Mike singing his country Gospel songs, and Scott on the camera. The team handed out the remainder of the 1,300 salvation bracelets that we brought from the U.S.A.

That last Sunday afternoon the team decided to do another GTS show down the street from the church for the locals. This time it was in a small chicken coup that was converted into a one table pool room. Forty-five people jammed in from the small neighborhood to see what was going on and each one clearly heard the Gospel, many for the first time. The local pastor served with us and invited all to come to his church and indicated that he would follow up on this outreach. The GTS team unexpectedly found a few more salvation bracelets and took others off their wrists to give to the people as a gift reminder of what they had just heard.

Those salvation bracelets again are made by the dedicated ladies of the "Serving Hands" group at the Hawthorne Gospel Church which has been a supporter of Gospel Trick Shot since the beginning of the ministry back in 1996. GTS has distributed tens of thousands of these bracelets all over the world for the past 16 years. Thanks ladies! The bracelet corresponds to a specific Gospel Trick Shot that is shaped exactly like a bracelet with all five colors of the Gospel presented using the pool balls: the black 8-Ball for the darkness of sin, red 3-ball for the blood of Jesus, white cue ball for the cleansing from sin, yellow 1-ball for the promise of heaven, and the green 6-ball to grow in grace. The shot is executed with all five balls disappearing on one stroke of the cue after a clear Gospel presentation is done with the colors representing the message like the "wordless book" used by missionaries around the world for decades.

In summary, the 27-day Gospel Trick Shot (GTS) tour included 24 Gospel Trick Shot shows in 15 different cities on three different islands. Wonderful Gospel Trick Shot sponsors McDermott Cues from the USA, Butch Puyat and Puyat Sports of the Philippines, ESPN Asia made the trip possible. Pro Filipino players Francisco Bustamante, Dennis Orcollo, and Marlon Manalo, various Christian ministries, churches, pastors, and evangelists all contributed. Thanks to all for helping Mike Massey, Tom Rossman, and yours truly, Steve Lillis, minister to the precious people of the Philippines using our wonderful sport of pool and billiards.

Most of all, thanks to our precious Lord and Savior Jesus Christ for dying on the cross in our place so that we can have forgiveness and salvation. Thanks be to God that He has made us to be His Gospel Trick Shot RACK team. RACK stands for Recreational Ambassadors for Christ's Kingdom. What would our Lord have you to do to help advance His Kingdom around the world for the glory of God?

**End of Article.**

After this Philippines trip in 2012, I returned to the USA. Mike and Tom headed out to China for an international artistic pool event with six other GTS RACK team friends including Jason "The Michigan Kid" Lynch and Wayne Parker from South Africa. The GTS RACK team was growing. In China, Tom ran that event with Mike as MC. Jason handled the technical support with Wayne serving as GTS chaplain. GTS Bible studies were held as a source of edification and encouragement. Jason shared his testimony which helped lead a person to Christ. We all sensed something special as God continued to open doors around the world.

Three years later in 2015, a return trip to the Philippines was planned. We noticed that on our last trip in 2012 hundreds of people responded to the Gospel, but we did not have sufficient follow-up in place to disciple all of them. We knew from the Bible that our Lord Jesus instructed His disciples in Matthew 28:19 (ESV), "Go therefore and make disciples of all nations." We were not to just make converts but more importantly disciples. That is the real work of ministry as it involves time and effort to invest in other people's lives.

My heart was heavy as I felt we needed to improve in that area internationally as a ministry. Back home on college campuses, it was much easier since we worked with campus ministries who would facilitate the follow-up. Rob Boswell, who helped with our last trip in 2012, returned home to care for his aging parents. He joined the GTS Board of Directors and began serving with a new Filipino ministry called the (CMC) Church Multiplication Coalition [71]. They specialized in follow-up. GTS decided to partner with CMC in a return trip to the Philippines in 2015. Here is the story of what happened on that trip taken from our GTS newsletter files.

---

[71] "S.E. Asia – Philippines," CMC International. Available at: https://www.4cmcinternational.org/countries/#se-asia. © Copyright 2018 CMC International

**GTS Newsletter August 2015** - What a tremendous move of God in the Philippines July 9-20.  We had a team of 18 Americans embedded with 35 Filipinos in a base camp in the province of Cavite.  We first visited and prayed for the governor and then the mayor and police chief.  We always went first to the authorities to greet them and get permission to minister in their area.  The Scripture says in Romans 13:1 (ESV), "Let every person be subject to the governing authorities."

After, requesting a visit to the local jail, we had the opportunity to lead all the prisoners to Christ.  The police chief then summoned his police force and we then led them to Christ as well.  This came about after the Burklow brothers, Ben and Morgan, asked the mayor if they could visit a local jail.  So, Ben and Morgan, Tom and I, along with Pastor Jill Boyonas, the CMC leader, went to see the Police Chief.  Tom did some tricks with pool balls and cue sticks as we had no pool table, and then I shared the Gospel with the salvation bracelet with the policemen.  Ben and Morgan shared the Gospel with the inmates behind bars.  What a day as the police officers and those who they locked up all put their trust in Jesus.

With favor from the government, we proceeded to reach out to schools and villages. Everywhere we went people responded to the Gospel to receive Christ.  We went to five schools, held sixteen crusades, and had five billiard presentations by Tom "Dr. Cue" Rossman and myself.  Entire pool rooms prayed to receive Christ.  Also, on the two Sundays we were there, we split up and preached in different churches. Those churches also partnered with the Church Multiplication Coalition (CMC).

A typical day included a visit to a school in the morning with follow up in the afternoon from the previous night's crusades. The evenings were devoted to crusades as we split into two teams to do two villages per night.  Nine Americans were placed on each team with team captains assigning roles in the crusades. Rob Boswell and I were team captains.

A crusade consisted of a band concert, greetings, comedy skit, testimony, drama skit, evangelistic preaching, altar call, and prayer for healing. Those who came forward received prayer. After they gave their contact information, they received a booklet to fill out for homework. They would work on the booklet questions to be sure they understood what salvation by grace meant. They brought the booklets back the next day to the same location to receive a free Bible and be placed in a home Bible study group or church.

On one follow-up, 250 children showed up to receive a snack, Book of Hope (shortened Bible), and a salvation bracelet. There were also over 100 adults who brought 60 of their unsaved friends. One of the Filipino missionaries preached from the bumper of our van and led 60 more adults to Christ at what was supposed to be a follow-up meeting. Daytime Gospel Trick Shot shows served to generate excitement for the nightly crusades.

The totals for the crusades as published by the CMC [72]:

| | |
|---|---:|
| Crowd ministered to | 11,671 |
| Salvations | 10,709 |
| People prayed for in healing lines | 2,615 |
| Bible Studies started | 49 |
| Churches planted | 8 |
| Villages where crusade was done | 16 |

---

[72] "Statistics - Jill Boyonas," CMC International. Available at: https://www.4cmcinternational.org/statistics/. © Copyright 2018 CMC International

| | |
|---|---|
| Churches preached at | 26 |
| NT Bibles given | 2,000+ |

There were 53 people in all who served. We had 18 Americans and 35 Filipinos helping to make all this possible. It was wonderful seeing Americans and Filipinos working together for the Kingdom of God. We had 2 full bands with equipment, 4 large vans to transport the two teams, cooks to serve breakfast, lunch, and dinner, and housekeepers who stayed back at the base camp to clean up every day.

We would wake up early every morning to the sound of roosters crying. It was loud, and it reminded us of the suffering hearts in the Philippines. The roosters are used for sport in cockfighting which is a national pastime among men for gambling purposes. The roosters are in bondage and so are many of the people. We learned on this trip how to effectively follow-up on each soul that came forward for salvation and help. Our prayer for the Philippines is that the crying would stop and be comforted by the love of Jesus.

**End of Article.**

# Chapter 21 – Ella

Pain and suffering will always be part of the human experience. I have heard preachers say that when you speak to pain you will always have an audience. Many times, in my Gospel Trick Shot shows through the years, I referred to my own challenges from the 19 1/2-year separation from my wife Camille. The pain of watching my children grow up without their father in their house had its own unique level of suffering for all involved. My first book chronicles that entire experience. In 2009, my wife Camille came back to me after our daughters Amanda and Sarah were grown and out of her house. However, there is one backstory I need to share.

Before Camille and I separated in 1989, we appeared to be on track to have a normal Christian married life. Back in 1988 with two small children in tow, we attended a mission's conference at the First Presbyterian Church in Chattanooga, Tennessee. Both of our daughters, Amanda and Sarah, were born in Chattanooga. After leaving professional full-time pool in early 1985, I had been working for the Krystal Corporation as a restaurant manager after graduating for the University of Tennessee in 1986. I must admit that after a 15-year career of playing pool, working in the real world for a living was, to say the least, a challenge. I was so thankful for my family and wanted to support them financially. In the back of my mind, I was looking for a way to serve God and earn a living at the same time.

At that mission's conference, a Coca-Cola heiress from Lookout Mountain, Tennessee offered a full one year of financial support to a group of families who were willing to go to France to minister the Gospel as part of a large mission team. Pastor Ben Hayden shared this opportunity and asked for volunteers who felt led of God to go. Immediately, I stood up but Camille remained seated with our two small girls. I encouraged her to stand up, but she refused. I became frustrated and could not understand why she was not jumping at this opportunity.

When we got home, I again expressed my disappointment. Camille responded, "I am having enough difficulty here in the USA raising two small children, I do not need to go to France and make it more difficult." I gave her some very "spiritual" answers but to no avail. I then proceeded to call Pastor Ben and shared my complaint. He politely listened and then wisely remarked, "Steve, God does not call the husband into ministry, He calls the husband AND the wife." He went on to explain that if she is not being led to go then I should accept that as God's will. I half-heartedly agreed. Looking back, I did not accept that and began to become angry. This is probably one of the reasons that we separated less than one year later in 1989. God would now begin to teach me for the rest of my life to accept His will over mine. He did not force His will on me, I asked and prayed for it. Almost 20 years later, Camille returned! The story of our marital separation and her eventual return is chronicled in detail in my first book, "But You Must! The Steve Lillis Story."

Having Camille back in my life in 2009, meant I had a helper not only in life but in the ministry of Gospel Trick Shot. Before we started our family, Camille and I had traveled around the country as professional pool players for the first 8 years of our relationship. She knew me better than any other human being. Pastor Thomas Fox, who presided over the rededication of our vows in 2010 said to me, "With Camille back in your life, you will live longer." How true this is as she speaks so much wisdom into my life and helps prevent a lot of potential difficulties. At that rededication ceremony, daughters Amanda and Sarah gave us back to each other at the altar of the Ringwood Baptist Church. We had never divorced so this simply marked a turning point in the history of our family. The ceremony took place on April 26, 2010, which marked exactly 30 years of marriage as we wisely did not emphasize the 19 1/2 years of marital separation.

Little did we know that in the year 2014, our family would need each other to get through the tragedy that God allowed. In 2012, our pregnant daughter Sarah and her son Jayden came to live with us after she experienced marital difficulties that ended in a divorce. Ella was born soon after they moved in. After two years of living with our daughter and her two precious children, they moved out in January 2014 to get on with life. Those two years were challenging but rewarding. Sarah finished her college degree at William Paterson University. Jayden began his school career at age four on a scholarship to a Christian pre-school and then at age 5 kindergarten at the Haledon Public School in the town we rented an apartment. Ella was like a daughter to us in those first two years of her life as we watched the final trimester of Sarah's pregnancy with great anticipation and then welcomed her birth with open arms.

God really had a sense of humor. Because Camille and I were separated all those years, I was unable to be the kind of husband to my wife and the kind of father to my daughters that I wanted to be. Now, I had the opportunity for two years to be a husband, father, and grandfather all at the same time in our small, 3rd floor, one-bedroom, attic apartment in Haledon, New Jersey.

My Mom Ellie, not to be confused with my granddaughter Ella, died of stroke complications in January 2014 after living a wonderful Christian life of 86 years. In March 2014, I did a special Gospel Trick Shot show at the annual Hopkins Super Billiards Expo in the Philadelphia Expo Center in the McDermott Booth in memory of my Mom and the founders of McDermott Cues, Jim and Marilyn McDermott. They also both happened to die in January 2014 after living a wonderful Christian life.

However, later that same year in October 2014, our family would face something the likes of which we never had experienced.

Here are two GTS newsletters describing what God did in the face of tragedy.

**GTS Newsletter November 2014** - "In Memory of Ella" by Steve Lillis. On October 12th our dear granddaughter Elizabeth "Ella" Rose Fuehring, 2 1/2 years old, went home to be with the Lord Jesus. My Mom Ellie Lillis Arntson, 86 years old, went home to be with the Lord in January of this year and today, as I write this, it is October 29th which would have been Mom's 87th birthday. The picture that my niece Christina had in her mind was that Mom was holding Ella in her arms in heaven the day Ella departed this earth. What a beautiful picture that all of us who know Christ will be reunited with loved ones.

From an earthly perspective, the colliding of two shuttle buses with Ella, our daughter Sarah, and her friend Joanna crushed between them was a total disaster. It will perhaps be six months before Sarah can walk again, and Joanna is about in the same condition having damage to their hips and legs. We rejoice that our grandson Jayden six years old was lagging far enough behind that he was not struck by the shuttle buses. However, he did see the whole thing including seeing his sister Ella lying on the ground having instantly departed from this world. Again, from an earthly perspective, this was a disaster! However, knowing Christ, we can be assured that God has a plan to cause all things to work together for good (Romans 8:28).

The good has already started as in the past two days, I was privileged to do my Gospel Trick Shot shows at two locations with a new show entitled "In Memory of Ella." The first show was arranged by the Searchlight Men's Fellowship of Toms River, NJ. When they heard what happened, they suggested that I postpone coming until the spring. Initially, I agreed, but then I had a dream the next night on October 22nd. In my dream, I was performing trick shots while speaking about Ella. While dreaming, I saw that I was up on a platform in a pool room performing as people were looking up at me doing this show. I woke up halfway through the dream and sat up in my bed continuing to visualize shots and thinking about what I would continue to say. Immediately the next day, I called the leader of the group and shared the dream. We both concluded that I must come and do the show as scheduled.

On October 27th, just 5 days later, I went to the Players Billiards Café in Eatontown, NJ. When I walked into the pool room the owner asked me where I wanted to do my show. Looking across the room, I noticed a pool table up on a one-foot high platform just like in my dream. I asked the owner for that table and he said that would be fine. That night, I did the "Ella" show on that platform for the 25 men from the men's group. Additionally, there were about one hundred APA pool league players competing in league matches. As the show continued, most of them stopped and listened. I felt an inner healing knowing that God was working and blessing others too. One pool player remarked, "We are having church right here in the pool room and I feel the presence of God!" Conversations broke out that night as many of the pool players came forward to receive helpful Christian literature and talk with the men from the church group.

The next night, October 28th, I went to the Crossroads Ministry Center in Paterson, NJ to do the same "In Memory of Ella" show for about 25 young boys and leaders in a Royal Rangers church group with another five friends of mine in attendance. This show was performed on the very pool table I started my ministry on some 18 years ago when I lived, worked, and ministered in Paterson. Back then, a friend of mine helped to repair the table and we both chipped in for the cost. And now here we are some 20 countries later, 30 states later, and over 1,000 Gospel Trick

Shot Shows later, returning to Paterson with a new show entitled "In Memory of Ella." People were deeply moved once again as I shared. Lives were touched by the Lord Jesus Christ as an invitation to join my Mom and Ella in heaven was given. God has put in my heart to continue to share this message in memory of Ella and by His grace, I will.

**GTS Newsletter May 2015** - The "Ella Tour" continues to impact lives all over the country! Who would have thought that God would use the death of our precious 2 1/2-year-old granddaughter Ella to help Gospel Trick Shot change hurting lives? This past month the GTS portable pool table was rolled into a Paterson public elementary school for two assembly programs in a school filled with 560 students. GTS helper Ken Neill played music as the students filed in and out. I shared the "In Memory of Ella" GTS presentation.

The students stood speechless watching the shots fall as they listened to the story of God's amazing grace during tragedy. They were challenged to have faith in God when life does not make sense. One-week later, I returned to the school and received news from the school counselor that there had been a deadly drive-by shooting in that Paterson neighborhood days after the show. The counselor said that students remembered and were encouraged by what I said and that some were directly affected. The counselor also remarked that God had sent us to prepare the hearts of the students for that tragedy! We have just received an invitation to go to another Paterson school which is a high school. Praise God!

**End of Articles.**

"In Memory of Ella" GTS shows are still used on occasion. In that first year following the tragedy, it not only helped me to grieve but I found that there were many other grieving people who needed to hear encouraging words. Our daughter Sarah and her son Jayden are doing great. She is re-married to Gregg, and they have two precious daughters, Isabelle and Chloe, as Jayden is the big brother. Camille and I love to visit their house to share in the busy lives of our grandchildren.

In the "Ella" GTS show, I mention that it took the death of Jesus to give us life. Just as a seed goes into the ground and dies, eventually life springs forth. Ella represents a new chapter in the life of our family as so many other things have worked out for the better. Trying to figure out why it had to be this way is fruitless. The Scripture from Isaiah 55:8-9 (KJV) says it best, "For my thoughts are not your thoughts, neither are your ways my ways, saith the Lord. For as the heavens are higher than the earth, so are my ways higher than your ways, and my thoughts than your thoughts."

# Chapter 22 – The Arab World

Like many Americans, the events of September 11th, 2001 caused me great hurt and resentment. Growing up in the suburbs of Northern New Jersey did not prepare me to understand Arab Culture. However, in the late 1990's, God began exposing me to Arab Culture through my Gospel Trick Shot Ministry.

In 1998, a friend of mine Matt DeLorenzo [73], youth pastor at Jacksonville Chapel in Lincoln Park, New Jersey, recommended me to the Mideast Evangelical Church in Jersey City, New Jersey. Matt had helped launch a youth group in this Middle Eastern Christian church of Egyptians. They came to the USA to escape discrimination and persecution by Muslims in their home country of Egypt. The year before, I had a very successful Gospel Trick Shot show for Matt's youth group at Jacksonville Chapel with over 200 young people attending. The Mideast Church youth leader, Nash Salib, contacted me and extended an invitation to come and minister. At the first Gospel Trick Shot show for this Egyptian church, I sensed a special bond.

At the time, my two daughters Amanda and Sarah were about the same age as most of the Egyptian young people. The church continued to have me back every few months until finally, I asked my daughters if they would like to go with me. They were already familiar with inner-city young people as they had previously attended the Greater Grace Church back in Paterson. There they sang and danced in many church skits and plays with

---

[73] "Matthew Peter DeLorenzo - Obituary," Stellato Funeral Homes. Available at:
https://www.stellatofuneralhomes.com/obituaries/Matthew-DeLorenzo/#!/Obituary. August 25, 2008

other inner-city youth. My daughters got involved in helping form a band with the Egyptian young people. Since I was still separated from my wife Camille, this became a wonderful opportunity for them to see my ministry with Gospel Trick Shot. I was so proud to have my daughters' partner in ministry.

The relationship with my Egyptian friends grew. My Hawthorne Gospel Church friend Ken Rezstak, who earlier inspired me to start Gospel Trick Shot in 1995, decided to move and donated his pool table to GTS in 2000. I immediately knew what to do with it. The wood top pool table that I had been performing on at the Egyptian church was poor quality. Ken's table was slate and rolled perfect. The pool table was delivered and my visits to the Egyptian church became more frequent.

Nash Salib wanted me to meet more of his Egyptian friends in the Northeast. In July of 1999, Nash invited me to be the featured speaker at the Mideast Evangelical Conference at the Holiday Inn near the airport in Philadelphia, PA. About 250 people from a number of Egyptian churches, met once a year to encourage each other. Upon arriving at the conference, I immediately proceeded to ask where the pool table was assuming, I would do one of my Gospel Trick Shot shows. The event coordinator looked at me and said, "What pool table?" I responded that I do Gospel Trick Shot shows. He said that there was no pool table in the building but asked me to do anything I wanted, and the people would be happy.

My mind began to churn as I thought of a way to do a GTS show without a pool table. I went out to my car and got several different balls that I used with the young people. I had golf balls, tennis balls, pool balls, ping pong balls, softballs, and baseballs. I remembered how my mentor Peter Everett at the Hawthorne Gospel Church, explained to me that you can use anything to share the Gospel. I had six baseball gloves and I brought them inside and placed them around the stage area that was shaped like a rectangular pool table. The gloves became the pockets and the different size and different weight balls allowed me to do trick shots.

I took out my cue stick and began to hit the balls around the stage (pool table) and into the gloves (pool table pockets), all the while talking nonstop illustrating spiritual principles. When the show was over, the people expressed their gratitude with some mentioning that they had never seen anything like that before. They were genuinely impressed. I responded that I had never seen anything like that either! God taught me that He certainly did not need my pool playing prowess to share the Gospel. I probably was getting spoiled by that perfect pool table back at the church. This lesson sure came in handy as you will see in the next chapter when I go to the Middle East and back to Albania.

My Egyptian relationships have continued through the years. Even when I stopped going to the Mideast Evangelical Church in Jersey City in the early 2000's, I would meet Nash Salib and others at the (JFM) Jesus for Muslims Banquets each year starting in 2003. JFM became a tremendous source for networking as (MBB's) Muslim Background Believers from all over the world were part of what God was doing here in the USA with Muslims. In 2010 and 2011, I received invitations to go to Egypt to be part of the KDEC sports festival in Wadi, Egypt [74]. Since I was unable to go because of my teaching responsibilities at William Paterson University, I sent my partners Tom "Dr. Cue" Rossman in 2010 and Mike Massey (2011) to take my place. The sports festivals had 17,000+ Muslim attendees each year and

---

[74] "KDEC – KASR EL DOBARA EVANGELICAL CHURCH – Wadi Sports Camp," North Coast Calvary Chapel. Available at: https://northcoastcalvary.org/kdec/. North Coast Calvary 2018

were broadcast by SAT-7 TV [75]. Later, SAT-7 became a GTS ministry partner when I went to Lebanon in 2017.

In 2009, I received a phone call from missionary Mark Engel. He had an Arab Cultural Center in Chicago and searched on the internet for someone who did billiards and the Gospel. My name came up and seeing that I had some experience with Muslims, he asked me if I would accompany him to the Arabian Peninsula. Mark was a missionary cue stick salesman for Schuler Cues. A worker for Schuler Cues went to the same church as Mark. His way of donating to Mark's ministry was to give him cue sticks to sell on his many trips to the Arabian Peninsula. Mark concluded that he needed a trick shot artist to help increase his sales. This was a perfect fit for me as I was in between cues and not quite ready to start playing with a cue from my eventual sponsor McDermott Cues. Schuler made a specific cue for the trip cut to my favorite dimensions. We were off to the Arabian Peninsula in the Spring of 2009.

This was my first trip to the Arab world. I had been to Albania and worked with secular Muslims, but these were Arab people who practiced their faith. Only my Christian Egyptian friends back home along with those I met at JFM activities were Arabs. This was an exciting culture shock as I went to Kuwait first with the landscape dotted with mosques and signs of Arabian culture everywhere. My travel partner Mark Engel knew the Captain of the Kuwaiti National Billiard Team Khalid Almutari. I was off to a good start with Khalid and we had much in common

---

[75] "Televised Conference in The Desert Energizes Faith in Egypt," SAT 7. Available at:
https://www.sat7uk.org/televised-conference-in-the-desert-energises-faith-in-egypt/. October 2015

with billiards. I felt at home in the Kuwaiti pool room playing with Khalid and doing my trick shots.

After billiards, Khalid loved to talk intelligently about our different faiths. From my previous training with STOP (Summer Training Outreach Program) in 2006, I not only learned how to converse with a Muslim but enjoyed discussing the differences. I also taught World Literature at William Paterson University and each semester my students read parts of the Koran and studied the Life of Mohammad.

After Kuwait, I was excited to see more. Mark and I went to Bahrain next on this same trip where I did a Gospel Trick Shot show for the USA 5th Naval Fleet of the Arabian Peninsula. I worked with the U.S. Navy chaplains and shared the love of Jesus with the fleet. Having been in the U.S. Navy, this was indeed an honor. Next, a show was done for the American Mission Hospital with CEO Dr. Paul Armerding [76].

This was held on hospital property in Bahrain, so it was legal for me to preach the Gospel to the many Muslims in attendance. A Christian Indian ministry called R11 (Revelation 11th Hour) did the follow-up. We had 80 positive responses by way of response cards out of the hundreds of people that were there. Next, we went to the UAE (United Arab Emirates). I did a Gospel Trick Shot show in a pool room in the more liberal emirate of Dubai but could not do one in the more conservative emirate, Abu Dhabi. I ended up going to 2 out of the 6 emirates which are like states. The country of the UAE was the last stop, so I ended up going to 3 of the 6 Gulf countries. I came home with a renewed excitement to go back to the Arab World.

---

[76] "Paul Armerding," LinkedIn. Available at: https://www.linkedin.com/in/paul-armerding-44817a8/. LinkedIn Corporation © 2018

Again, I sent Tom Rossman and Mike Massey to Egypt with Gospel Trick Shot in the fall of 2010 and 2011 respectively because my teaching responsibilities limited my travel overseas until I retired from teaching college in 2016. I could only travel in the summers. At a Hawthorne Gospel Church missions conference in October 2015, a seed was planted in my mind. The speaker Keith Baker asked who would be interested in pursuing BAM (Business as Mission) in North Africa. My ears perked up as I knew from the Arabian Peninsula (AP) how popular billiards was in the Arab World. Furthermore, I knew that the AP countries were the big brothers of the Arab world with all their money and influence.

After observing that the World 9-Ball Championship had taken place each year in the AP since 2010, I knew it was only a matter of time before American pool would catch on in a big way in the Middle East and North Africa. The English, of course, were there first with the English versions of billiards, but the AP had converted to American pool and this was a good sign of things to come for the rest of the Arab world. The idea of doing BAM with an American billiard café was launched. My church was sponsoring "vision trips" to North Africa to investigate doing BAM. At first, Morocco was the preferred country of choice because of its promise economically. I retired in 2016 and then signed on to go to Morocco in 2017.

God once again began to move pieces together to confirm my return to the Arab World. I found out that in Tangier, Morocco the first sanctioned WPA world class 9-Ball tournament was set for March of 2017. I discussed the dates with my church and it was a good fit for our team of four. Our objective was to gather information about establishing an American style billiard café in Morocco.

The trip was a success as we gathered the necessary information. I competed in the tournament and managed to finish in the money. I had a very competitive match with the 2014 World 9-Ball Champion Neils Feijen of the Netherlands which was live streamed by a French company throughout the world. The tournament host, MYcherif Zine Elabidine of Morocco became a good friend and allowed me to do a Gospel Trick Shot show right before the finals of the event [77].

The success of this Moroccan event led to an invitation to go to Lebanon the following month of April. Apparently, the live streams combined with Facebook got my name out there in the Arab world. I had friend requests coming in from all over the Arab world. I was honored that they would call me their friend. After accepting the invitation, I thought that a good follow-up would be to investigate BAM in Lebanon to see if a billiard café would be feasible there as well.

They had another world class 9-Ball tournament in Beirut. I was an honored guest and was invited to do my Gospel Trick Shot show. In both Arab countries, I was the only American to accept their invitations to come and compete. I did three shows in Lebanon and won two matches in that tournament, but more importantly made some very important Arab friends.

My sponsor was McDermott Cues for both Morocco and Lebanon. They had given me some cue sticks to bring as gifts to give to our hosts and for others as door prizes in the shows. In return, the tournament promoters made McDermott one of their sponsors for the tournaments. As a result, the top player in Lebanon, Mohammad Ali Berjaoui, eventually requested to become a McDermott team member and representative for McDermott Cues in the Middle East. Thus, he became the first Arab player to represent McDermott, one of the largest cue

---

[77] "MYcherif Zine Elabidine," Facebook. Available at: https://www.facebook.com/mycherif.zineelabidine. Facebook © 2018

makers in the world. These two trips to Morocco and Lebanon in 2017, help set the stage for the biggest trip ever for Gospel Trick Shot in November 2017 to four war-torn and key countries in the Middle East. More preparation for that trip in the next chapter!

# Chapter 23 – Preparing for Middle East in Canada

God prepared us for a trip to the Middle East using our summer trips to Canada in 2016 and 2017. My dear friend and fellow missionary from the Hawthorne Gospel Church, Jim Percy, gave me contact information for a summer outreach to French Speaking Quebec City, Canada. Jim, a missionary to France, decided that he would join a group coming over from France. The group, France Pour Christ [78], was sending over 30 missionaries. Every year, Jim usually would team up with them on a summer campaign in France. Realizing that French was the most popular language in the Arab World besides Arabic, I decided to join the outreach and offered my portable pool table to help. I invited Tom Rossman and GTS RACK team member Chuck Dutcher to join us. The project was called 100% Connect and was hosted by French Quebec ministries Aujourd'hui l'Espoir and SEMBEQ [79]. Chuck lived in Upstate New York close to the Canadian border, so the plan was to pick him up after Tom and I did some campground shows on the way.

Here is an article that I wrote about the trip in 2016 that was published in the national billiard media [80].

---

[78] "Who We Are," France Pour Christ. Available at: http://www.missionfpc.fr/en/presentation/. 2018
[79] "About," SEMBEQ. Available at: https://sembeq.qc.ca/en/the-seminary/about/. © 2017 SEMBEQ. All Rights Reserved
[80] "And the Ball Stopped Here," AZBILLIARDS.COM. Available at: https://www.azbilliards.com/news/search/. August 9, 2016

### "And the Ball Stopped Here" by Steve Lillis with Tom "Dr. Cue" Rossman

Tom "Dr. Cue" Rossman and Steve Lillis journeyed through Upstate New York to Quebec, Canada to be part of an evangelistic outreach. They brought with them a portable pool table invented by Fred and Devra Robledo of Wildlife and Wood in Anaheim, California. The trip started with a Gospel Trick Shot show at a Christian youth camp in the Albany, New York area for about one hundred and fifty underprivileged inner-city New York/New Jersey junior high school youths. It ended 16 days later with a Gospel Trick Shot show for another one hundred and fifty 9th and 10th-grade high school youth from Newfoundland, Canada attending a summer French training program on a college campus in Quebec City, Canada. Tom and Steve have journeyed to 21 countries over the last 15 years to minister on pool tables with trick shots and instruction with a Christian message of hope and encouragement.

Here is our story entitled "And the Ball Stops Here"!

To begin our story, we need to back up about two weeks to Illinois to a training site where Tom "Dr. Cue" Rossman teamed up with BCA Hall of Famers and superstars of American pool Nick Varner, Johnny Archer, and Jeanette Lee to work with the Billiard Education Foundation (BEF) in training young American pool players for the upcoming Atlantic Cup Challenge. Tom's responsibility was to work on the mental and emotional side of the game. Back in February of this year, he published a training manual entitled "Student of the Game and 'Life,'" that also included the spiritual component of the game and came away from that event with a burning desire to touch the lives of more young people. It just "so happens" that Steve Lillis was attending a Christian youth camp at the same time with his grandson Jayden age 8. Jayden had just performed his first Gospel Trick Shot with "Pop Pop" on the Gospel Trick Shot portable pool table the week before at an outreach to underprivileged inner-city young people in Paterson, NJ.

Now back to that first Gospel Trick Shot show with Tom and Steve at the Christian camp in the upstate Albany New York area on July 20, 2016. This outreach was scheduled by Steve many months before totally unaware of the sequence of events that would follow. Additionally, Gospel Trick Shot Ministries, Inc. (GTS) had donated a slate top pool table to that same camp two years before! Steve picked up Tom at Newark Airport on the afternoon of July 20th and they headed north.

Thy intended to do a Gospel Trick Shot show that same night and they still had to set up the GTS portable pool table. Running late, they arrived only 30 minutes before one hundred and fifty young people would file into the building. Because of steps, the terrain, and other obstacles, there was no time to back in the truck and trailer, unload the portable pool table, and roll it into place. Normally the table sets up and is ready to go in about 20 minutes. Tom looked at the GTS donated slate top 900-pound pool table in the other room of the building. Based on his years of experience of owning a retail billiard store and billiard room back in the 1970's and 80's, he declared that we can move the table on rollers in a matter of minutes. Rollers were provided, and setup was completed with 10 minutes to spare to warm up for the show.

The amped group of one hundred fifty junior high campers filed into the building, Tom and Steve wondered what they would say during the show. The trick shots would be routine. Combined, they have done many thousands of shows, but what do you say to young people who hear gunshots almost every night back home with gang violence all around and with maybe only one parent or grandparent to care for them.

Tom usually leads off with his vast array of rapid-fire shots tempered with witty phrases and instruction while sharing the joy of the roll combined with stories of hope and faith. Early in the show, a ball "accidentally" fell out of a pocket and began to roll on the hardwood floor. Tom declared to the young people, "wait and watch where it stops." In unison, the entire group of one hundred fifty young people rose to their feet and watched every turn of the ball until it stopped, some 10 feet away from the table. Then Tom prophetically said, "and the ball stopped here!" He began to explain that in the expanse of the universe the ball stopped there and similarly each person in the room at that moment had stopped exactly where they were at an appointed place in time and space.

The young people got it as they realized that it was no accident that they were there. Every one of them had been given scholarships by a multitude of people who wanted them to get out of the city for one week to experience God, peace, and joy in the woods of Upstate New York.

This set the stage for Steve to be the closer with his thought-provoking array of trick shots which are illustrated messages using the position, colors, numbers, and direction of the billiard balls. This illustrates life lessons with Christian applications of hope and encouragement. Steve felt led that night to share the story of Ella with the pool balls. Ella was his 2 ½-year-old granddaughter who died tragically in a shuttle bus accident over two years ago. This story had moved the hearts of many before and tonight these one hundred and fifty young people were deeply touched.

For Steve Lillis and his family, the passing of Ella was a representation of, "and the ball stopped here." What do you do when "life happens" to you like that? This amazing story caused the young people to look to Jesus for hope and encouragement because of their desperate situations back home. This night became the pattern for a sequence of amazing events over the next two-plus weeks.

Steve and Tom did three billiard room shows with one televised to the people of Canada. There were outdoor shows on the GTS portable pool table by the St. Laurence Seaway and in old downtown Quebec City in the city center square. They also did park shows on the GTS portable pool table in and around Quebec.

The last show was for one hundred and fifty youth on the campus where they stayed with one hundred and twenty outreach team members. These team members came from all over the world to give hope and encouragement to the people of Quebec. On that last day in the parking lot outside the cafeteria, they set up the portable pool table and students filed out and circled the pool table to see the show.

Tom and Steve had a special guest Gospel Trick Shot artist traveling with them named Chuck Dutcher from Salem, New York. Chuck had performed with them the prior two weeks and was in training to hone his skills. So, when Steve set up a six-ball trick shot representing his family of six, Chuck approached the table with confidence having made that shot many times before. Chuck got down and stroked the cue ball and only one ball went in disappearing from the table. Chuck was perplexed and went to grab the balls to make a second attempt. Steve yelled stop, "and the ball stopped here." That was a "perfect" illustration that Ella is gone, and the other five family members remain with hope. Not one of those young people in the audience that day moved as they held their position in time and space to hear the eternal message of hope and faith through Jesus Christ!

**End of Article.**

Tom and I had one more very important trip back to Canada again through Upstate New York in the summer of 2017. This would again help us prepare for the biggest trip to date to the Middle East. Here below is another article I wrote summarizing that Canadian trip. Again, it was published in the national billiard media.

**"Dancing Angels and Gospel Trick Shots" – by Steve Lillis**

On Wednesday, July 19, 2017, a very unusual thing happened on the Gospel Trick Shot portable pool table. Tom "Dr. Cue" Rossman and Steve Lillis were performing their usual Gospel Trick Shot (GTS) presentation in front of 250 inner-city young people at Inspire Sports Camps in the Taconic Retreat Center in Upstate New York. Tom and Steve had just performed a similar GTS show on that same table the day before at the Solid Rock Day Camp in West Milford, NJ for 150 campers. Little did they know at the time, that 12 more GTS shows on this GTS portable pool table would follow in Canada with the usual expected results. However, on July 19th, at the Taconic Retreat Center, something very strange was about to happen. With a combined total of 113 years of billiard experience between them, Tom and Steve had no apparent explanation for the events that night.

It all started at lunchtime on July 19th when Tom and Steve arrived at the Taconic Retreat Center. The camp director had to scold the 250 inner city youth campers about the toilets being stopped up and it appeared to be "no" accident. After threatening to close the bathrooms, the campers were told to put both hands in the air and clap on the count of three if they agreed to report any suspicious activities in the bathrooms for the rest of the week. And on the count of three, all 250 young people agreed for obvious reasons. Tom and Steve left dinner early to set up the GTS portable pool table for an 8:00 pm show in the gym.

They were all set up and with one hour to spare. However, there was one big problem that 113 years of combined billiard experience between Tom and Steve could not solve. The trick shots for no apparent reason would not go in! As a matter of fact, the balls came off the rails at different angles even after hitting the balls in the same direction with the same spin and at the same speed. There was no way to adjust! The camp director came by 15 minutes before the show and asked if everything was all right to which they responded, "everything is fine except the balls will not go in the pockets". The camp director began to panic and asked if they wanted a different location to set up. Tom and Steve replied stoically that since they had done well over 100 shows together, and "everything would be just fine!"

Two hundred and fifty campers filed in and after the camp director announced, "fresh off their international pro tour 2017 BCA Hall of Famer and legendary billiard entertainer Tom "Dr. Cue" Rossman and world renown Gospel Trick Shot artist and professional pool player Steve Lillis are both here tonight just for you." The show started with a bang! Tom, as usual, led off with his fantastic array of shots but many were not falling into the pockets. As a matter of fact, he used one of his famous lines that almost never fails, "if this shot does not go in this time, I will buy everyone pizza." Well, guess what? The shot did not fall, and 250 inner city kids began to chant PIZZA, PIZZA, etc. Tom decided to not shoot his last shot and left his props of big pool balls, medium pool balls, and small pool balls on the table and said, "now Steve will come out and explain how God took care of a big problem in his life."

Steve came to the table and, to say the least, was not too excited about trying to execute his shots under these difficult circumstances. However, he pressed on with his real-life story of the death of his granddaughter Ella in 2014 and how God worked everything out for good in the life of his family. The shots were not falling but the story pressed on! Then Steve realized that the 250 campers were no longer interested in two pool players with 113 years of billiard experience between them, who could not fully execute the trick shots. So, Steve proceeded to bring the story to a close followed by an invitation to trust Jesus for whatever problems they were encountering in their lives.

The camp director, sensing the moment, came out of the audience and asked Tom and Steve to pray for the 250 campers. Steve led the prayer on one side of the room, while Tom followed in leading the campers on the other side of the room in a prayer of commitment to God. Remembering lunchtime and the commitment the campers made concerning the bathrooms, Steve and Tom asked the campers to raise two hands over their heads. On the count of three, they were to clap their hands together to make a commitment to Jesus to give their lives and their problems over to God. And on the count of three, about 100 campers clapped their hands and made that commitment. After that prayer, the camp director asked the campers to come down and thank Steve and Tom personally. One by one, they came and shared how the message encouraged them as they had lost loved ones, struggled with gang violence, wrestled with addictions, contemplated suicide, and have been overwhelmed with feelings of hopelessness.

The next morning before Tom and Steve left for Canada to do 12 more GTS shows on that same portable pool table, they wanted to have one last talk with the camp director. He stated the night before that he was surprised by so many missed shots. Tom wanted to give the camp director a copy of his new training manual "Student of the Game and Life", which talks about his trademark philosophy that "a miss is a make in disguise". It became obvious to Tom and Steve that the misses defied billiard physics and that they served to get them out of the way, so the message could be fully received by the campers. After our brief discussion with the camp director, he understood all the missed shots and that the bathrooms clogging up were part of God's plan. Two days later, Tom and Steve met with a pastor in Canada who remarked after hearing the story, the Lord placed "dancing angels" on the pool table to prevent the shots from going in so the campers could focus on the message. That is indeed beyond our natural understanding and something that only God can do!

**End of Article.**

Tom and I concluded that we need to be open to whatever God would do on our Middle East trip which was only months away. Tom mentioned to Steve to not be surprised "if we see a ball fly into 'outer space'!" Steve added that "God would allow it for the sake of the Gospel!" Little did we know that our speculation would come true, in some sense, on our first stop in the Middle East that November in Lebanon. More on that in the next chapter.

There was one more very important item of preparation for the Middle East that God provided while we were in Canada that summer of 2017. While on outreach in Canada, Edgar Reich, a former GTS board member came and met us in the Montreal, Quebec area. Edgar had moved back to Canada after leaving the USA upon retirement in 2013 as his work visa expired and his family was in the Toronto area. Edgar and I were well familiar with each other as for years we had been accountability partners.

When Edgar arrived, he sensed some friction between Tom, Chuck, and myself. He suggested that we all meet every day for two hours for group discipleship with him as the leader. This turned out to be very beneficial as one of the highlight verses he shared with us from the Bible was Luke 17:10 (NLT) where Jesus said, "when you obey me you should say, 'We are unworthy servants who have simply done our duty.'" This was truly humbling! Tom and I needed that spiritual principle as we continued to prepare for the Middle East.

Back in April of 2017, Jim Percy had accompanied me to Lebanon as my French translator. As mentioned in Chapter 22, this was a very important trip as key contacts were made. One such contact was a Lebanese Christian, Bernard Abi Nadar. Jim met him while I was playing one of my matches in the Lebanon 9 Ball International Open Championship [81]. Bernard had entered the tournament hoping to meet a fellow Christian as many of the players in the event were Sunni Muslims. Bernard was so excited about Gospel Trick Shot that he is now one of our GTS RACK team members. Bernard greatly helped us later in the year on the trip to the Middle East.

---

[81] "May 11, 2017 posted video - Lebanon 9 Ball International Open Championship," Facebook. Available at: https://www.facebook.com/Lebanon9BallIntelOpen/. Facebook © 2018

# Chapter 24 - Building Bridges in the Middle East and Beyond

God had been preparing Tom and me for a lifetime for this Middle East trip. The missing pieces were falling into place right on God's timetable. The initial plan was to go to Lebanon, Palestine, and Israel, but that expanded. In Lebanon, my new Arab friends that I met on my first trip with Jim Percy months before, extended a formal invitation to come as guests of the Lebanese Billiard Federation to the Arab World Team Championships in Beirut, Lebanon in November 2017.

Sixteen Arab countries met with their respective teams and Tom and I did special Gospel Trick Shot shows and teaching clinics. Our Sunni Arab hosts had arranged other shows in Beirut in Palestinian and Syrian neighborhoods. The Shia Muslims of the north asked if we would come to Tripoli as their guests. This was not in our original plan. Also, the US State Department does not recommend going to this part of Lebanon [82]. However, we realized that Jesus loves all people and as stated before in the words of Jesus that we are just unworthy servants, who are simply doing our duty (Luke 17:10).

Our Sunni Muslim friends escorted us to the north and we were honored to do a show for the Shia Muslims. They had 250 pool players gathered at a banquet to honor the champions

---

[82] "Security Message for U.S. Citizens: Lebanon Travel Warning," U.S. Embassy in Lebanon. Available at: https://lb.usembassy.gov/security-message-u-s-citizens-lebanon-travel-warning/.
By U.S. Embassy Beirut | 29 July, 2016

of their billiard league. Tom and I were their special guests and we did a special Gospel Trick Shot show for them.

After that one-night show in Tripoli, we returned to Beirut by bus. On the bus were two brothers, Mohammad and Mazen, who are professional pool players. Mohammad was already touched by our message back at the Arab Championships but Mazen was not until that bus ride back from Tripoli. Tom was asked to share his thoughts and ended up sharing his testimony about how he came to Christ. Mazen listened to every word and the next day Mohammad reported that after losing his match, Mazen realized that he now has the victory in his heart even though he had lost on paper.

In a friendly gesture during one of the shows back at the Arab Team Championships, I brought an Arab pool player to the table to help me with a shot. The shot was the famous Mosconi butterfly shot with two balls placed in front of the cue ball to create what I call an obstacle shot. Tremendous force is needed to get through the two object balls and then pocket all eight balls. I knew that not only would our Arab friends appreciate this acknowledgment of his pool playing prowess, but the crowd would then pay more attention to what was being said in the show.

That Arab player not only made the shot but launched the cue ball high in the air off the bottom cushion as if it was part of the show. He then nonchalantly caught the ball when it flew back through the air to him. Tom and I looked at each other in amazement, reflecting back on Tom's prophetic comment about a ball flying into "outer space." We have both been doing that same shot for years, thousands of times, and knew that the physics of that shot would not allow that to happen. The Arab player, after receiving a rousing ovation, wanted to do the shot again for the audience. I asked him to wait until I finished my message which was the most important part of the GTS show.

After the show, our Arab friend tried over and over unsuccessfully to duplicate that shot. Tom and I both realized that God had intervened so that the message of the Gospel could be most effectively delivered.

A country that I did not initially figure on visiting was Jordan and that was next. Because we flew into Lebanon, we could not fly from there into Israel. These two countries do not cooperate with one another. They were at war with each other in 2006 and there is still much tension. We had to fly into Amman, Jordan so we could enter Israel through Palestine. Because of my network of Arab billiard connections, I had our Arab friends arrange to have a cab driver pick us up from the airport to take us to a hotel in Amman. The cab driver was a pool player, of course, and he asked us if we would be willing to do a show in an upscale billiard room in Amman. Again, Tom and I realized that this was our duty and the show that night touched many Jordanians with the love of Jesus.

Now it was on to Palestine. This was one of the most difficult parts of the trip as we had to go through three walls and three military checkpoints. We had to take a taxi from our hotel in Amman to the Jordanian border and then go through our first wall and military checkpoint. Our passports were taken away and we had no photocopies. That produced an uneasy feeling as we boarded a Jordanian bus and headed to the Israeli wall and another military checkpoint.

With our passports and luggage returned, we thought we might be interrogated knowing how tight security is at the Israelis checkpoint. The fact that we had a Lebanese stamp on our passports, produced another level of concern. Before arriving from the USA, I asked our cue sponsor McDermott to compose a letter stating that we were representing them as McDermott Ambassadors. We also had a letter from the President of the Israeli Billiard Federation stating our business with them as well.

I thought we were in for a long wait but to my pleasant surprise, after a few short questions, they let us through.

Now we were back on another bus to the final wall and military checkpoint controlled by the Government of Palestine. Our passports were again removed, and luggage taken for inspection. Again, there was tension, as this next checkpoint seemed very different from the first two. Not many people come this way as usually tourists fly into Israel and travel on an Israeli bus to Jordan and easily return the same way. We were now heading into Palestine with Palestinians.

We stood around in a building without our passports and luggage with nobody to direct us. The signs were in Arabic so that was no help. As we were confused and not knowing where to go or what to do, three Palestinians, a Mom and her two daughters, asked if we needed help. We told them our situation and they warmly greeted us and welcomed us to Palestine. They said follow us and you will get through. Tom said to me, "God provided three angels."

We got on another bus with our angels and were delivered to yet another building where our passports and luggage were waiting for us. On the way over, we had a pleasant conversation. They were coming in from the USA. They left Palestine years ago to live and work in California and were returning to visit Grandma.

Mom further explained that her two daughters were entering school in England and that she was going with them for the first year to help them set up. One daughter was studying international law to defend the humanitarian rights of Palestinian people worldwide. The other daughter was studying politics to understand how governments work so that she can help her people on the world stage. They were on a mission for Palestine and we felt honored to meet these crusaders who were working to help solve problems in a peaceful way. Once we got through these final checkpoints and entered Palestine, we took a taxi to Jericho to meet my friend Monther.

My Palestinian friend Monther Salah Awartani, who I met in my last trip to Lebanon, was anxiously awaiting our arrival to Palestine. He had invited me the previous April to visit his country. We had become good friends as he was the official referee while I played as the only American in the Lebanon 9-Ball International Open Championship. He asked me questions back then about American 9-Ball rules and I was delighted to help. He was excited that I accepted his invitation and we had planned this visit to Palestine months before.

Monther was a Palestinian government official and a representative for the Palestinian Billiard Federation. He is also a world-class certified English snooker referee. Tom and I stayed in his home in Nablus with his wife and two precious children. The hospitality we received was so kind and gracious as he arranged all the Gospel Trick Shot shows and drove us to Holy Land spots in Palestine as our special tour guide.

One of the highlights of our visit to Palestine was Bethlehem, the birthplace of Jesus. We had the honor to do a show in Bethlehem as Monther made the arrangements. He brought along a pool player who was crippled by a bullet wound in his leg in a scuffle with Israelis. At the Bethlehem Gospel Trick Shot show, that pool player and a teenage young man received the message of Jesus with joy and they took part in the show by shooting some of the shots with us.

While visiting the birth site of Jesus, Monther insisted that we not only wait on the line to see the actual spot where Jesus supposedly was born but also take part in the lighting of candles and communion with all the other Christian pilgrims. Tom and I decided not to wait on the long lines and informed

Monther of our desire to leave as we had seen enough. He was shocked that we did not care to do what all the other Christians were doing. We explained to him that the most important thing in our life was to have Jesus in our heart.

Monther, feeling that he was not doing his job as a tour guide, went around the back of the birth site, and because he knew the Muslim attendant, he went in and snapped a picture for us. He proudly came back and presented us the picture of the birthplace. Again, I said, Jesus is not there, He is here, as I pointed to my heart. From that moment on, our Muslim friend Monther became intrigued and wanted to know more about this Jesus in our hearts. Monther now understands that religion is not about rituals and promised to read about Jesus in the Gospel of John in Arabic.

After Palestine, we were excited to go on what we thought was the final leg of our journey, Israel. However, because we flew into Lebanon we had to return through Palestine, then fly out of Amman back to Beirut, and finally, from Beirut, we could go home. At this point arriving in Israel only marked the halfway point in our journey.

Another wall awaited us to leave Palestine to enter Jerusalem. For us, this turned out to be easy as we were already cleared on the other side of Palestine when we entered through the three checkpoints while leaving Jordan. In Jerusalem, we took another bus and headed to Haifa to meet new friends. We had invitations in Israel to be on a live TV sports talk show and do a special Gospel Trick Shot show and teaching clinic for members of the Israeli National Billiard Team. Our cue stick sponsor, McDermott Cues, helped with these arrangements as they had a sales representative in Israel. Through my Gospel Trick Shot contacts with Operation Mobilization (OM), a Christian based ministry, we were scheduled to stay part of the time in Haifa in the OM team house. Then, we would move on to Tel Aviv for TV and GTS shows with our Israeli billiard friends.

We enjoyed staying with our Muslim friends in Lebanon, Jordan, and Palestine, and now we would be with Christian friends in Haifa. Dave McBride, the director of the OM team house, planned for our lodging and took us on a Holy Land tour as our personal guide. He also contacted a Messianic Jew named Yossi who was planting a new Calvary Chapel Church in Haifa and happened to be from my hometown of Wayne, NJ. Yossi was raised Jewish and went to the same Wayne Valley High School as I did. Later he converted to Christianity against his parents' wishes.

Yossi had contacted a pool room owner in Haifa to set up a show the month before. To our surprise, when we arrived, we found out that the previous owner had left. However, the new owner was having his grand opening. He was delighted to have us come and do a Gospel Trick Shot show and informed us that he had become a Christian just two weeks ago. We had a wonderful night as God touched the hearts of many young people through the show. The owner was excited and agreed that he would use his pool room in the future as a RACK (Recreational Ambassadors for Christ's Kingdom) room to hold Bible studies and outreach. Later, another RACK room was planted on our return to Lebanon the following week with our Christian pool player friend Bernard Abi Nader as we did a show in his home pool room in Beirut. Bernard remarked that he now understands what God wants him to do as a pool player for Christ.

After our GTS show in Haifa, Dave McBride, our Christian friend, and OM Director took us on a Holy Land tour to the Sea of Galilee. The highlight for me was when he took us to the possible place where Jesus healed a man with demons by casting them out into a herd of pigs who then rush down a steep bank into the lake and drowned (Luke 8:33). The amazing part of the story was that Jesus left the other side of the lake in Capernaum, where he started his ministry and was becoming famous, to come five miles across the lake in a boat to heal just one man. Jesus then returned across the lake to continue his ministry. Dave remarked, "What did Jesus have to do to find you?" This became another reminder to Tom and I of the importance of sharing the love of Jesus with just one person. This trip was not about accomplishments, but about touching the lives of individuals.

Tom and I had the honor on a Sunday morning to preach at a Messianic Jewish Church located right at the Valley of Armageddon. Our hosts at Operation Mobilization had been helping to build this church congregation. What a joy it was to look out the window and see the actual place where the end times battle will occur right before Jesus returns. We shared how God was using us to build bridges in the Middle East with our cue sticks. Knowing that the time is short we encouraged our brothers and sisters to be busy sharing the Good News of Jesus Christ.

After Haifa, we went to Tel Aviv for the TV special, GTS show and teaching clinic. We were on a live TV sports show and right after did a Gospel Trick Shot show and teaching clinic for members of the Israeli National Billiard Team and other guests. We were told later that the TV show got great reviews and good exposure. Tom and I discussed what material we would use in the Gospel Trick Shot presentation. We agreed that it was time for me to do the "In Memory of Ella" GTS show. Hearts were moved that night as it became clear in conversations after that many have had loss in their lives. They expressed heartfelt appreciation for the show. In the teaching segment, Tom did his famous banks and kicks clinic. He has teaching DVDs and manuals on this material. I did my science show knowing how Israelis love science and technology. I have done this show at

Princeton and MIT, dazzling students with 25 principles and concepts taken right out of their college physics book. I had college physics myself and learned how to apply my billiard experience with the technical understanding.

After our time in Tel Aviv, we returned to Jerusalem to visit the place where Jesus died and was buried. Later, we would re-enter Palestine to begin our return home back through three countries. An Israeli couple served as tour guides in Jerusalem. As we found out later, they were not married, and the man had a wife and children back home. The tour of Jerusalem was everything I thought it would be and more. We saw the Mount of Olives, the Garden of Gethsemane, the Wailing Wall, the Dome of the Rock in the background, and then proceeded through the Stations of the Cross. Our guide had shared that he was an atheist and without apology. However, he knew the Bible both Old and New Testament and had many times before been a tour guide.

When we arrived at the tomb, our guide asked us if we would like to light a candle and take communion as is the custom of many Christian pilgrims. Tom and I prayed the night before for an opportunity to share our faith. Sensing the need for this couple to meet the real Jesus and remembering what happened in Bethlehem with our Muslim tour guide, we declined the opportunity to light candles and take communion. I said to the couple that Jesus is not here at the physical tomb but here in our hearts as I pointed to my heart and Tom's. Tom agreed.

Then I further said that we have freedom from rituals and the burden of sin. I asked them to give all their sins, problems and cares to Jesus who died for them and meet Jesus right here in their hearts. Tears began to flow from the woman's eyes as her heart received the message. Our male guide did not accept but the seed was planted for him to hopefully think about that experience at the tomb of Jesus. We ended up walking back down the Via Dolorosa and back out to his car. Our Israeli guides dropped us off outside the military checkpoint and wall leading back into Palestine. We were on our own again.

I still had the phone number of our Palestinian friend Monther, so our mission was to find him. With no problem, we got through the wall and when we came out the other side, there many Palestinian taxi cab drivers who apparently all spoke Arabic. I sensed tension in the air as it turned out this was just two weeks before the December 2017 announcement by President Trump of moving the US Embassy to Jerusalem [83].

Then, apparently out of nowhere, one unknown driver came up and asked us in English if he could help. I gave him Monther's phone number and they spoke on the phone. The cab driver handed me his phone and Monther instructed us to get in the car and drive about 90 minutes with him to Nablus and not say a word. Halfway to Nablus, the cab driver drilled us with questions and we tried to say as little as possible. Then, when he heard the word billiards, he perked up and said that he was a pool player. The conversation somehow turned to God. Before long, I was sharing the same message of Jesus with him that we had shared in Bethlehem and Jerusalem. Again, I shared that we are free from rituals and the bondage of sin. He accepted the message and agreed to read the Gospel of John in Arabic just like our Muslim friend Monther had done in Bethlehem. We made it to Nablus and our friend Monther scheduled another Gospel Trick Shot show in Palestine before we departed.

---

[83] "Trump Recognizes Jerusalem as Israeli Capital, Says Final Borders Up to Israel, Palestinians," Haaretz. Available at: https://www.haaretz.com/us-news/trump-recognizes-jerusalem-as-israeli-capital-says-final-borders-up-to-israel-palestinians-1.5627953. © Haaretz Daily Newspaper Ltd. All Rights Reserved

We left Monther's house by shuttle to go through the three walls again to fly out of Amman, Jordan to return to Beirut. For some reason, we got held up at the Jordanian checkpoint and we had a plane to catch. Again, God sent another "angel" in the form of a Palestinian lady who was waiting there with us. She explained that not many buses come this way as most people are tourists on Israeli buses and they go through right away. Finally, a bus arrived and took us to the airport in Amman. Another "angel" in the form of a Jordanian flight attendant, noticed that we had Israeli inspection stickers on our bags. He said that our luggage would be confiscated in the Beirut Airport as people coming from Israel are highly interrogated. In addition to destroying our temporary Israeli passport card, we needed to remove all evidence that we had been in Israel. That was just another reminder of the tensions in the Middle East and our need to help build bridges with the love of Jesus.

Arriving back in Beirut, we met our Christian Lebanese friend Bernard Abi Nadar at the airport. We ended up doing another Gospel Trick Shot show in his home pool room in Beirut. Bernard remarked that in Lebanon he had much frustration dealing with people in the billiard rooms. After that show in his home billiard room, he now understands what he must do to love and be a witness to others. He said that this pool room will now become a RACK room. Bernard continues to be our Gospel Trick Shot RACK team representative in Lebanon. After this short time with Bernard, we returned to the airport in Beirut and headed back to America. What a joy it was to arrive home and marvel about all that God did!

In conclusion, as mentioned earlier, we needed much preparation for this trip. The billiard tables differed in each country. In Lebanon, we played on American pool tables and even did one show on a carom table in a Palestinian neighborhood. In Jordan, they had snooker, carom, and

American pool tables. In Palestine, we played on English pool tables. Finally, in Israel, they had every kind of billiard table: American pool, carom, English pool, English and Canadian snooker tables, and even Russian pyramid pool tables. The Russian game served as a reminder that the first Jewish settlers back in Israel were Russian Jews from the late 1800's [84]. The Russian pyramid game is played on the large size 6 x 12-foot pool table with large 3-inch size pool balls which require special cue sticks. Our American pool is played on 4 1/2 x 9-foot tables with 2 1/4-inch object balls. With all our equipping through the years, Tom and I were able to do shows on all these type tables for the glory of God.

I remembered the lessons learned with the Egyptians and the Albanians. The show that I did on the stage back in 2002 for the Egyptian retreat in Philadelphia taught me that I did not even need a pool table if God so willed. In Albania in 2003, I remembered my hands freezing as I did shows in the villages in the middle of winter on tables that had almost no cloth as the pool table bed felt like an ice cube. As a result, I developed blisters on my hands which made it very difficult to perform. God reminded me that the message was most important.

Now in the Middle East, the message of the Gospel would have to cross over into different cultural barriers. God showed me that the most important part of the Gospel was to be set free. In the Middle East, each of the three major religions has rituals. It was no coincidence that we would tour the Holy Land with a Muslim in Palestine, a Christian at the Sea of Galilee, and an Israeli in Jerusalem. The message remained the same across all boundaries as Jesus came to set us not only free from the legalism of religious rituals but more importantly from the

---

[84] "Mass emigration," Wikipedia. Available at: https://en.wikipedia.org/wiki/History_of_the_Jews_in_Russia. 9 December 2018

bondage of sin. This message resonated with all our new Middle Eastern friends. God is truly the Master of Irony!

Here is a press release below of an article published by the national billiard media [85].

## Press Release for December 2017 – "Building Bridges with Billiards in the Middle East"

BCA Chaplain Steve Lillis with Gospel Trick Shot Ministries, Inc. and BCA Hall of Famer Tom "Dr. Cue" Rossman with Dr. Cue Promotions toured the Middle East for over two weeks to help build bridges in the name of Jesus using the wonderful sport of billiards. Four war-torn countries were visited including Lebanon, Jordan, Palestine, and Israel. A total of 13 Gospel Trick Shot shows were performed with 2 teaching clinics that included national billiards teams. Shows were done on American pool tables, English pool tables, English and Canadian snooker tables, a carom table, and a Russian pyramid pool table. Also included in the trip was a Holy Land visit with Muslim, Jewish, and Christian tour guides.

Steve and Tom were special guest performers for the Arab Championships in Beirut, Lebanon which included national teams from 16 Arab nations. In Israel, they did a live TV interview, a Gospel Trick Shot show, and a teaching clinic for members of the Israeli billiard team. They also spoke at a Messianic Christian Church and helped start two billiard Bible study groups in two different billiard rooms which are now called RACK rooms (Recreational Ambassadors for Christ's Kingdom) with one in Lebanon and the other in Israel. Travel was challenging as transportation was provided by 9 private cars, 7 taxies, 4 buses,

---

[85] "Building Bridges with Billiards in the Middle East," AZBILLIARDS.COM. Available at: https://www.azbilliards.com/news/search/. November 29, 2017

6 planes, all of which included travel through 20 military security checkpoints.

Steve and Tom are also McDermott Ambassadors and McDermott cue sticks were brought and distributed as gifts to some of their special hosts and friends. Special thanks to all our billiard friends across the region who helped build bridges across different cultural, religious, ethnic, and national backgrounds. Billiards is alive and well in the Middle East and is a strong bond to bring people together. Tom and Steve went as men of peace with cue sticks in hand with the message of Jesus who is the Prince of Peace!

**End of Article.**

After returning home from the Middle East, God began to put the pieces together for a return trip to Albania. This would be the first time for Tom and a fourth time for me. Tom had an opening in his schedule for February 2018 and was looking forward to God using him once again. He also made a prior commitment to me to go overseas three times per year wherever I felt the Lord was leading us. He knew that I had years of contacts and experiences overseas and felt that God had gifted me in the area of administration. This also freed me up to make plans knowing that I would have my reliable traveling partner on GTS trips. As I began to contact my old Albanian friends the Christian Farmers, Open Air Campaigners (OAC) in Korce, the International Church in Tirana, and pool players from the Albanian Billiard Federation, plans began to fall in place fast. Within one month after returning from the Middle East, we had a full itinerary ready to go. Below is a press release that I prepared for the billiard news media after we returned from Albania.

**Press Release in February 2018 – "Hope and Billiards for Albanians" – by Steve Lillis**

BCA Hall of Famer Tom "Dr. Cue" Rossman and BCA Chaplain Steve Lillis went on a Gospel Trick Shot/RACK team tour from 2/10/18 – 2/24/18 to minister with billiards to ethnic Albanians in the countries of Albania and Kosovo. The trip included 14 Gospel Trick Shot presentations in 10 villages/cities working with 12 local churches. Some of the Albanian villages/cities like Durres and Feir where Tom and Steve shared the Gospel on the billiard table were along the ancient road called Via Egnatia constructed by the Romans in the 2nd century BC [86]. That road crossed Illyricum (present-day Albania), Macedonia, and Thrace where the Apostle Paul preached the Gospel some 2000 years before. Tom and Steve went briefly into Kosovo and shared in the city of Gjakova, an Islamic cultural center at the crossroads of the trade routes in Eastern Europe. Despite the scars of the 1999 Kosovo war with Serbian Christians, the hope of the Gospel was welcomed by our Kosovo Albanian Muslim friends.

After returning from Kosovo, there were more village shows in the south and the north of Albania with one last show in the capital city of Tirana located in the center of the country. That final show included gut-wrenching testimonies of what God did in the personal lives of both Tom and Steve's families. Eklent Kaci, the 2017 (WPS) World Pool Series Champion [87], was in attendance along with the President of Snooker Albania Ogert Shkrepa. Eklent turned the pool world upside down last year at the age of 18 years old by defeating a host of world-class players in New York City at Darren Appleton's World Pool Series. That

---

[86] "Via Egnatia," Wikipedia. Available at: https://en.wikipedia.org/wiki/Via_Egnatia. 29 November 2018
[87] "World Pool Series 2017 – Grand Final," Wikipedia. Available at: https://de.wikipedia.org/wiki/World_Pool_Series_2017_%E2%80%93_Grand_Finale. 14 March 2018

host billiard room in Tirana, Albania, called Snooker Albania, is Eklent's home room and the youngster was greatly encouraged by what Tom and Steve had to share on the pool table.

Special thanks to McDermott Cues and (GTS) Gospel Trick Shot Ministries, Inc. for sponsoring the tour as McDermott cue sticks were given to the billiard room owners and the winners of various youth tournaments held in the different villages as Gospel Trick Shot organized the tour.  Leaving Albania was difficult as various projects were presented including renovating a new church and an orphanage for homeless street children in the south along with expanding a school for handicapped children in the north.  These projects are in predominantly Muslim villages where the people have great needs.  Please join us in prayer and support as we hope to go back with laborers to help meet some of these needs and share more on the pool table of the hope that is in our hearts. God bless you!

**End of Article.**

One event in which we saw God's hand at work occurred as we were heading out of Albania to Kosovo with one of our dear pastor friends in his car.  We were faced with a traffic jam and could not see up ahead to learn what was blocking the road.  Our pastor friend decided to jump out of the line to see what was going on and got stopped by the police.  They pulled him out of his car and threatened to arrest him and severely punish him.  It turns out that the President of Kosovo was coming through and this was a high-security situation.  Tom and I prayed fervently as panic gripped the face of our pastor friend and we were also faced with the possibility of going to jail with him.  God had mercy on us all as one of the top officers decided to let us go as the pastor continued to plead with him for mercy and explained that he was a man of God.  Once again, the Lord answered our cry for help and protected us.

Another interesting story that took place in the northern part of Albania involved our dear friend Sajmir. He planted a church in the Village of Burrel and he has two missionary farmers from Vermont helping him for six months each year during the winter. We got connected with him from our Fellowship of Christian Farmer friends George and Julie Holmes from Upstate New York. They go to Albania from January to early March each year to work in the villages in the Tirana area. Tirana is the Capital City of Albania and one-third of the country's population reside there. Our schedule was tight, but we had a small window of opportunity to go up into the mountains in the North where there are 17 Muslim villages and no churches except for Sajmir's.

Sajmir had built a school for the handicapped in Burrel, to minister to the handicapped children of the region and show them the love of Jesus. His wife and their two daughters serve at the school. Sajmir's father years before was a member of the Communist Party when Albania was communist and declared itself to be an official Atheist State in which all religion was banned [88]. His Dad enforced strict policies of no religion and the people feared him. The penalties were harsh as many people were sent to concentration camps for their faith prior to 1989. Sajmir grew up watching his father rule with an iron fist. As a result, he learned many of his father's harsh character traits and later used them when dealing with people.

Sajmir had a life-changing experience during an (OAC) Open Air Campaigners men's conference in the early 2000's. He heard the Gospel for the first time and realized that he was a sinner and needed Jesus to help him change. God called him into ministry right after to help the people in the North, whom his

---

[88] "Irreligion in Albania – History," Wikipedia. Available at: https://en.wikipedia.org/wiki/Irreligion_in_Albania. 18 November 2018

father had treated poorly. He shared this testimony with me on one of our long car drives up into the mountains.

I shared with Sajmir the vision I had about bringing pool tables into Albania to equip churches so that they can have billiard cafes to draw men into the church. As I mentioned earlier in the book, ten years prior I had a list of 15 churches and a sponsor to purchase all the pool tables. However, when I found out that I had to submit to a bribe to get the tables into the country, I suspended the project. Sajmir perked up and said that it will be no problem to get the tables into the country, as he has many connections because of his father. I began to dream again of the billiard café project. However, currently I do not have that pool table sponsor. I believe God can and will supply. Maybe someone reading this book will meet this need.

While there in Burrel, Tom and I did two shows with Sajmir. At the first show, I forgot to give an invitation to put their trust in Christ. Tom and I were involved playing partner challenge matches against our Albanian friends. We were having a lot of fun and a wonderful time of fellowship. At the end of the show, Sajmir came over to me and barked out the command, "share the Gospel right now." I immediately snapped to attention and shared. The young men responded as Sajmir told me later that some said to him that they would be in church next Sunday. It really amazed me at how God uses Sajmir with all those rough edges. One thing I know is that he has a tender heart and is a servant to his people. He loves them with the love of Jesus.

Two months before, Tom encouraged me to join him in producing a PowerPoint presentation after our trip to the Middle East. We had many pictures and much to share. At first, I hesitated as I knew Albania was coming up in February 2018. After returning from Albania, I realized that I must. The title became obvious as I had already written an article about building bridges in the Middle East, so I simply added the words, and beyond, to include Albania and Kosovo.

In the months after, I would do 23 of these PowerPoint presentations entitled "Building Bridges in the Middle East and Beyond." The life-changing message of the Gospel that all people can be set free became the theme of the DVD. Included with the pictures was evidence that God indeed is building bridges in the Middle East and beyond with the Gospel and in our case using billiards. Closing every DVD presentation, I would ask people what they can use to share the Gospel and help build bridges. As important as a bridge is from person to person, the ultimate bridge and the need of all people is that they have the bridge to God through Jesus Christ.

# Chapter 25 – Viva la France!

In the beginning of the book, I mentioned that France is where the game of billiards first originated. It then spread to the crown heads of Europe and eventually the entire world through the Age of Colonization. It became known as the sport of kings and the noble game of billiards.

In November of 2018, I finally fulfilled a lifelong dream of going to France. When I was in high school, I completed three years of French. I thought that I would take a fourth year of French in my senior year which would have entitled me to go to France with my fellow classmates. However, based on my father's suggestion, I took calculus instead of French as it would be more useful for a major in Electrical Engineering at Georgia Tech where I was headed for my freshman year of college. I was disappointed that I did not go to France.

Fast forward 20 years to 1988 and Chattanooga, Tennessee. My wife Camille, our two small children, Amanda age two, and newborn Sarah, and I were attending a mission's conference at First Presbyterian Church which was our home church. An offer was made to the congregation for volunteer couples to consider going to France as part of a church planting team. There was a substantial amount of money that was donated to this cause and all it required was a willingness to go for one year. After the call was given, I immediately stood up in response. I encouraged Camille to stand up but she refused! She said that she had enough of a challenge raising two small children here in America and that going to France would make it even more difficult.

When we got home, we began to argue. I told her that I was willing to quit my job at the Krystal Corporation where I served as restaurant manager, and that she should be an obedient wife and follow me. I got so frustrated that I called the head pastor Ben Hayden and explained my predicament. He calmly said the me, "God does not just call the husband into ministry, he calls the husband and the wife!" I knew in my heart that these words of wisdom were true, but I was angry! About one year later, Camille and I separated. I know that this incident and my poor attitude contributed to the separation. Thank God years later we did get back together and I went to France!

By 2018, I had already been to some French speaking Arab countries on my Gospel Trick Shot outreaches. My good friend, Hawthorne Gospel Church missionary Jim Percy, had been with me to Morocco and Lebanon in 2017 to serve as my French translator. In 2016, Jim and I along with many others went to French Quebec, Canada as discussed in a previous chapter. At the time, I did not realize the importance and the rich history of billiards in French Quebec resulted from the love and influence of the sport back in the home country of France [89]. At that outreach a group of 30 French short-term missionaries from France Pour Christ (FPC) came over from France to partner with us in Quebec City. They saw Tom and I do our Gospel Trick Shot shows and asked if we would like to go to France to do our shows.

I had been sharing with Jim about the rich history of billiards in France and told him that I had dreamed of going to France for some fifty years since high school. The opportunity to go to France finally came in God's timing. After contacting FPC to consider their invitation, a formal invitation with proposed itinerary came from Guy Leduc who was planting churches for FPC in the north of France in and around the town of Lille. Jim

---

[89] "HISTORY OF BILLIARD IN QUEBEC (NEW-FRANCE)," Le billard dans les bois. Available at:
https://actu.fondationlionelgroulx.org/Le-billard-dans-les-bois.html.
14 August 2013

Percy and Tom Rossman were both excited to go to France and we did.

An added bonus of this trip for me was that I was possibly going back to my family routes. According to some histories of my sir name Lillis, decedents of mine might have come from Lille in France. They eventually moved to Ireland perhaps some 800 years ago and changed their name to Lillis. Finally, they moved to New York City during the potato famine in Ireland in the 1850's. My grandfather William Joseph Lillis was a New York City fireman.

Here is the article below that was published in the national billiard media in **November 2018** of our exciting trip to France [90].

### "Viva La France and Billiards" by Steve Lillis

Tom "Dr. Cue" Rossman and Steve "Leapin" Lillis embarked on a teaching and trick shot tour of Northern France in conjunction with Gospel Trick Shot Ministries (GTS) and France Pour Christ (FPC) sponsored in part by McDermott Cues. The tour included eleven shows with two on carom ball tables, four on English pool tables, and five on American pool tables from November 13 – 20, 2018. Tom and Steve partnered with various churches, billiard cafes, and billiard clubs in France.

France has a rich history of billiards dating back to the 15th and 16th century [91]. Billiards was used in the Royal Palace of France and places where both men and women assembled to engage in the finer things in life. Billiard academies were formed and used for training in the education of military officers and in higher

---

[90] "Viva la France and Billiards," AZBILLIARDS.COM. Available at: https://www.azbilliards.com/news/search/. November 26, 2018
[91] "History of Pool," pooltables.com. Available at: https://www.pooltables.com/history-of-pool. © pooltables.com

education. The royal families of Europe were all inter-connected and so out of France the game spread to all the crown heads of Europe and then to the New World in the Age of Colonization or Exploration depending on your politics. Steve "Leapin" Lillis will be publishing a new book in 2019 that will include a history of billiards and how Gospel Trick Shot Ministries (GTS) in conjunction with Tom "Dr. Cue" Rossman's RACK Vision (Recreational Ambassadors for Christ's Kingdom), retrace the steps of the European colonizers who brought billiards to the entire world. The next two tour stops for Tom and Steve will hopefully be Scotland and Turkey in February 2019!

This recent tour of France included teaching clinics on physical technique, mental aspects of the game, and finally how all are brought together by matters of the heart. Much of this can be found in Tom's 2016 training manual entitled "Student of the Game and Life." Steve, a former college professor, shared some of the "deeper" aspects of the game using physics, math, psychological and sociological principles, while including life lessons and spiritual principles, as "Dr. Cue" in his own famous unique style shared the simple or "shallower" aspects of the game to produce pure joy! All this was brought together by an assorted array of traditional and unique trick shots and so much more! Special thanks to our friends in France and to McDermott Cues.

**End of Article.**

Finally, going to France reinforced a very valuable life lesson! My nickname by no coincidence is "Leapin" Lillis. I got that nickname in my mid-twenties because I leaped into things with reckless abandon. It took fifty years to finally get to France. I waited 19 ½ years for my wife to come back. There are other important things in my life that I am still waiting for God to answer. For me, this has been the grace of God to teach me patience and to move in His timing! How about you my friend?

Will you trust God to bring about the things that you are waiting for in your life?

The Bible says in Isaiah 40:31, "But those who wait on the Lord shall renew their strength; they shall mount up with wings like eagles, they shall run and not be weary, they shall walk and not faint." One of my favorite Gospel Trick Shots is based on the Psalm 46:10a, "Be still and know that I am God." In this particular shot four balls are struck with three balls rapidly moving into three different pockets while one ball in the middle remains completely still. I share this visual illustration with the pool balls to remind us all to be still before God before proceeding with the decisions of life. I then offer Christian reading material and especially Bibles to meditate on to enhance their time of being still. I am so thankful for the Word of God which serves as our road map!

# Chapter 26 – When God Says NO!

In February of 2019, I was scheduled to go to Turkey with Tom "Dr. Cue" Rossman. This possible outreach resulted from our trip to France in November 2018. Guy Leduc, our team leader in France working with France Pour Christ, asked us if we wanted to join him on a trip to Turkey in 2019. He had worked 15 years in Turkey with Operation Mobilization (OM) and spoke perfect Turkish. Tom and I had an opening in our schedule for February 2019 so we began to make plans.

Guy Leduc connected us with the Operation Mobilization (OM) team leader in Turkey who was home in the USA for the Holidays. After I shared by phone what we do and how we do it, the OM leader said, without hesitation, that this would be a good fit for an OM outreach in Turkey. He contacted his team in Turkey and plans began to develop. They eventually lined up billiard cafes and even contacted the Turkish Billiard Federation for us to do a teaching clinic and a special show much like we have done in other countries.

On the home front, I was dealing with a number of physical challenges. In the summer of 2018, I had knee problems. But during a New Canaan Society (NCS) 2018 Fall Retreat in early October 2018, I received healing in my knees after requesting prayer. When the 2018 fall season began, I was feeling so good with my "new" knees that I planned to play in two major professional pool events in January 2019, the Joss 9-Ball Turning Stone event and the Derby City Classic. I also had my traveling partner Mike Martin scheduled to join me as we secured sponsor money and a venue booth at the Derby City Classic to do Gospel Trick Shot shows. We were both very excited as it had been almost two years since we last traveled together to pro events and shared GTS outreach ministry.

Weeks before the France trip my back began to bother me as I had doubled my weekly swimming activities over the summer. Later my back was diagnosed by a Veterans Association doctor as a muscle strain. Additionally, when I returned from France in November, I began to experience near fainting episodes which suggested that I might be having heart problems. More on that later!

In December 2018, my physical challenges continued as plans for Turkey had not yet been completely confirmed. The OM leader asked me to hold off on purchasing plane tickets until he felt confident that his team had secured all the arrangements. He was not scheduled to return to Turkey until February 6, 2019, so communication with his team in Turkey was slow and unclear. We had tentatively set up dates for the outreach to be February 9-21, 2019. I went to the eye doctor in December 2018 and found out that I had the beginning of cataracts. My new glasses apparently were not able get my vision back to 20/20 and for a pool player this presents a challenge. I also went to a cardiologist in December and had four kinds of tests to check out my heart which included an EKG, an echo cardiogram, a nuclear stress test, and a heart monitor attached to me for three weeks.

After New Year's Day 2019, questions began to surface in my mind about going to Turkey. Money came in to cover Tom's portion of the trip and I felt that if we went GTS would have enough funds for me to go as well. However, my health concerns were looming large. I went back to the cardiologist and found out that I passed three out of four tests. The heart monitor revealed that I might have the beginning of afib. Right after that diagnosis, I developed pain in my jaw so that I could not chew my food. I went to an urgent care clinic and was diagnosed with TMJ (temporomandibular joint and muscle disorder). I had to go on a liquid diet and stop talking for one week. For me, not talking was extremely difficult!

Where is God in all this? At 3:00 am on Monday January 7, 2019, God showed up! I could not sleep and as I often do when this happens, I take out my Bible and begin to study. I have been systematically studying the Bible for years while using my Wycliff Bible Commentary that my mother gave me about 50 years ago. I was now in Ezekiel Chapter 3 as I had started with Genesis a couple of years ago. I have studied through the Bible this way about 6 times in the last 30 years.

As I studied this chapter 3 episode in Ezekiel's life, I realized that God was talking directly to me. The Prophet Ezekiel had been preaching to the people of Israel for years trying to warn them about impeding disaster if they do not repent of their evil ways. Now, God wanted Ezekiel to stop! God allowed him to be bound up (commentary suggests that it was physical challenges) with his tongue stuck to the roof of his mouth so he could not talk. Then the Lord told him to stay home with his wife for two years and his only ministry would be to the people that God would bring directly to his house. It hit me like a ton of bricks that God was trying to tell me through my physical challenges to stop and stay home. My wife Camille had been suggesting that for weeks. I called my partner Tom and he agreed that it was time to stop for a period of time. I then contacted the OM leader and postponed going to Turkey and he understood.

Even though I felt like I did the right thing in postponing the trip to Turkey, there was that little voice of doubt from the enemy suggesting that I misunderstood God in all of this. I struggled in my mind for one month as I went to those two professional tournaments in January vowing that they might be my last. I had already paid the money up front before all this happened, so I felt that God wanted me to go. I did not do well in the tournaments. When I got home, I was frustrated with all that was happening. Then, I received an email that changed my thinking in a heartbeat.

Guy Leduc, from France Pour Christ, who was going to travel with us as our Turkish translator, sent me an email in the middle of February 2019. This was about the same time we would have been in Turkey had we gone. He informed me that the OM team leader was stopped at the border and blacklisted for life from Turkey. He was now cut off from his possessions and his team in Turkey. I realized that God was protecting us all the time as we were originally scheduled to arrive three days later with this same team leader picking us up at the airport. God sure has his own way of saying "NO" to a trip!

In conclusion, my physical challenges seemed to all disappear after that email from Guy. My knees and back are fine and I am swimming again but not overdoing it. I finally got eyeglasses that work well when I play pool. It turned out that they put the old lens back in my frames by mistake. My jaw is completely healed and I am eating and talking as usual. As for my heart, maybe it all was about my heart all along but not my physical heart. My follow-up appointment with the cardiologist was good as he suggested that we do not have to take any action at this time. Thank you, Lord, "that your thoughts are not my thoughts, neither are your ways my ways, as the heavens are higher than the earth, so are your ways higher than my ways and your thoughts than my thoughts" (Isaiah 55:8-9).

# Chapter 27 - What's Next?

In my Gospel Trick Shot journey of being a follower of the Lord Jesus Christ, searching for the will of God and finding out what to do and where to go has obviously been extremely important. As administrator of the ministry, staying connected to Jesus in prayer and looking at His Word has been key. TV evangelist Pat Robertson [92], in one of his teaching sessions, used three factors in finding the will of God. I have used them to be my guide as well. Pat taught that first, what you are about to do must not violate Biblical truth. Secondly, the circumstances of your life are moving in a direction and you should pay close attention. Third, and last, after deciding, the peace of the Holy Spirit should follow. When these three principles line up, then proceed, trusting that your decision is the will of God. I have used this for the past 35 years and I have been blessed with the peace of God. Romans 8:28 (ESV) gives me added confidence, "And we know that for those who love God all things work together for good, for those who are called according to his purpose."

Sometimes decisions do not work out as planned. For example, ten years ago I printed up flyers to start Christian pool leagues around the country for a national billiard pool league association. This resulted in me losing privileges because of complaints from some pool league operators. However, a few years later, I was pleasantly surprised that a Christian pool league was started by Robin Dodson in California and she invited me to do my Gospel Trick Shot show for that league. Early on in the 1990's, I sought parachurch ministry endorsements by large organizations, only to be led back to the local level. However,

---

[92] "Pat Roberson," Wikipedia. Available at: https://en.wikipedia.org/wiki/Pat_Robertson. 25 December 2018

later, I had the privilege to partner with worldwide ministries like Chi Alpha at World SALT 2000, InterVarsity at Urbana 2009, Cru at Radiate 2010, and other regional events. A major disappointment occurred when an important outreach event was planned and canceled in 2005 in Upstate New York. However, a few years later, Tom, Mike, and I did two shows in 2010 and 2011 at the Hardrock Café in Universal Studios in Florida for the returning disabled US Vets from Iraq and Afghanistan. This was a major blessing to serve our military with the love of Jesus.

God led me to many wonderful people who caught the vision for Gospel Trick Shot. There were also some frustrations with people along the way. Disagreements, personality conflicts, and rebellion crept in at times even though I believed we were moving forward in the will of God. In Acts Chapter 15 in the Bible, the Apostle Paul and Barnabas had a "sharp disagreement over Jon Mark which caused them to separate. We are not immune from people problems because we follow Jesus.

Conversely, through the years, many people have stepped up to help Gospel Trick Shot. Coach Lonnie Smith at the Hawthorne Christian Academy had me do GTS Shows for his basketball team and then joined the GTS Board of Directors. Jane Brain, Director of Top O' the Hill Summer Day Camp, had me do five shows for the campers of all different age levels. We did GTS shows and partnered with Christian motorcycle gangs in Phoenix, AZ and Quebec City, Canada. My good friend Donny Christopher, with Down the Stretch Ministries, still brings me each year to Monmouth Park Racetrack in Oceanport, NJ to do GTS shows for the horse training staffers. I was asked to do a renewal of marriage vows in 2004 in Las Vegas and then married two pool players in Pennsylvania ten years later. We have had dozens of GTS board members through the years. Many short-term missionaries have partnered and traveled with us all over the world.

God has worked through wonderful people willing to serve. My Old Testament Bible school teacher Pastor Jim Richmond at the Hawthorne Evening Bible School where I earned my 4-year diploma in 1999, discussed during the semester many of the Old Testament Bible characters like Abraham, Sampson, David, etc. Pastor Jim would not only mention their successes but also their failures. At the end of the semester, he remarked as he looked out over the class with a penetrating gaze, "God goes with who He's got." Those words hit me back then and still do! We now have 35 Gospel Trick Shot artists in 10 countries serving the Lord with pool.

The question of what God wants to do next with Gospel Trick Shot is always in the forefront of my mind and heart. In 2017 and 2018, we investigated having billiard cafés in Morocco, Lebanon, and Albania while partnering with churches and/or ministries. That idea is still under consideration with the ministry platform model called (BAM) Business as Mission [93]. We have presented a billiard café franchise proposal to Diamond Pool Tables and McDermott Cues and both are interested in partnering with us. We have trusted on the ground contacts in Morocco, Lebanon, and Albania to secure good workers for the billiard café(s). We are looking for investors to start the project(s), God willing.

We have ministries like Horizons International and Sat 7 Tv interested in working with us in the Middle East and North Africa (MENA) region. We share a common interest in helping the Syrian, Iraqi, Palestinian, and African refugees displaced because of war and economic hardship. Building projects and evangelistic outreaches in Albania with three different ministries are still on the table. A Gospel Trick Shot billiard training

---

[93] "Business as Mission," Lausanne Movement. Available at: https://www.lausanne.org/networks/issues/business-as-mission.

academy in the Philippines is a possibility with all the billiard talent and GTS connections in that country.

In March of 2019, I went to do Gospel Trick Shot college shows in the great state of Virginia working with Chi Alpha Campus Ministries. After hundreds of shows through the years on college campuses, I had yet to experience an outreach on an historically black college and university campus (HBCU). As part of this tour I had the privilege to minister at Virginia Union an HBCU campus. It was such a blessing to minister to my African American friends at Virginia Union as it brought back fond memories of my ministry beginnings in Paterson, NJ in the 1990's in the African American community. The outreach was so successful that Chi Alpha leadership is working with me to possibly go to the other 18 HBCU campuses in the southeastern region.

Planning is underway to have a conference called "Woodstick" at Tom and Marty Rossman's one-acre home property in Indiana. GTS partner Pastor Michael Hewitt is assisting in the planning. Michael is prayerfully considering coming on board full time in the future with Gospel Trick Shot to help with the administration of the ministry. GTS helper Brian Pauley will also help spearhead this effort as he serves on the Board of Directors for the WPA Artistic Pool Division and is a top ten WPA world-ranked Artistic Pool competitor. Woodstick will bring together Gospel Trick Shot artists and helpers from all over the world for a week of refreshment, encouragement, teaching. They will also share in the vision of what God wants to do to further use billiards while being a (RACK) Recreational Ambassadors for Christ's Kingdom.

Young people are the future of any ministry. GTS has an 18-year-old young man named Florian training in France with Dr. Cue's manual for a GTS trip to Scotland. Joey DeMarco, a 27-year-old member of the Hawthorne Gospel Church, is now my assistant and apprentice working with me in the New York Metro Area. Albanian Eklent Kaci, number one ranked player in the world at 19 years-old, is in touch with an Albanian pastor right here in New Jersey. Young Arab players like Mohammad Ali Berjaoui, the number one ranked player in Lebanon, and others from the Middle East and North Africa stay in touch with me on a regular basis by social media.

In the 1930's there were thousands of billiard rooms in Manhattan and by 1986 there were only two billiard rooms left in the city [94]. According to billiard historian Mike Shamos, the sport of billiards did not look like it would make it to the end of the decade of the 1980's. Temporarily retired from the billiard industry in 1985, God called me back into pool in 1996 with Gospel Trick Shot Ministries. In 2019, billiards was seriously considered to be a part of the 2024 Paris Olympics [95]. Last report was that it will not be a part of 2024, but we can still hope for 2028. This would attract more young people around the world to the sport of billiards. GTS is planning to be there when it happens, Lord willing, as this has been a personal dream of mine since I turned professional in the 1970's.

---

[94] Shamos, Mike. "Forward," The Complete Book of Billiards. Published by Gramercy Books, New York, NY. 1993, p. viii. Print. Copyright 1993 by Michael Ian Shamos.
[95] "Billiards 2024 Olympic Campaign Launches," AZBILLIARDS. Available at: https://www.azbilliards.com/news/stories/14316-billiards-2024-olympic-campaign-launches/. WCBS Press Release Dec. 4, 2018

# Chapter 28 – Final Thoughts

To accomplish anything for Christ, we must be Kingdom minded. Our allegiance must be to Jesus Christ and him alone. As believers, we are in God's army. The Bible says in II Timothy 2:4 (ESV), "No soldier gets entangled in civilian pursuits, since his aim is to please the one who enlisted him." Jesus said in Matthew 6:24 (ESV), "No man can serve two masters, for either he will hate the one and love the other, or he will be devoted to the one and despise the other. You cannot serve God and money."

I have found that our culture strongly resists the message of Jesus. There are spiritual forces seeking to keep us from following Him. When I do Gospel Trick Shot shows, I use my billiard gift to draw people into the show. One particular shot called "Be Still" encourages people to stop and listen to what God is trying to say through the trick shot and the message. Mike Massey in his well-known trick shot book called "Mike Massey's World of Trick Shots" makes mention of my "Be Still" shot [96]. At some point in the show, my goal is to become invisible and make only Jesus visible. John 3:30 (ESV) says, "He must increase, but I must decrease." This is the work of the Holy Spirit as we yield ourselves to the will of God.

The induction of Tom "Dr. Cue" Rossman into the BCA Hall of Fame in December of 2017 brought many people together for the glory of God. Here is an article I wrote for the billiard news media in **May of 2018**.

---

[96] Massey, Mike and Phil Capelle. "Bachnine 10-Cent Special," Mike Massey's World of Trick Shots. Published by Billiards Press. ISBN 9649204-6-8. Copyright 2003 Mike Massey, p. 65. Print.

## The Witness – by Steve Lillis

The billiard industry came together last December 2017 to witness the induction of Tom "Dr. Cue" Rossman and Darren Appleton into the BCA Hall of Fame. In the largest turnout of (HOF) Hall of Fame players, manufacturers, fans, and friends to date, Tom gave a speech giving glory to God for all his achievements as he has served the billiard industry since 1974. In response, sponsor McDermott Cue Company made 20 signature cues with crosses representing Tom's faith and to honor his HOF accomplishment.

Additionally, cue maker and dear GTS friend Curtis Robertson made two very special cues called "The Witness Cue." These cue sticks have crosses, biblical images, and some of Tom's favorite Scripture verses. Tom asked me to do a special show at the Hopkins Expo this past April 2018 in honor of the "Witness Cue." This was done on a Saturday night in the McDermott Booth before many Hopkins Expo attendees. I also did a special tribute to the passing of my granddaughter Ella which tragically happened in 2014. The people there that night witnessed a special journey of faith and hope!

Tom and I have partnered the past year to go to six war-torn countries in the Middle East and beyond representing Gospel Trick Shot Ministries, Inc. to help build bridges of hope and share our faith while using billiards.

Gospel Trick Shot Ministries, Inc. (GTS) is a (BCA) Billiard Congress of America associate member and this year is celebrating our 20th anniversary of incorporation on June 8th. I have served as official BCA Chaplain since 2007. GTS has been to 26 countries, performed more than 100 college shows, attended more than 100 billiard industry events, and visited most of the states in the USA while doing about 1,500 presentations since 1996. For more information please go to www.gospeltrickshot.org.

Tom currently serves on the GTS board of directors and his website is www.drcuepromotions.com. Brian "Superman" Pauley, a WPA world ranked Artistic Pool player, also serves on the GTS board with seven other men. Tom "Dr. Cue" Rossman recently published a training manual called "Student of the Game and Life!" I published my life story in 2013 entitled "But You Must!" Both are available on our respective websites. Together Tom and I and others are planning to go to ten more countries, Lord willing, with Gospel Trick Shot shows and teaching clinics.

The story of Tom and myself is a journey of faith and witness that started separately as both of us believe that God has brought us together for such a time as this. Tom's faith journey started in 1984 with the RACK (Recreational Ambassadors for Christ's Kingdom) vision. You can read about it on his website.

In 1976, I met Mike Massey and we became road partners and friends in the faith. In 1993, Loree Jon Jones (now Hasson), a lifelong friend and fellow New Jersey native, along with then-husband and pool player Sammy Jones, encouraged me to use my gift for pool as I had quit playing in 1985. In 1998, Robin Dodson called me to do the same and the ministry was incorporated that same year. And finally, in 1999, Tom, who started the modern-day Artistic Pool movement, invited me to Las Vegas for the first WPA World Artistic Pool Championship in 2000 that was won by who else but Mike Massey.

In 2001, Mike, Tom, and I combined forces along with Loree Jon and Robin and began to do Gospel Trick Shot shows together at various major billiard events to be a witness to what God had done in all of our lives. The witness goes on as many other younger pool players are now stepping up and sharing their faith! To God be the glory!

**End of Article.**

# Chapter 29 – Conclusion: "The Journey" - For those who want to become God's pool player or .......!

Do you remember the first time you experienced the game of pool? The first time your eyes were filled with the vast array of rainbow colors ROYGBIV? Remember the first time your ears experienced the rhythmic and methodical click of the balls as their surfaces collided on the green but silent bed of the table? How about the gentle thud of the rails as the colorful spheres seem to rebound at the exact same speed? Most likely we did not understand the Physics of the game at that juncture with the principles of inelastic collisions, friction, momentum, and the like. Nor did we understand the mechanics of execution with stance, bridge, stroke, and pendulum motion. Nor did we understand the inner mental game necessary to consistently execute on the green felt with a high level of proficiency.

Yes, we were utterly fascinated with a childlike faith to trust that the game of pool could give us hours of fascination and enjoyment. We launched out at that point on a "journey". A love affair, an adventure, a journey into the world of pool not knowing where it would take us, only believing that at the end of the journey we would be satisfied. Yes, that childlike faith in the game that set-in motion for most of us, a lifelong journey seeking to understand, experience, and relate to all this wonderful game had to offer. We really did not know where we would end up when we started; we only set out to "enjoy the roll".

There was another man in History who set out on a journey and his name was Abram, better known as Abraham. His story is found in the first book of the Bible called Genesis and specifically in Chapter 12. You see Abraham's story is about a man who had to learn to live between the promise and the fulfillment. When we were first attracted to the game of pool it offered us the promise of sensory excitement, the thrill of unpredictable outcomes, and an infinite number of possibilities on the green felt which promised us a lifetime of fascination and interest. But then there is the fulfillment of the promise which at times did not seem to pan out. Times in which we questioned why we ever picked up a cue stick to play this game in the first place. Instead of feeling satisfaction we felt deceived, disappointed, and discouraged. Abraham felt the same way on his life journey. God had made him a promise that his decedents would form a great nation and that he would be blessed with the favor of God. Abraham was to follow God out into the unknown. With childlike faith he began to chase the promise. In his journey and in our journey, three questions seem to scream out at us on the way. First is where am I going? Second is how will I get there? Third is who am I becoming?

You see Abraham did not know where he was going on this journey, for he was going by faith, faith in God, and faith in the promise. It was a childlike faith, the kind of faith Jesus talked about some 2,000 years later. He said in Matthew 18:3; "I tell you the truth, unless you change and become like little children, you will never enter the Kingdom of Heaven". Yes, that is the childlike faith we embraced at the beginning of our pool journey. That faith was the promise that this game would give us a lifetime of fascination and enjoyment. But how will we get there? This is the next question Abraham wrestled with.

In his story, he encountered obstacles along the way. There was a famine in the land, so he headed down to Egypt. In the Bible, Egypt usually represents the world system or man's way as opposed to God's way. So, it is with us that when we experience a famine in our game or life, you or I will resort to other means to be successful. Abraham did exactly that when he lied to the Egyptians and said that his wife Sarai, better known as Sarah, was his sister. He feared that they would kill him and take his wife who was very beautiful.

We sometimes resort to unscrupulous or ungodly tactics on the pool table to win or be successful in the eyes of the billiard community or for monetary gain. You might say I'm not like that or I would never stoop to anything that was wrong to get ahead. Please let me remind you that not one of us can say that we are perfect. Our Lord Jesus successfully encountered the three basic temptations we all unsuccessfully face. In Matthew Chapter 4, the Devil confronted Jesus in much the same way he confronts us. First, it was with possessions and fleshly needs. The Devil told Jesus to turn stones into bread as Jesus had been fasting for 40 days. How many of us at one time were tempted to hustle someone out of their money or gamble to quickly solve our desire or need for money? You might say, well I never did that with the game of pool. Consider the second temptation in which the Devil told Jesus to throw himself down from the cliff and command his angels to rescue him. This would be a spectacular show, gratifying the now with a show of power.

How many of us have pranced around the pool table showing off our ability and being full of ourselves? Maybe it was to impress a member of the opposite sex or maybe just simply an ego trip. Then there was the third temptation where the Devil took Jesus to a very high mountain and showed him the kingdoms of the world. He then said that they would all be his if only he would bow down and worship the Devil. Who of us is not tempted to control, conquer, and subdue? It starts as a little child when one might say to a little sister or brother, that's my toy, give it to me, as opposed to sharing. In our journey through life, we are tempted to control perhaps friends, family members, or even the entire pool world when we get a taste of power and control. I know many people at the top jockeying for position to control and I know people in the poolrooms looking to rule their little kingdoms as well. You see none of us are immune from these temptations.

Now back to our story of Abraham. He was in a real-life struggle trying to live between the promise and the fulfillment of the promise. Where was he going and how was he to get there? You see he not only failed in the "how" when he went to Egypt during the famine and lied about his wife Sarah, but later he got tired of waiting for the promise and with his wife Sarah concocted a plan to do it themselves. Remember the promise was a great nation that would come from them but there was no child and they were getting older.

How many of us lose our patience in waiting for the promise that we had as a child? The promise is that we would, with the game of pool, "enjoy the roll" all the days of our lives. We begin to take matters into our own hands.

Abraham and Sarah did exactly that when they hatched a plan to have a child through their maid servant Hagar. This has resulted in a 4,000-year-old struggle between the Arab peoples who are the descendants of Abraham and Hagar and the Jews who are the descendants of Abraham and Sarah. You see God did fulfill the promise but not on Abraham and Sarah's time schedule.

The "where am I going" and the "how will I get there" questions actually answer the question of "who am I becoming". Psychologists tell us that we make about 500 choices per day. Everything from when I decide to get up after I hear the alarm ring, to what I will wear, to what I will eat, and whether I will brush my teeth and floss, or not. You get the idea! Where you will end up in one year, five years, ten years, will be the product of the sum total of the choices you make starting right now.

You are on a journey and today is the first day of the rest of your life. Who we will become will be determined by whether we live for ourselves or for God and others? Will we live for others and become a blessing and an encouragement to them?

Pool is a game and even more can become a tool to display the Godly character of humility and service to others. World Champion and ESPN "Trick Shot Magic" star Tom "Dr. Cue" Rossman and his life helpmate Marty "Ms. Cue" Rossman say that "Artistic Pool" is a "Gift" and the foundation of their belief lie in the RACK stewardship vision. Tom has a fantastic testimony of how God gave him this vision directly and you can read more about it at www.drcuepromotions.com.

Artistic Pool is an umbrella term for all the various types of shots that can be executed with a cue stick. The "Gift" is from God and the opportunity is to be a Recreational Ambassador for Christ's Kingdom (RACK) so states Tom and Marty.

There is a battle on planet earth between good and evil, between God and the Devil. Consequently, there is a wrestling match for the minds and hearts and souls of men and women. Just like in all areas of life, it is going on in the world of pool.

As Joshua said in the book of the Bible after his name in chapter 24 and verse 15, "chose for yourselves this day who you will serve". God wants us to choose him and his way of faith. David Nasser in his book entitled "A Call to Die" says that, "If we have that kind of simple faith (child), God will use us in incredible ways, but if we are plotting to get power and recognition, God will oppose us". In the Bible, in I Peter 5:5, he says, "God opposes the proud, but gives grace to the humble."

Nasser also said in his book, "Christianity is littered with stories of men and women who had great talents but lusted for more power and more prestige until God pulled the plug on them. He is patient. He gives us plenty of warning and plenty of opportunity to repent of our desire for fame, but if we refuse, we lose." So, Nasser says!

Likewise, the world of pool is littered with stories of men and women who had great talents but lusted for more power and more prestige until God pulled the plug on them. I know many of my generation who started out like me with a childlike faith in the game and thought that it would deliver a lifetime of fascination and enjoyment.

Many who embarked on this journey did like Abraham and lied not only to themselves and others, but to God and used the gift for their own self-seeking desires instead of using it to bring glory to God and service to others. They now are bitter with disappointment, angry with the game, and too proud to admit that they have made a series of poor choices. Is there hope? Is there forgiveness? Is there a future? The answer is yes.

You see there is One who like us did battle with Satan but he made all the right choices, because he could. He was Jesus Christ, God in the flesh. We cannot nor do we make all the right choices all the time. In the book of Romans in the Bible in Chapter 3 in verse 23 it says, "for all have sinned and fall short of the glory of God." Does that sound like you and me and our beloved pool world?

There is good news in Romans chapter 5 and verse 8 where the one Who did not succumb to Satan's temptations "demonstrated his own love for us in this; while we were still sinners, Christ died for us." To reject this and embrace a life of selfishness and poor choices, hurts the game of pool, people, and yourself and has sad consequences. Yes consequences!

For example, if you were caught stealing you would probably do time in the slammer. There is good and evil and so there is reward and punishment. Again, in the Book of Romans this time in chapter 6 and verse 23 the Bible says, "the wages of sin is death, but the gift of God is eternal life in Christ Jesus our Lord." The good news is "that if you confess with your mouth, Jesus is Lord, and believes in your heart that God raised him from the dead, you will be saved" according to Romans 10 verse 9, and verse 13 says, "Everyone who calls on the name of the Lord will be saved." It's your choice who you want to be, a child of God or a child of Satan. How do you want to get there, by God's way or your way? Where do you want to end up, eternally with God or eternally separated from him in eternal punishment?

In the pool world, you are living perhaps somewhere between the promise that the game offered to you as a child with all of its fascination and charm, and the fulfillment of that promise. You will find fulfillment only as you lose the false promise of the game and use it as a gift to serve others in the billiard industry and beyond. The promise to Abraham was to "walk by faith and not by sight" (I Corinthians 5:7). God will take you to a better place free from pain, free from worry, free from care. That promised better place is heaven. Are you willing to walk this journey by faith in God and not by the natural sight of man? Only you can make that decision. Do you want to become God's pool player? As Tom and Marty Rossman say on their telephone message recording at the end, "RACK up a victory in your game and life."

If you are reading this chapter and your gift is something other than pool, for example art, do you want to use it for God's glory? My good friend and fellow Gospel Trick Shot Ministries board member, Ian Grinyer, uses spiritual themed canvas oil painting to share the love of Jesus. He has held art classes to teach and inspire many inner-city youths on how to paint as many of the local schools have abandon art education. His paintings hang in many places all over the Paterson, New Jersey area including one on my kitchen wall. That painting has me in the center of the picture in front of a pool table on one of the islands in Lake Victoria in the Country of Tanzania. I am surrounded by many Africans who are standing, sitting on the ground, and also sitting on the branches of a large tree hovering over the pool table. People who come to my home are inspired by that painting as they hear the story of our Gospel Trick Shot "pool safari" to Africa in 2010. After suffering 4 months in intensive care for congestive heart failure in 2018, Ian is back painting for Jesus in 2019. God gave him that gift and he continues to use it to bring glory to God! You can do the same!

**End of Book Chapters.**

# Epilogue

When I was an up and coming young professional pool player in the early 1970's as a twenty-something-year old, I acquired the name "Leapin", as in Steve "Leapin" Lillis. Some of the reasons could have been because I would leap from one pool room to another and I also leaped up after my shots on the pool table. Another reason could have been my totally unpredictable behavior resulting from my drug and alcohol abuse. Now when I leap it is for Jesus. He tells me where to go and what to do. It used to bother me when people would bring that name up because of the negative connotations. I do not mind anymore being called "Leapin" Lillis because I leap for the joy of the Lord with the game of pool.

When I started my ministry in 1996, I had a mentor from my home church, the Hawthorne Gospel Church, named Peter Everett, who was a Gospel magician. He took me aside one day and showed me his deformed fingers as he was up in age and struggled with arthritis. He said to me that when he was younger, he asked God to make him the best ten-fingered Gospel magician he could be. Then as he began to age, he lost the use of two fingers and asked God to make him the best eight-fingered Gospel magician he could be. In 1996, when he was in his 70's, he had the full use of only three fingers. His prayer, as I sat there listening back then, was that God would make him the best three-fingered magician that he could be. I got the message then and I realize it even more now as I approach 70 years old.

My fingers are fine, my eyesight is good with the help of glasses, and my nerves are still steady, thank God. I have all the ingredients to still play competitive pool with some of the best players in the world even at age 68. However, in the past year, I developed knee problems. At first, I looked for a quick fix and went to the doctors insisting that I needed to get back on the pool table with healthy knees. It was not happening, and I began to ask God why. Out of necessity, I began to cut my schedule of pool playing at tournaments and accepted only invitations to do GTS shows.

About the same time that my knee problems began, God put on my heart to write this book. I procrastinated for months. My knee problems worked out for good so that I can start this book and now it is finished. My knees are healed as well. Praise God! What a lesson I learned through pain. God will get me to do His will even if being afflicted is needed.

Now I have a vision for a third book to complete a trilogy. This third book, Lord willing, will be about reflections on doing ministry all these years. I hope to share in more detail what God has taught me so that the next generation of believers in Jesus will have some sort of guidebook to hopefully help encourage them to use their gifts and talents for the glory of God. God specializes in the unexpected! He is constantly changing our plans to accomplish His goals. Our job is stay connected to Him and open to His plans!

What about you my friend? Are you in the will of God? It starts by asking Jesus to set you free from the consequences and the bondage of your own sin and rebellion against God. Ask Jesus to be your Savior because He died in your place for the penalty of your sins, and then make Him Lord over every area of your life. Then you can live for the Kingdom of God by the power of the Holy Spirit that will live inside you upon receiving His free gift of salvation for you. Just ask and then just receive, Romans 10:13 (NIV) says, "Everyone who calls on the name of the Lord will be saved."

# Appendix I – Credits and Accomplishments

## GTS Show Credits:

8/1998 – Steve Lillis did a GTS Show as a part of the 1998 Hawthorne Gospel Church Summer Bible Conference in which such people as Billy Graham of BGEA, Jack Wyrtsen of Word of Life Ministries, Ron Hutchcraft of RHM Ministries, and other Worldwide Christian Statesmen have appeared in years past. This was the first major public GTS Show.

5/2000, 5/2001, 5/2002, 5/2003, 5/2004, 5/2005, 5/2006, 5/2007, 5/2008, 5/2009, 5/2010, 5/2011, 5/2012, 7/2013, 7/2014 – GTS RACK Team appeared at the BCA (Billiard Congress of America) National Eight Ball Championship and Expo in the Riviera Hotel in Las Vegas, NV for shows and outreach. Mike Massey, Tom "Dr. Cue" Rossman, and Steve Lillis were the featured performers for most of BCAPL events.

2000, 2001, 2002, and 2012 – Steve Lillis did GTS Shows at various Joss Northeast Pro Tour events in such states as Connecticut, Maine, New York, and Massachusetts.

2001 - 2004 - Steve Lillis served as the Chairman of the World Pool and Billiard Association (WPA) Artistic Pool Division (APD)

2001 – 2004 - GTS RACK Team appeared at various WPA (World Pool and Billiard Association) World Artistic Pool Tour events for shows and outreach in both the USA and overseas.

3/2002, 3/2003, 3/2004, 3/2005, 3/2006, 3/2007, 3/2008, 3/2009, 3/2010, 3/2011, 3/2012, 3/2013, 3/2014, 4/2015, 4/2016, 4/2017, 4/2018, 4/2019 – GTS RACK Team appeared at the Hopkin's Super Billiard Expo in the Valley Forge Convention Center in Valley Forge, PA for shows and outreach.

8/2002, 8/2003, 8/2004, 8/2005, 8/2006, 8/2007, 8/2013 – GTS RACK Team appeared at the APA (American Pool player's Association) National Championships in the Riviera Hotel in Las Vegas, NV for shows and outreach.

10/2002, 10/2003, 9/2004, 9/2005 – Steve Lillis did GTS Shows at the NJ State 14.1 Straight Pool Championship in Parsippany, NJ. 12/2002 – Steve Lillis did GTS Shows for the Southeast Pro 9 Ball Tour in Florida.

7/2003, 4/2004, 4/2005, 4/2006, 8/2006, 6/2007, 6/2008, 6/2009, 7/2010 – GTS RACK Team appeared at the BCA (Billiard Congress of America) Trade Shows at various venues for shows and outreach.

2003 – 2009 - Steve Lillis did GTS Shows at various UPA (United States Professional Pool Player's Association) Tour events in such cities as Phoenix, Philadelphia, Los Angeles, Atlanta, Jacksonville, New York, and Chesapeake, VA at the U.S. Open 9 Ball. Steve has been consistently ranked in the top 32 players in the world on the UPA Tour which was the top professional men's tour from 2003-2008.

10/2003 – GTS RACK Team appeared at the Midwest Billiard Expo in The Pheasant Run Resort in Chicago, IL for shows and outreach. 6/2004 – GTS RACK Team appeared at the (VNEA) Valley National Eight Ball Championships in the Riviera Hotel in Las Vegas.

9/2004, 9/2005, 9/2006, 10/2007, 10/2008, 10/2009, 10/2010, 10/2012, 10/2015, 10/2016 - Steve Lillis did a series of GTS Shows at the U.S. Open 9 Ball Championships in the Chesapeake Convention Center in Chesapeake and the Sheridan Hotel in Norfolk, VA. In 2006 and 2007 Steve was given permission by tournament promoter to eulogize fallen pool players, share, and pray over the PA system.

10/2004 - Performed Gospel Trick Shot Show at Grand Central Station in New York City.

6/2005 - Steve Lillis did 14 trick shot shows at 16th Annual International Sports Show in Shanghai, China.

1/2006 - Steve Lillis was invited by the President of the Albanian Billiard Federation to start a billiard academy with a focus on artistic pool. Steve's title was the "Professor of Bilardo Artistica". The academy was attended by an elite group of players and their coaches called Team Albania.

1/2006 - Steve Lillis performed a Gospel Trick Shot Show on the campus of the University of Tirana in Albania and partnered with Campus Crusade for Christ.

10/2006, 5/2008, 12/2015 - Steve Lillis did featured GTS presentations at the Hawthorne Gospel Church in Hawthorne, NJ in the "new" gym as part of their 2006 Fall Missions Conference and 2008 Spring Outreach.  In 2015 Steve did three "In Memory of Ella" shows on the GTS portable pool table for the junior/senior high chapel services of the Hawthorne Christian Academy in the "new" gym and one other for the "Serving Hands" group in the Chapel formally known as the Bible House Bookstore.

1/2007 – Steve Lillis did a series of GTS Shows at the "Derby City Classic" in Louisville, KY working in conjunction with GTS/RACK team member Robin Dodson in her booth called Robin's Pro Shop in 2007.

11/2007 – Steve Lillis did a series of GTS Shows at the Qlympics Billiard Event in Louisville, KY produced and directed by the BCA Pool League.

1/2008, 12/2013 – Steve Lillis did a series of GTS Shows working in conjunction with Dr. Cue Promotions and the "Classic Cup" event and the Derby City Classic produced and directed by Diamond Billiard Products. Steve also helped organize and direct the first RACK Room Sunday morning service for pool players and by pool players. GTS/RACK team members Mike Massey, Tom Rossman, and Steve Geller.

12/2009 - Steve did GTS Shows as part of "Urbana 2009" in St. Louis, MO produced and directed by InterVarsity Christian Fellowship which was attended by 17,000 college students.

6/2010 – Steve Lillis was on a "pool safari" on the islands of Lake Victoria in Tanzania, Africa conducting pool tournaments and doing a series of Gospel Trick Shot shows for the island people in conjunction with missionaries from the Hawthorne Gospel Church in Hawthorne, NJ.

12/2010 - Steve did GTS Shows as part of "Radiate 2010" in Baltimore, MD produced and directed by Campus Crusade for Christ which had 1,500 students in attendance.

8/2011, 9/2013 - The GTS RACK Team of Mike Massey, Tom "Dr. Cue" Rossman, and Steve Lillis, launch "RACK Up A Victory" world tour with first stop at the Hard Rock Hotel at Universal Studios in Orlando, Florida to honor our abled and disabled U.S. Vets and Military who are stationed there.

Appearances at the (CSRM) The Christian Sports and Recreation Ministry Summit in Phoenix in 2009, Atlanta in 2010, Indianapolis in 2011 and Dallas in 2012

Summer 2013, 2014, 2015 - Gospel Trick Shot did a series of shows with the GTS portable pool table in Jones Beach Boardwalk in New York, the Asbury Park and Ocean Grove Boardwalks in New Jersey, and four times in Central Park at the band shell off 72nd Street in NYC.

8/2014 - Saturday night GTS show at Sandcastle Billiards in Edison, NJ as part of the "Classic Cup VIII" artistic pool event with a RACK Room Sunday morning service.

2014, 2015, 2017, 2018 – GTS shows at the Monmouth Park Race Track in NJ for the jockeys, trainers, and staff.

5/2015, 9/2018 – GTS "In Memory of Ella" show at the Alexander Hamilton Public School in Paterson, NJ on the GTS portable pool table for the entire school of 700 students.

5/2015 – GTS "In Memory of Ella" show on the portable pool table for the Anaheim, CA public school "Released Time" for religious instruction program end of the year banquet celebration.

7/2016, 7/2017 - NJ and NY campgrounds and Quebec, Canada portable pool table tours with Steve Lillis, Tom "Dr. Cue" Rossman, and Chuck Dutcher with 30 total shows at various venues including campgrounds, parks, and churches,

3/2017 - Steve Lillis was the first and only American professional pool player to compete in Morocco in the Morocco 9 Ball Open in Tangier and did a Gospel Trick Shot show before the finals of the event.

4/2017 - Steve Lillis was the first and only American professional pool player to compete in Lebanon in the Lebanon 9 Ball International Open in Jounieh, Lebanon and did three Gospel Trick Shot shows.

11/2017 - Steve Lillis and Tom "Dr. Cue" Rossman on tour in the Middle East including Lebanon, Jordan, Palestine, and Israel doing 15 Gospel Trick Shot shows and teaching clinics working with billiard federations in each country and ministries including OM and Calvary Chapel in Israel.

2/2018 - Steve Lillis and Tom "Dr. Cue" Rossman on tour in the countries of Albania and Kosovo doing 14 Gospel Trick Shot shows in 10 cities working with 12 churches, McDermott Cues, and Snooker Albania.

11/2018 - Steve Lillis and Tom "Dr. Cue" Rossman toured Northern France doing 11 Gospel Trick Shot shows in 4 cities working with 3 churches and McDermott Cues.

## **Media Credits:**

9/2000 and 9/2001 – Steve Lillis was featured on 270 worldwide radio stations as part of RBC's Ministries broadcast entitled "Words to Live By".

2000-2009 – GTS RACK Team members have appeared numerous times on the ESPN broadcast entitled Trick Shot Magic for competition and interviews.

2001 – 2012 – GTS RACK Team appeared in many newspapers, magazines, brochures, flyers, and other printed material both inside and outside the billiard industry. Steve Lillis appeared on the front page of the June 2004 issue of Professor Q Balls Nationwide Billiard Newspaper.

2/2002 - GTS RACK Team did a show that was taped in Willingen, Germany and broadcast on German Television at the conclusion of the 2002 WPA World Artistic Pool Championship.

3/2002 – GTS RACK Team featured in "Inside Pool" magazine article entitled "GTS RACK Power Team Hits the Road".

6/2003 – GTS RACK Team did a show that was taped in Kiev, Ukraine and broadcast on Russian Television and aired to potentially 290 million people in the former Soviet Union.

12/2003 – Steve Lillis did a GTS Show and interview that was taped by Telesports in Tirana, Albania and aired throughout the country of Albania.

8/2004 – Steve Lillis appeared on ESPN TV as the Master of Ceremonies and Head Referee for the 2004 Men's International Challenge of Champions at Mohegan Sun.

8/2004 – Steve Lillis appeared on ESPN TV as the Master of Ceremonies and Head Table Judge for the 2004 Women's International Trick Shot Challenge at Mohegan Sun.

6/2005 - Steve Lillis interviewed with trick shot show taped for broadcast on Chinese National TV.

1/2006 - Steve Lillis choreographed an artistic billiard show for Telesports TV using his own Gospel Trick Shots and included 10 Albanians demonstrating shots they learned at the academy. RACK Team members Tony "The Comic" Anthony, Marcel Kaiser of Germany and Christian Coffey of Canada participated. The three-hour broadcast received about 40 hours of air time in Albania.

12/2006 - Steve Lillis was interviewed by David Virkler of Dedication Evangelism for the national radio broadcast of "Word and the World".

12/2006 - Steve Lillis appeared on the national TV broadcast of the "700 Club" on ABC Family and other affiliate television stations. The show was rebroadcast in 2007.

5/2009 - Steve Lillis was featured in billiard publications highlighting a GTS tour of the Arabian Peninsula which included working with mission organizations, U.S. Navy, and the National Billiard Teams of Kuwait, U.A.E., and Bahrain.

6/2010 - Steve Lillis and Jason Lynch was featured in billiard publications as part of GTS Africa Tour in conjunction with Thomas Aaron Billiards and McDermott Cues. A GTS team of three Kenyans was formed to minister in East Africa.

6/2012 - GTS RACK Team World Tour continues in the Philippines as Mike Massey, Tom "Dr. Cue" Rossman, and Steve Lillis perform 24 shows in 15 cities on three islands with local, national, and world TV and newspaper coverage. Special interview was done by the 700 Club in their TV studios in Manila.

3/2013 - The life story of Steve Lillis "But You Must!" published by Gospel Trick Shot Ministries, Inc. and released on Amazon.com.

7/2016, 7/2017 - Canadian tour advertised on Canadian radio and articles published in national billiard publications in the USA including Professor-Q-Ball's National Pool & 3-Cushion News, Pool & Billiard Magazine, and AZBilliards.com.

3/2017 - Steve Lillis did a live streamed Gospel Trick Shot Show before the finals of the 2017 Morocco 9 Ball Open in Tangier, Morocco.

4/2017 - Steve Lillis did 3 Gospel Trick Shot Shows for the Lebanese Billiard Federation at the Lebanon 9 Ball International Open and a video was published and released worldwide through Facebook.

9/2017 - Steve Lillis did a Gospel Trick Shot Show for the K Love Radio Single Moms event at the Montclair Community Church in NJ.

11/2017 - Steve Lillis and Tom "Dr. Cue" Rossman were on live sports talk TV and had a Gospel Trick Shot show taped for TV both in Tel-A-Viv, Israel along with two different articles published on their Middle East GTS Tour in various American based billiard publications.

## GTS Countries Visited Around the World:

England 2001

Germany 2002, 2004

Ukraine 2003

Albania 2003, 2006, 2007, 2018

Taiwan 2004

Korea 2004

China 2005, 2012

Greece 2007

Russia 2007

Kuwait 2009

Bahrain 2009

Dubai and Abu Dhabi of the United Arab Emirates (UAE) 2009

Tanzania 2010

Kenya 2010, 2012

Egypt 2010, 2011

Iraq 2012

Honduras 2012

Guatemala 2012

Philippines 2012, 2015

Canada 2016, 2017

Morocco 2017

Lebanon 4/2017, 11/2017

Jordan 2017

Palestine 2017

Israel 2017

Kosovo 2018

France 2018

# Appendix II – Personal Credits & Titles, Campus Ministries and Colleges

## Steve Lillis

## Personal Credits and Titles:

1977 - represented the U.S. Navy in world championship competitions and finished in the top ten in the World 14.1 Straight Pool and the World 9 Ball Championships

1979 - BCA Colorado State 8 Ball Champion

1980 - BCA Georgia State 9 Ball Champion

1981 - Miller Lite Tennessee State 8 Ball Champion

1981 - Miller Lite Tennessee State 9 Ball Champion

1981 - Miller Lite Southeastern 8 Ball Champion

1981 - Miller Lite Southeastern 9 Ball Champion

1982 - BCA Florida State 9 Ball Champion

1985-1996 - in retirement from playing professional pool

2000 – came out of retirement to compete in the first ever BCA North American Artistic Pool Championship, which was a "world qualifier" for the first ever WPA World Artistic Pool Championship.

2001 - 2002 – served as Chairman of the World Pool Billiard Association (WPA) "General Artistic Pool Committee."

2002-2004 – served as Chairman of the World Pool Billiard Association Artistic Pool Division (WPA APD)

2003 - 2008 - ranked in the top 32 according to the UPA (United States Professional Pool Players Association) rankings with sanctioning by the BCA (Billiard Congress of America)

2004 - Picked by the BCA to represent the United States in Taipei City, Taiwan at the WPA (World Pool and Billiard Association) World 9 Ball Championships

2006 - invited by Albanian Billiard Federation to teach 12 pro Albanian pool players and coaches and design and perform a TV pool show for Telesports, their major sports network

2007 - selected to be the UPA Chaplain of the men's professional tour and confirmed by the BCA

6/2008 - Steve Lillis ranked in the top 32 players was invited to play in the BCA GenerationPool.com 9 Ball ESPN TV tournament in Charlotte, NC and performed a Gospel Trick Shot Show for the live TV audience

3/2009 - semi retired from professional billiard competition

# Gospel Trick Shot Ministries, Inc. - Colleges and Universities Visited

## Campus Ministries partnering with Gospel Trick Shot Ministries, Inc.

InterVarsity Christian Fellowship (IVCF)

Campus Ambassadors (CA)

International Student Friendship Ministries (ISF)

Campus Crusade for Christ (Cru)

Chi Alpha Christian Fellowship (XA)

## New Jersey Colleges:

William Paterson University

Farleigh Dickenson University

Essex County Community College

Montclair State University

New Jersey Institute of Technology

Passaic County Community College

Drew University

Ramapo College of New Jersey

Rutgers University in New Brunswick

Rutgers Newark

Princeton University

Kean University

New Jersey City University

Caldwell College

## New York Colleges

State University of New York SUNY Plattsburgh

State University of New York SUNY Cortland

Nassau County Community College

Ithaca College

Nyack College

Fashion Institute of Technology

Rensellear Polytechnic Institute

## Virginia Colleges

Virginia Commonwealth University

Virginia Union

Virginia Tech

Radford University

University of Richmond

## Minnesota Colleges

University of Minnesota

North Central University

Saint Mary's University

Winona State University

## Texas Colleges

University of Texas El Paso

Texas A & M University

Lamar University

## Illinois Colleges

Southern Illinois University

Bradley University

## Georgia Colleges

Georgia Tech

Columbus State University

## Other Colleges and Universities:

Arizona State University

San Diego State University

University of South Florida

University of Louisville

University of Maryland

University of New Hampshire

Massachusetts Institute of Technology

Valley Forge Christian College in PA

# Appendix III - Gospel Trick Shots – Glossary, Diagrams, and Explanations

This section will present a few examples of some Gospel Trick Shots. Some of them have been used since the ministry began back in 1996. If you are not a pool player the "Glossary of Terms" below will be helpful even though you may still not be able to understand all the concepts involved. To my pool playing friends, this will hopefully be a tool to not only learn a few shots, but how to incorporate the message as well. The first 12 shots are performed using standard billiard equipment. The bonus shots need special equipment. It is my hope and prayer that others will learn these shots and be inspired to invent other Gospel Trick Shots so that the message of Jesus can be shared around the world through billiards.

## Glossary of Terms

**Pool Table** – always the length is twice the width with 6 pockets and usually 4 ½ x 9, 4 x 8, or 3 ½ x 7.

**Side Rails** – 4 total side rails containing the felted rubber cushions and placed on the longer sides. In the diagrams they are rails AB, BC, DE, and EF.

**Head Rail and Foot Rail** – rails containing felted rubber cushions and noted on diagrams as AD and CF.

**Diamonds** - 6 spots on long side rails and 3 spots on short side rails to provide aiming direction.

**Props** – other objects needed in some Gospel Trick Shots. For example, a scarf is used in #3 to cover the balls.

**Triangle** – used to rack the balls and also can be used as a prop in trick shots.

**Cue Ball** – solid white with a line through center in the diagrams and noted as such under diagram.

**Object Balls** – solid white in diagrams with explanation of what balls to use in some Gospel Trick Shots.

**Eight Ball** – solid black in the diagrams and usually used as a key ball in some Gospel Trick Shots.

**Cue Stick** – used to strike cue ball or as a prop to jump over or help pocket balls on certain shots.

**English** – hitting left or right-side spin on the cue ball altering the path of the cue ball and object balls.

**Running English** – striking the cue ball on the left or right to cause the cue ball to run off the rail in a natural motion.

**Frozen ball(s)** – no gap between the balls and/or the rail.

**Combination Shots** – straight line through the center of two frozen balls in a trick shot indicates direction of outer ball.

**Directional Throw** – altered direction of the natural path of the balls due to applied physical forces.

**Symmetrical** – set up of object balls in a trick shot that looks like a mirror reflection when divided in half.

## Gospel Trick Shot #1

### Obstacles

**History of the Trick Shot:** This is a spin-off of the "Butterfly Shot" made famous by Willie Mosconi on the Ed Sullivan Show in the 1960's. I saw Jim Rempe add two balls in the front of the cue ball creating an obstacle. I concluded that this shot would now represent the obstacles in my life. My good friend, Pastor Scott Packard in Albany, NY, used a video tape of me doing this shot and 10 others as part of his weekly APA church league's 15-minute devotional. At the time, Scott owned that APA Mohawk Valley franchise.

**GTS Name and Why:** Obstacles - My personal life was full of obstacles. Having been separated from my wife for 19 $^1$/2 years taught me to go on and go through the obstacles of my life!

**Scripture References in NIV Translation:** Romans 5:3-5; II Corinthians 4: 17; James 1:2-8; Proverbs 3:5-6; John 14:27; and Psalm 31:24. Each one is worth reading in any translation.

**Cue Ball Placement:** Place the cue ball as shown and shoot directly through the center of the butterfly.

**Object Ball(s) Placement:** Place the six object balls on the table first as shown allowing for directional throw in each pocket. Lay your stick-on table to make sure the center two balls of the butterfly (6 balls) are centered and about 2/3 of a ball width apart. Place the two remaining object balls frozen to the cue ball and headed to the inside of the side pockets.

**Objective:** Pocket all eight balls as shown thereby going through the obstacles of life.

**Special Notes:** Focused concentration on firm center cue ball hit, straight stoke, and follow through.

**Crowd Reactions Through the Years:** This shot has always been a crowd pleaser as people love to see many balls fall in the pockets. More importantly they really begin to think about the obstacles in their lives!

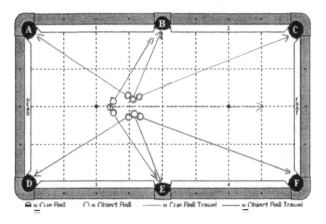

## Gospel Trick Shot # 2

## Deception

**History of the Trick Shot:** The first time I saw this shot was the early 1970's when a road player came to my pool room in Verona, NJ and set up the shot to show off after beating up on some of the locals. I tried the shot unsuccessfully until years later when my road partner Mike Massey gave me some pointers.

**GTS Name and Why:** Deception - When I finally mastered the shot, I realized that the shot was very deceiving as the cue ball heads in one direction with the 8-Ball going in the side pocket moving in the opposite direction. I thought about situations in life that appear to be headed in the wrong direction and people who mislead you. I realized that we must rely on God's Word and what He will do!

**Scripture References in NIV Translation:** Jeremiah 29:11; I John 1:8; Proverbs 12:19-22; Philippians 1:6; Galatians 6:3; Romans 10:9,13; John 3:16; Romans 8:28.

**Cue Ball Placement:** Place cue ball as shown moving no more than a diamond width from that position.

**Object Ball(s) Placement:** Place object balls as shown frozen with the two pairs of balls on rail with the top ball in the pair about ½ ball over the other. The pair of balls on the bottom rail are the key balls in the six-ball combination with the other two pairs of balls clearing out for the 8-Ball to pass towards the side pocket. The 8-Ball is pocketed after kicking off the single object ball sitting in front of side pocket E.

**Objective:** Pocket only the 8-Ball using all the object balls (see note below) in the set-up of the trick shot.

**Special Notes:** You can add or remove one or more object balls from side rail DE combination to adjust for proper contact from the pair of balls on head rail DA. Split first pair of balls on rail DE with slight low draw English on the cue ball so it does not collide with the 8-Ball coming up rail DE.

**Crowd Reactions Through the Years:** I ask people to guess where the 8-Ball will be pocketed. Usually it takes five guesses to pick the correct pocket. I then remind the people that the shot is called Deception. Then I remind them about life and how things are not always as they appear. Something to think about!

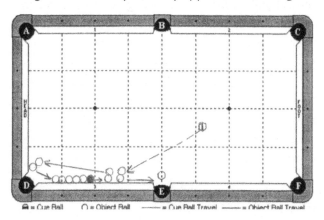

A = Cue Ball     O = Object Ball     ———— = Cue Ball Travel     ———— = Object Ball Travel

## Gospel Trick Shot # 3

## Peer Pressure

**History of the Trick Shot:** The first time I think I saw this trick shot was in an exhibition by the late great BCA Hall of Fame pool player Jimmy Caras. There are many other names for this shot as it has been around for a long time. One other name for the shot that I am aware of is the Rosebud.

**GTS Name and Why:** Peer Pressure - Having been a teacher for 23 years to mostly college freshmen, I often thought about the tremendous peer pressure imposed on them. In many of my college shows, I almost always include this shot to remind students about choices in life. I ask them to pick one of the four pockets ABDE which represent four possible directions in life. I remind them that their Creator has a special plan for them as each person is uniquely different. Peer pressure can take them out of God's good plan for their life. Be careful who you keep company with!

**Scripture References in NIV Translation:** Romans 12:2; Proverbs 22:24-25; Proverbs 4:14-16; Proverbs 22: l; II Corinthians 6:8; I Corinthians 15:33.

**Cue Ball Placement:** Depending on designated pocket ABED, the cue ball will be placed accordingly.

**Object Ball(s) Placement:** Place six balls frozen around the black 8-Ball as shown with four ½ inch gaps.

**Objective:** Hit the object ball closest to cue ball full and firm and watch 8-Ball go in designated pocket.

**Special Notes:** Continue to reposition cue ball same distance from closest object ball so that you can make 8-Ball in all four pockets around the symmetrical shape. Place scarf over the object balls for special effect. Then position cue ball so that the line to strike the object ball is directly to the opposite pocket. In diagram you would aim for pocket D and 8-Ball would come out from under scarf to pocket A.

**Crowd Reactions Through the Years:** People are deeply moved by this shot with the scarf as it represents faith because you cannot see what will happen. So, it is the same in life as we walk by faith. I have used this shot many times in the "Ella" story (see Chapter 21) to illustrate choices when tragedy hits home. I personally chose to trust God and then share some of my other impulses which would have led to other problems. Crowds have been silenced by this shot, hearts have changed, and Jesus Christ glorified!

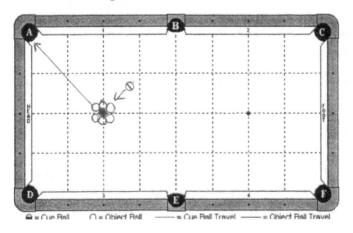

◨ = Cue Ball     ○ = Object Ball     ——— = Cue Ball Travel     ——— = Object Ball Travel

## Gospel Trick Shot #4

## Proud/Humble

**History of the Trick Shot:** The first time I saw this shot was in a show in Chattanooga, TN performed by the great BCA Hall of Fame pool player Nick Varner after he won his first World Championship in 1980. Thirty years later, I did a show with Nick in Arizona as his special guest. He remarked after the show that he never saw that shot and others used that way. I thanked Nick and shared that my shots are GTS shots.

**GTS Name and Why:** Pride/Humble Shot - When I was looking for GTS shots, I remembered seeing the balls in this particular shot fall to the table. My mind went to Proverbs 16:18 that "pride comes before a great fall." Many times in my life I have become prideful and suffered the painful consequences.

**Scripture References in NIV Translation:** Proverbs 16:5, 18; our example Jesus in Philippians 2:5-1 1.

**Cue Ball Placement:** Place cue ball directly in line with pocket B as shown.

**Object Ball(s) Placement:** Suspend two object balls on two different coin wrappers with one cut about two-thirds the size of the other placed closest to cue ball so that when the object balls crash to the table they will collide and travel into pockets B and E. Place a third object ball in front of pocket B.

**Objective:** Shoot the cue ball and pocket the third object ball in front of pocket B. Hit about half of the ball so that the cue ball gets out of the way of the other object ball headed to that same pocket.

**Special Notes:** Must hit both coin wrappers as cue ball passes under suspended balls while heading towards third object ball. Lift hands off table to avoid obstructing the path of object ball moving to pocket E.

**Crowd Reactions Through the Years:** Simple shot that can be done by a child and that is exactly what I try to do in my shows as I bring out a young person to execute the shot. When the shot goes in the crowd cheers wildly for the youth. This also demonstrates humility by putting others first as I get out of the way! The goal of GTS shows is to make Jesus more visible and this is one technique that enhances that!

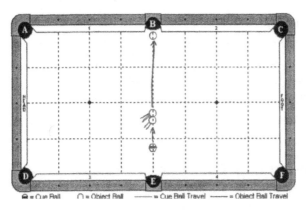

⊜ = Cue Ball    ○ = Object Ball    ——— = Cue Ball Travel    ------- = Object Ball Travel

## Gospel Trick Shot # 5

## Walls

**History of the Trick Shot:** In 1983 in Tupelo, Mississippi at a pro 9-Ball event, Minnesota Fats did this shot five times missing the first four in his special trick shot show. Each time he missed he told a better story to the delight of the crowd. Earlier that day he had invited me to do the show with him to be his caddy. I got to witness first hand not only the shot but the art of telling stories during a trick shot show!

**GTS Name and Why:** I never forgot that night with Fats. Years later I would name the shot "Walls" because it looked like a wall as I related it to matters of the heart. We build walls with people when we get angry, don't forgive, are jealous, or lack self-control. This shot became a GTS favorite as stories about my own walls revealed the need to take down the walls and have healthy relationships with people.

**Scripture References in NIV Translation:** Proverbs 27:4, 15:18, 27:4, 3:31, 14:30 and James 1:19, 20.

**Cue Ball Placement:** Place cue ball as shown but its position can be adjusted forward or backward slightly.

**Object Ball(s) Placement:** Start with the first object ball closest to side pocket E as shown. Then place the other three in a straight line in front of the first object ball. Notice balls are slightly to the right of side pocket E. Place an object ball in corner pocket C as shown.

**Objective:** Pocket four object balls (wall) near side pocket as shown with cue ball coming back to pocket final object ball near corner pocket C.

**Special Notes:** Hit cue ball in the center aiming to split the middle two balls. You can go slightly forward or back with the cue ball after you see the direction of the cue ball. You can also place the triangle in front of the object ball hanging in pocket C to make a larger target area for the cue ball to pocket the ball.

**Crowd Reactions Through the Years:** I ask the audience if they have any walls in their life and explain that we are all being tested by God through people. All of us at times fail our test and need to make adjustments. People usually get very quiet while I talk about this shot as I can tell God is speaking to them personally. That final ball being pocketed represents having a relationship with somebody after the wall comes down! How are you doing with your test today?

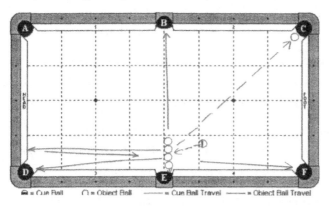

🌑 = Cue Ball      ◯ = Object Ball      ------ = Cue Ball Travel      ——— = Object Ball Travel

## Gospel Trick Shot # 6

## Be Still

**History of the Trick Shot:** The first time I saw this shot was probably in a trick shot show by the great Hall of Fame pool player Irving Crane from Rochester, NY. I had the privilege of playing in the 1977 World 14.1 Straight Pool Championship with him where he took 4th in his mid-sixties and I took 9th as a 26-year-old. This classic shot was used by many of the game's greatest players in their trick shot shows.

**GTS Name and Why:** When I observed that the cue ball in the center of the shot does not move, I thought about how God wants us to be still and reflect on Him. My nickname is "Leapin" and I did not get that name by being still. This shot always reminds me to spend time being still as I seek the Lord.

**Scripture References in NIV Translation:** Psalm 46:10 says to "Be still and know that I am God;" and also Proverbs 8:34 and Psalm 131:2 say more on the subject.

**Cue Ball Placement:** Place cue ball in between the two object balls as shown. Use another object ball to replace the cue ball as the ball you strike to set the shot in motion.

**Object Ball(s) Placement:** As shown in the diagram below.

**Objective:** Hit center ball on the third object ball to the outer edge (1/4 ball) of the object ball closest to pocket A. If hit at just the right angle the balls will go in as shown with the cue ball remaining still.

**Special Notes:** Some cushions play shorter or longer so you can move the three balls left or right on the head rail to make an adjustment. They must always be frozen to the bottom rail and to each other to be successful. A variation to this shot is to place a dime 1/4 inch on the cushion in front of the object ball closest to pocket A. Place a coffee cup 2 inches behind the dime and standing upright on the rail. Shoot the "Be Still" shot in the same way and watch the dime pop up into the cup for added affect.

**Crowd Reactions Through the Years:** This shot is simple but yet profound. People see the shot and immediately can relate to the principle. When the dime and cup are added it becomes a crowd favorite!

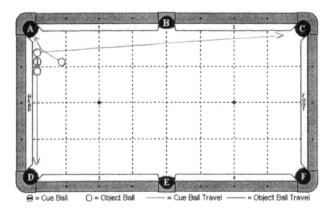

## Gospel Trick Shot # 7

## Salvation Bracelet

**History of the Trick Shot:** My former road partner in the 1980's, Mike Massey, used this classic shot in his fabulous repertoire for years. He is still considered by many the greatest trick shot artist of all time. Mike called it the "Smiley Face" and later when we traveled together with Gospel Trick Shot, I used the five specific Gospel colors and renamed the shot the "Salvation Bracelet."

**GTS Name and Why:** The five Gospel colors in order are black for the darkness of sin, red for the blood of Jesus, white for the cleansing of sin, gold for the promise of heaven, and green for growing in grace. The Serving Hands group at the Hawthorne Gospel Church has made tens of thousands of these bracelets for Gospel Trick Shot. They have been distributed all over the world as the shot was being performed.

**Scripture References in NIV Translation:** Romans 3:23, 6:23, 5:8, 10:9-10, 10:13 and II Peter 3:18.

**Cue Ball Placement:** Place cue ball in between the other four colored object balls – black, red, gold, and green. Use another object ball or another cue ball to perform the shot.

**Object Ball(s) Placement:** As shown in the diagram below with the black eight ball first, then red three ball, white cue ball, gold or yellow one ball, and green six ball.

**Objective:** Using another cue ball or object ball hit the eight-ball firm full in the face and directly in line with pocket A. All five Gospel colored balls will be pocketed as shown in diagram.

**Special Notes:** If the cue ball is a different size and weight then adjust the tangent line accordingly on the red, white, and gold balls to successfully pocket all balls. Observe that the last two balls are a combination into pocket F and the green six ball will throw about two ball widths because of the directional force.

**Crowd Reactions Through the Years:** As the shot is being set up and explained each person in the audience receives a free bracelet from a Gospel Trick Shot helper. Similarly, the Gospel is a free gift because Jesus did it all for us as our Savior and salvation cannot be earned.

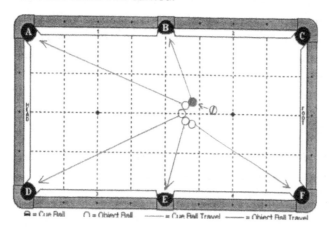

## Gospel Trick Shot # 8

## Titanic

**History of the Trick Shot:** My Gospel Trick Shot road partners Mike Massey and Tom "Dr. Cue" Rossman worked with me on this shot. Mike was the first trick shot artist I saw use this shot in his show.

**GTS Name and Why:** The first thought I had about this shot was that everything must be sunk and hence the name Titanic. I later realized that there was another boat called the Ark, built by God, that was designed to float and save humanity. The comparison about which boat to be on as we travel through life crossed my mind! I realized that for years, I was on the Titanic. When I met Jesus, I switched to the Ark.

**Scripture References in NIV Translation:** Genesis 6:1-11:32; Hebrews 9:27; and Acts 4:12.

**Cue Ball Placement:** Place cue ball as shown and hit firm through the middle of the six object balls.

**Object Ball(s) Placement:** Place two balls each hanging near pockets B and E as shown. Follow set-up of Gospel Trick Shot #1 but move the two balls with the cue ball back about 1.5 inches. Aim those two balls frozen to the cue ball directly at the balls closest to pockets B and E. Place one ball near each of pockets A and D as shown. You can adjust to other sides of pockets A and D if needed. Place 8 Ball on rail on a cube of chalk.

**Objective:** Stoke hard with good follow through to make 14 balls in one shot. For added affect, you can place the eight ball on a cube of chalk nearby and after the shot simply drop it in your side pants pocket.

**Special Notes:** Remove six balls in the middle and test with a firm stroke the cue ball with the two frozen object balls and the two hanging balls in each of pockets B and E. If this works then do the complete shot.

**Crowd Reactions Through the Years:** I start building the boat (pockets B, E, A, and D) and share that my Dad and I were in the U.S. Navy. I bring out the passengers in the middle, the captain (cue ball), and the first and second mate (frozen to cue ball). Before I shoot, I challenge the crowd to switch to the Ark like I did years ago. I shoot, 14 balls sink, and fifteenth ball the eight ball goes in my pants pocket from sitting on a cube of chalk on rail! Cover line if you miss the shot can be that there were survivors on the Titanic! After applause, I encourage people to take our free literature to get more information about Captain Jesus!

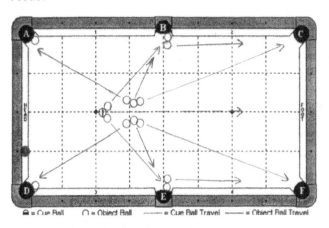

● = Cue Ball ○ = Object Ball ------ = Cue Ball Travel ------ = Object Ball Travel

## Gospel Trick Shot # 9

## Joy

**History of the Trick Shot:** This is one of those oldies but goodies! A very simple l, 2, 3 shot that I had seen BCA Hall of Fame players Nick Varner and Jimmy Caras use along with a few others.

**GTS Name and Why:** After practicing the shot, the thought came to me that I can use the balls to represent the letters J, O, and Y spelling the word joy. I further thought about a Bible lesson I learned years before about putting Jesus first, others second, and yourself last if you want to have lasting JOY. Since I was an English professor, the letters in the right order form the acronym JOY.

**Scripture References in NIV Translation:** Nehemiah 8:10 and Psalm 73:26.

**Cue Ball Placement:** Place cue ball as shown but it can be adjusted to accommodate the shooter.

**Object Ball(s) Placement:** Place the one-ball frozen to the rail as shown. The two-ball is in front about one half ball width away from pocket A. The three-ball is set up for a combination into pocket D as shown allowing for directional throw.

**Objective:** Hit the cue ball to pocket the one-ball with inside English hitting the rail and the ball at the same time. Ignore the other balls as if they were not there. All three balls will go in order with the one and two balls going in pocket A and the three-ball following across in pocket D.

**Special Notes:** This configuration can be adjusted by moving the one-ball slightly in either direction alongside rail AB. The other balls will remain in approximately the same formation.

**Crowd Reactions Through the Years:** This is yet another shot that is so simple but yet profound. People see the shot and immediately understand the principle. I usually share with the folks that years ago I had it backwards where I put myself first, others a distant second, and Jesus was not even on my radar screen. For years, I wondered why I had no joy! When I found Jesus, I found true joy. I challenge those in the audience that if they are not experiencing true joy, try putting Jesus first!

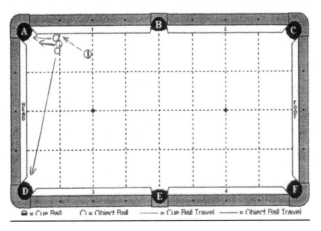

◨ = Cue Ball    ○ = Object Ball    ——— = Cue Ball Travel    ——— = Object Ball Travel

## Gospel Trick Shot # 10

## Parting of the Red Sea

**History of the Trick Shot**: This shot has been used by many of the legends of pool. There are many variations to this shot and they can be found in many other published trick shot manuals. Mike Massey's "World of Trick Shots" is the best in my opinion. My attempt to explain and diagram the shot is below.

**GTS Name and Why**: Naming the shot "Parting of the Red Sea" idea was suggested to me by Mike Massey. When you read the objective below, it should be obvious why the name was given. However, the message is the most important thing in this shot. I added a bag to the shot and added the name "Free Gift."

**Scripture References in NIV Translation**: Exodus 14 and Ephesians 2:8-9.

**Cue Ball Placement**: Place the cue ball approximately one ball width from the side rail diamond as shown. If needed move cue ball back from frozen two balls on rail another ½ diamond.

**Object Ball(s) Placement**: Place the two balls frozen to each other on the side rail one inch to the right of pocket E. Use the eight ball to be the ball frozen on the rail. Measure two balls width from outer frozen ball and place a third object ball ½ ball to the left. Now freeze another object ball ½ ball up from that third object ball. Repeat the process three more times with a two-inch gap between the pairs of balls.

**Objective**: Hit cue ball firm catching about ½ of the outer ball in the two frozen balls on the side rail by side pocket E. Make sure you have a good follow through to catch about half of that third ball. The four pairs of balls will separate as the black eight ball slides across the table into side pocket B.

**Special Notes**: Place a small "gift" bag (slightly larger than an object ball) on the table about one diamond width from side pocket B with the opening of the bag facing the path of the oncoming eight ball. It will enter the bag on its way to the side pocket and flip over and be deposited in side pocket B.

**Crowd Reactions Through the Years**: There is much movement on this shot and with the gift bag people are amazed that the eight ball goes in. The parting of the Red Sea was for the salvation of the Jews from the advancing Egyptian army who was chasing them. The gift bag represents our salvation which is a free gift from God because of what Jesus did for us on the cross! We cannot earn salvation but simply receive it!

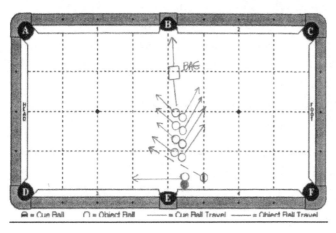

## Gospel Trick Shot # 11

## Rainbow

**History of the Trick Shot**: The first time I saw this shot was by the late great Lou "Machine Gun" Butera. This was his signature shot. He would shoot this shot in rapid fire and he was one of the fastest pool players on the planet. I had the privilege to play and notch a win again this legend! Years later, he attended our Gospel Trick Shot Bible studies and shared that he was a believer in the Lord Jesus Christ.

**GTS Name and Why**: Some trick shot shooters use the seven solid colored object balls in this shot. While teaching 4th and 5th grade back in the 1990's, I used the acronym ROY G BIV (red, orange, yellow, green, blue, indigo, and violet) to remember the seven colors of the rainbow in the correct order. In the Bible, the rainbow represents the first promise from God never to flood the world again!

**Scripture References in NIV Translation**: Genesis 6-9, Hebrews 13:5, and I Corinthians 10:13.

**Cue Ball Placement**: Cue ball is not needed, however can be included to represent a cloud.

**Object Ball(s) Placement**: As shown in the diagram below in the correct color order ROY G BIV.

**Objective**: Place a cue stick with the butt of the stick near corner pocket A on the table alongside rail ABC. Shoot the balls in the correct color order, with top right (running) English, so that they hit the 3 rails. The red ball should strike diamond 1 near pocket C and then each successive ball will strike one ball width above that. After 3 rails, the balls will hit cue stick on the table and slide into corner pocket A.

**Special Notes**: After you strike that first (red) ball, which is the first ball on the right in diagram, and it goes 3 cushions and passes you, then strike the next ball the same way and repeat the process until all balls are pocketed. You can learn to increase your speed by shooting two balls before one passes you and so on!

**Crowd Reactions Through the Years**: The crowd loves this shot and the faster the better. Again, the message is most important and what I do before shooting the shot is mention several promises from the Bible to build on that first promise that God made with the rainbow. "Promises of God" is another name that I gave to this shot to emphasize that the Bible contains many promises from God to us.

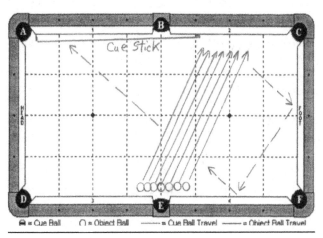

## Gospel Trick Shot # 12

## Showing Off

**History of the Trick Shot**: This shot was made famous by my friend and former New Jersey native Steve Mizerak who is a BCA Hall of Famer and legend of the game. Steve did this shot on a Miller Lite beer commercial back in the 1980's and went on to become larger than the game of pool as an international celebrity. I had the privilege to successfully compete against Steve many times in my professional career.

**GTS Name and Why**: This shot has always been a favorite of mine. For years, I combined it with the Pride/Humble Gospel Trick Shot #4 for obvious reasons. My good friend and GTS helper, Pastor Michael Hewitt, put an interesting twist on the shot and I will use that below for an explanation.

**Scripture References in NIV Translation**: Ecclesiastes 4: 9-12.

**Cue Ball Placement**: Place the cue ball about one diamond from pocket E and one ball from rail EF.

**Object Ball(s) Placement**: Place an object ball as shown in line vertically and diagonally with the left point on the side cushion of rail ED. Place another ball directly in front with a third ball pointed to pocket A on a combination shot allowing for directional throw. Then two balls will be placed frozen to each other and the cushion as shown about one inch from pocket E. Place the eight-ball hanging in pocket C.

**Objective**: Hit the cue ball firm with top left (running) English catching about 1/3 of the outer object ball of the two frozen balls on side rail EF. The cue ball should strike the first diamond on side rail AB before the outer ball of the combination shot reaches corner pocket A. All five balls will disappear with the cue ball coming around the table three rails before depositing the black eight ball in corner pocket C.

**Special Notes**: Steve Mizerak in the commercial placed a cup on the table and lifted it to drink before the cue ball came around to pocket the eight ball and said "this is what I do when I am just showing off."

**Crowd Reactions Through the Years**: People love this shot because it might be the most famous trick shot of all time. The message that Pastor Michael added is that it is not good to be alone as God created us to be in fellowship with one another. The two balls frozen on rail EF represent that two is better than one and the three balls near side pocket E represent that three is even better. The Scriptures listed above teach this principle. When we follow God's principles for living, we can then "show off for God."

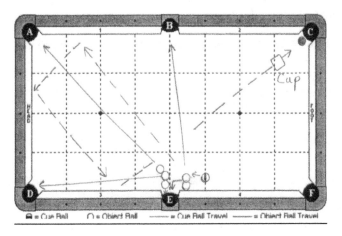

## Gospel Trick Shot Bonus 1

## Friend that Sticks Close

**History of the Trick Shot**: The only person I have seen use this shot is my Gospel Trick Shot travel partner Tom "Dr. Cue" Rossman. We have been to a dozen countries together and this shot has always been one of his signature shots while sharing the love and joy of Jesus in his portion of the show.

**GTS Name and Why**: When you see the outcome of this shot, the name and message become obvious. We joke around that I am deep (complicated) and he is shallow (simple). I have a math and physics explanation of Gospel Trick Shot #1 called "Obstacles" that covers about five chapters in my college physics textbook. After I am done, Tom breaks things down so even a child can understand.

**Scripture References in NIV Translation**: Proverbs 18:24 and John 15: 13.

**Cue Ball Placement**: The cue ball is placed as shown in the diagram.

**Object Ball(s) Placement**: Use only the special two prop balls that are bolted together which can be homemade or custom made to order. Make sure that the right ball is in line with the right side of pocket B.

**Objective**: Hit the center of the cue ball firm. The cue ball will strike the center of the right object ball. Shoot the cue and right ball in a straight line to the right side of side pocket B. Both balls will go in pocket B together at the same time. You can comment after the balls go in that you can't get any closer than that!

**Special Notes**: Make sure to hit this firm, as a softer hit will alter the direction of the twisting balls.

**Crowd Reactions Through the Years**: After you shoot the shot, ask if anyone has any questions. They will undoubtedly ask you how you did that. Take the two balls from the pocket made and show the answer for a great laugh, plus it can also be used to show deception in life again as a message point. I usually follow Tom's portion of the Gospel Trick Shot show as this shot is a good lead into what God wants me to say as Jesus is the one that sticks closer than a brother (Proverbs 18:24). This shot also helps to loosen up the crowd before I take the message a little deeper with the Gospel of our Lord Jesus Christ.

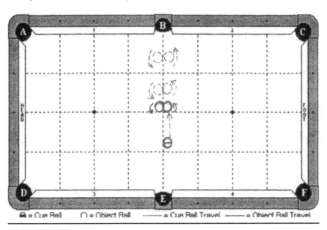

🅐 = Cue Ball    ◯ = Object Ball    ——— = Cue Ball Travel    ——— = Object Ball Travel

## Gospel Trick Shot Bonus 2

## Rise Up

**History of the Trick Shot**: This shot requires the use of a Bobble Ball invented in 2009 by Fred and Devra Robledo who also made the GTS portable pool table in 2013. The Bobble Ball can be ordered at bobbleball.com. The shot was invented by WPA top 10 world ranked Artistic Pool player Jason "The Michigan Kid" Lynch. It was later used by another WPA top 10 ranked Artistic Pool player Brian "Superman" Pauley, plus BCA Hall of Famer Tom "Dr. Cue" Rossman.

**GTS Name and Why:** Like most Gospel Trick Shots when you see the visual image of the shot, the principle becomes obvious. Gospel Trick Shots were created to give an illustrated message using billiards. It can be in story format or simply one spiritual principle that applies to the visual created by the shot. In this particular shot, the Bobble Ball will rise up when struck in just the right way!

**Scripture References in NIV Translation**: Philippians 4:8, Psalm 27: l, and Psalm 37:39.

**Cue Ball Placement**: The cue ball or any object ball can be used as the resistance ball as show.

**Object Ball(s) Placement**: Place Bobble Ball in front of resistance ball. Normally the Bobble Ball is placed with a gap of 1/8 to 3/16 of an inch between it and an object ball center to each other.

**Objective**: Hit the Bobble Ball straight into the "gapped ball" next to it and straight in line to pocket B and object ball will disappear into pocket B and Bobble Ball will remain spinning after it rises until it takes its rest (lying down) again.

**Special Notes**: You must hit the Bobble Ball very hard and as far to the right of the thin side as possible. This will generate maximum speed and spin. The record is about 30 seconds spinning like a top!

**Crowd Reactions Through the Years**: This shot has not been seen by most people. Because of its uniqueness like the Bobble Ball itself, there are a lot of oohs and aahs from the crowd when the Bobble Ball rises up. The performer of this shot can share a personal triumph over tragedy through Jesus or simply remind people that no matter what they are facing they can rise up with the help of the Lord. Another alternate meaning can include lying down to get your rest and rising up to do God's work.

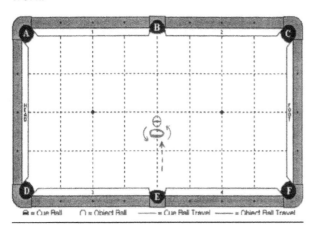

🏀 = Cue Ball    ◯ = Object Ball    ———— = Cue Ball Travel    ———— = Object Ball Travel

68149033R00156

Made in the USA
Middletown, DE
16 September 2019